THE MAKING OF THE SOVIET CITIZEN:
Character Formation and Civic Training in Soviet Education

THE
MAKING
OF THE
SOVIET
CITIZEN

Character Formation and Civic Training in
Soviet Education

Edited by GEORGE AVIS

CROOM HELM
London • New York • Sydney

© 1987 George Avis
Croom Helm Ltd, Provident House, Burrell Row,
Beckenham, Kent, BR3 1AT

Croom Helm Australia, 44-50 Waterloo Road,
North Ryde, 2113, New South Wales

British Library Cataloguing in Publication Data

The Making of the Soviet citizen: character
    formation and civic training in Soviet
    education.
    1. Education — Soviet Union
    I. Avis, George
    370'.947   LA832
    ISBN 0-7099-5105-1

Published in the USA by
Croom Helm
in association with Methuen, Inc.
29 West 35th Street
New York, NY 10001

Library of Congress Cataloging-in-Publication Data

The Making of the Soviet citizen.

    Includes index.
    1. Education—Soviet Union. 2. Communist education—
Soviet Union. 3. Political socialization—Soviet Union.
I. Avis, George, 1936-
LA832.M23 1987   370'.947   87-13566
ISBN 0-7099-5105-1

Printed and bound in Great Britain by Mackays of Chatham Ltd, Kent

CONTENTS

Contents

TABLES, APPENDICES AND FIGURES

Tables and Appendices

Figures

NOTES ON CONTRIBUTORS

Lynne Attwood is a research student attached to the Centre for Russian and East European Studies, University of Birmingham, and is just completing a doctoral dissertation on gender studies in the Soviet Union.

George Avis is Senior Lecturer in Russian Studies at the University of Bradford.

Dr John Dunstan is Senior Lecturer in Soviet Education and Deputy Director at the Centre for Russian and East European Studies, University of Birmingham.

Dr Nigel Grant is Professor of Education at the University of Glasgow.

John Morison is Senior Lecturer in Russian Studies at the University of Leeds.

Dr James Muckle is Lecturer in Education at the University of Nottingham.

Dr Felicity O'Dell is a former research student at the Centre for Russian and East European Studies, University of Birmingham, now teaching English as a foreign language in Cambridge and a course on Soviet education at Cambridge University.

Dr Jim Riordan is Professor of Soviet Studies at the University of Bradford.

Wendy Rosslyn is Lecturer in Russian at the University of Nottingham.

PREFACE

A distinctive feature of Soviet education since the
Revolution has been the crucial importance it gives
to the formation of a new type of person - the model
socialist citizen. Success in this endeavour is
regarded as essential for the creation of the
material and spiritual bases of communism. Soviet
educational establishments, accordingly, devote
immense effort and resources to a programme of
character-building which in Russian is called
vospitanie. Common English translations of this term
('upbringing', 'moral and social development',
'political education') do not fully convey its nature
and extent. For Soviet schools and colleges set out
to shape young people's knowledge and perceptions of
the world through an organised process which is all-
embracing and multifaceted. They attempt deliberately and systematically to instil in the young
officially-prescribed attitudes, values and habits
which will make them rounded, hard-working and loyal
members of socialist society. These attitudes and
attributes include: a sense of communist morality, a
scientific materialist world outlook, patriotism,
collectivism, a socialist orientation to labour,
internationalism, atheism, and hostility to
bourgeois capitalist regimes and imperialism. And
vospitanie is implemented on a wide front. It
permeates the content and teaching of all subjects in
academic curricula and is the underlying aim of many
school and extra-mural activities. Furthermore it is
reinforced by other agencies of socialisation in
Soviet society, in particular children's and youth
organisations.

In the 1970s and 1980s there has been renewed
emphasis on vospitanie in Soviet education. Several
developments have contributed to this. Manpower
shortages and a slowing down in the rate of economic

growth have underlined the need to direct the minds and energies of the Soviet younger generation more purposefully than before towards their obligation to work for the socialist motherland. Improved global communications, better education and greater affluence have in the view of many Soviet ideologues made young people more vulnerable to ideological subversion from Western propaganda, consumerism and imported lax moral standards. The upbringing of Soviet children is suffering, too, from a rise in social problems caused by alcoholism, divorce, one-parent families, delinquency and so on. If one adds to this set of trends the changes of political leadership in the 1980s following the deaths of Brezhnev, Andropov and Chernenko, it is not surprising that a climate has been created in which ideological, as well as economic and social, renewal is felt to be imperative.

This collection brings together for the first time the results of recent British research devoted to contemporary character formation and civic training in Soviet education. The contributors present detailed analyses of the aims and methods of various major components of the <u>vospitanie</u> process and examine the latest developments in their implementation. Most attention in the essays is understandably directed towards the theory and practice of such training in schools. But other sectors of the education system are not neglected, recieving particular attention in the chapters by Dunstan, Morison and Avis. The book contains detailed information and commentary which it is expected will be of considerable interest to a broad audience concerned with education in general, social and moral training, and Soviet affairs.

In the opening chapter of the book James Muckle offers a broad outline of <u>vospitanie</u> in general and then goes on to examine in detail one of its fundamental elements, namely the moral development of children. Schools, he argues, should be concerned with transmitting the best values of the society they exist in. It is inconsistent of Western commentators to agree with this principle and then to regard with dismay the defining and explicit imparting of such values in Soviet schools for being 'indoctrination'.

Soviet ideologists consider labour to be a basic need of all human beings. For the true socialist citizen it constitutes also a primary duty because it contributes to the establishing of the economic base of communism. The importance of the work ethic in Soviet upbringing is investigated by Felicity

'Dell. She analyses school textbooks to show how
pproved work values are presented in different
ubjects and for different age groups. Whether such
ocialisation is successful may be gauged by looking
t subsequent attitudes to employment and workplace
ehaviour. O'Dell concludes that in some areas Soviet
chools are failing to develop in young people an
nqualified respect for labour or dedication to
ocietal work goals.

Recent developments in political education are
he focus of the essay by John Morison. He
emonstrates how changes in the Soviet leadership and
he latest reforms in the education system have led
o increased stress being placed on ideological work
n schools, universities and institutes. The
ffectiveness of this work is impaired by the problem
hat genuine political commitment may only be
orthcoming if there is evidence of economic
rogress, but the latter is difficult to achieve if
olitical commitment is lacking.

A thorough grounding in scientific materialism
s regarded by Soviet upbringers as essential for a
orrect world outlook. Religious belief poses an
lternative philosophical explanation of human life
nd destiny and therefore constitutes a considerable
hreat to the young. In his overview of atheistic
ducation John Dunstan writes of the difficulties
acing Soviet teachers when they try to combat faith
ith rationalism and to instil positive atheistic
ttitudes in a generally apathetic audience.

The chapters on gender and pedagogy and on peace
ducation break new ground in the study of Soviet
ducation. Such subjects have been familiar, if
ontroversial, features of Western educational
ebate. In the Soviet Union, however, they play a
ole in the school curriculum which appears to run
ounter to general Western notions about their
unction and purpose. Why Soviet educators are now
romoting traditional sex-role stereotypes and why
hey combine peace education with military training
re paradoxes explored by Lynne Attwood and Wendy
Rosslyn respectively.

The all-embracing nature of <u>vospitanie</u> is well
illustrated by the contribution made to it by the
Pioneer and Komsomol movements to which virtually all
Soviet school pupils and students belong. A primary
oncern of these organisations is to carry on and
reinforce character and citizenship training in the
non-academic sphere. Through ritual and collective
activities they are able to harness the physical and
emotional energies of their members to fulfil

prescribed goals. More importantly, they ca
influence, perhaps more effectively than the school
the attitudes and behaviour of the young. The chapter
by Jim Riordan describes in detail how they go about
this and evaluates their impact on modern Soviet
youth.

The difficulty of determining and transmitting
a unitary set of values in any large industrialised
society is obvious. To attempt it in a multi-ethnic
federation in which numerous widely differing
cultural and religious traditions still live through
the medium of numerous different languages would
appear to be an impossible enterprise. Nigel Grant
explores the fundamental problem facing the Soviet
system of upbringing, namely that of establishing
unity of (socialist) content within cultural
diversity, by looking at the Soviet Union'
linguistic pluralism and relating it to educationa
policy and practice.

Of all the young people subjected to programmes
of <u>vospitanie</u> it is no doubt those who are destined
to be the future leaders of economic and political
life who are expected to assimilate them most
successfully. The final chapter in the collection
investigates communist upbringing among a future
Soviet elite, students in higher education
Extensive use is made here of the results of recent
major surveys of student attitudes and opinion to
estimate how far they conform to the approved model
of a Soviet graduate specialist in terms of
vocational commitment and socio-political activism.

Many of the contributions which follow were
first conceived at two one-day conferences held at
Bradford University in May and June 1986 on the theme
of <u>vospitanie</u> in Soviet education. I would like to
thank Professor John Green, Dean of the Board of
Social Sciences, and the Research Committee of the
Modern Languages Centre at Bradford for their moral
and financial support for these conferences. I am
grateful too for the generous help and advice given
by my colleagues in the UK Study Group on Soviet
Education who have encouraged me to bring this
publication project to fruition.

George Avis

Chapter One

THE NEW SOVIET CHILD: MORAL EDUCATION IN SOVIET SCHOOLS

James Muckle

An occupational hazard of writing about the Soviet education system is to be denigrated as a 'bourgeois falsifier'. A recent attack on some American and British educationists appeared towards the end of 1985. V. Mitina declared in the journal <u>Narodnoe obrazovanie</u> (Education) (1): 'What these people fail to realise is that the basic aim of Soviet education is to produce a new type of person'. The full extent to which the system sets out to develop children's personalities is perhaps not fully understood outside the Soviet Union, but Soviet educators have been concerned from the very beginning to create a 'new Soviet man'. The purpose of this chapter is to look at the content of the moral education, <u>vospitanie</u>, imparted to children, to discover what we can about the methods by which it is taught, to estimate what currently are the most urgent concerns of educators in this field. What qualities is the new Soviet child of the present day supposed to possess?

In the public debate following the appearance of draft guidelines for the reform of education in 1984, it is said that a prominent demand from ordinary people was that school should pay great attention to <u>vospitanie</u> (2). Just how this is to be interpreted depends, of course, on the meaning attached to the word, and to this we shall return very shortly. We see here an example of parents and adults generally trying, if not to shift the blame for poor standards of public conduct from themselves, at least to make teachers feel that it is their responsibility to bring about an improvement. There is nothing new and nothing Soviet in this. 'Where did you go to school?' is, after all, an English cliché used almost as often to express contempt for ill-bred behaviour as 'Where were you brought up?' Teachers in any country understandably feel resentful if they alone are held

1

responsible for the ills of society. In the Soviet Union the tendency of the middle-aged and elderly to bewail the poor behaviour, hooliganism or ill manners of contemporary youth is particularly strong, and this fact will prove useful to us in estimating what is felt to be wrong at present - since current concerns naturally find their way into the press, and into speeches by political figures.

Moral Qualities of the Soviet Citizen. Before going any further it will be necessary to establish just what vospitanie is (3). Perhaps the neatest formula for conveying the concept is 'character training and the development of personality': all those things which the pupil receives during education inside and outside school other than instruction in a subject within the curriculum. This is not an exact definition, since Soviet educators are quick to point out that vospitanie and instruction in school subjects are very closely connected, and in any case, ethics in one form or another has been and is being taught as a school subject. Nevertheless, the phrase will serve. 'Character training' is not sufficient on its own to convey the meaning of vospitanie, though there is a very great deal of character training within the development of personality as practised by Soviet teachers.

In a recent book (4) a Soviet educationist describes vospitanie as 'a creative process' and 'a complex art', and he adds that it is 'a very important part of the educational process. It has its own content, its own principles and is achieved with the help of specific ... methods.' (5) But what actually goes into it? There would seem to be eleven components:

> Socio-political awareness (to make citizens politically active and literate),
> Morality and ethics,
> Patriotism and internationalism (to encourage love of the socialist motherland and worldwide proletarian solidarity),
> Military-patriotic education (to develop the desire to defend the motherland),
> Labour education and professional orientation,
> Mental development and the raising of general culture (this would seem to take in everything in the school curriculum),
> Atheism,
> Knowledge of the law and the obligations of a

2

citizen,
Economic,
Aesthetic, and
Physical education.

There are, perhaps, a few surprises here. Why exactly is physical education seen as an integral part of the development of personality? It was, of course, and still is part of the British boarding-school ethic, but it is interesting to discover very similar reasons being given for its inclusion in the Soviet canon: it produces determined, disciplined and courageous people who have initiative and who are ready to work for and defend their native land (6). The stress placed on economic and labour education is connected with preparing young people for a role in working society and for an understanding of the place of their work within the scheme of the nation's production. Physical labour and the skills of the artisan have, as is well known, an honoured place in the socialist consciousness and they are not neglected in schools. But perhaps particularly noteworthy is the importance accorded to aesthetic education. Not every Soviet citizen or even every Soviet teacher fully understands or agrees about the importance of the arts in personality development, but at least the theorists at the top are emphatic that appreciation of beauty - natural and in the arts - is vital to every child. If only the same could be said in Britain! The humanising effect of literature recurs as a theme in books and articles on moral education.

An interesting document attempted 25 years ago to sum up in its entirety the 'moral code of the builder of Communism', in the Programme of the Communist Party of the Soviet Union published in connection with the 22nd Congress of the Party in 1961. The twelve precepts were: devotion to the communist cause, love of socialist motherland and of other socialist countries; conscientious labour for the good of society; concern for the preservation and growth of public wealth; a high sense of public duty, intolerance of actions harmful to the public interest; a collectivist attitude; mutual respect between individuals; honesty, truthfulness, moral purity, modesty, unpretentiousness in social and private life; mutual respect in the family and concern for the upbringing of children; an uncompromising attitude to injustice, parasitism, dishonesty, careerism and money-grubbing; friendship and brotherhood among all peoples of the USSR,

3

intolerance of national and racial hatred; an uncompromising attitude to the enemies of Communism, peace and the freedom of nations; fraternal solidarity with working people of all countries. (7) These principles are extended somewhat in articles 59 to 69 inclusive of the 1977 Constitution of the USSR, which deal with the obligations of a citizen. (8) In summary, they state that it is the duty of a citizen

> to uphold the Constitution and laws and comply with socialist standards of conduct (article 59),
> to work conscientiously and uphold labour discipline (60),
> to preserve and protect socialist property (61),
> to safeguard the interests of the Soviet state and enhance its power and prestige. 'Betrayal of the motherland is the gravest of crimes against the people' (62),
> to perform military service (63),
> to respect the national dignity of other citizens and to strengthen friendship between the Soviet nationalities (64),
> to respect the rights of others and to help maintain public order (65),
> to bring up children, train them for work and raise them as worthy members of society. Children are obliged to care for their parents (66),
> to protect and conserve nature (67),
> to preserve historical monuments and other cultural treasures (68),
> to promote friendship and cooperation with peoples of other lands and help maintain and strengthen world peace (69).

It has, rather unfairly, been pointed out that adherence to a very large number of these precepts would further the economic interests of the state. This again is not specifically Soviet; honesty is widely recognised as 'the best policy', even though moralists agree it should be followed as a principle, not a policy. Any country benefits economically by having conscientious, disciplined and conforming citizens.

Here we have, then, a profile sketch of the 'new Soviet person'. What does that person look like in detail, and how does he or she learn or receive the character traits that make him a rounded, harmoniously developed communist personality? We

4

shall investigate these two matters by looking at what interpretations and emphases leaders of Soviet society place upon the desired qualities of personality, and by looking at how, that is through which media and in what manner, the values are communicated. It is convenient to take the two issues together in order to avoid repetitiousness, and as they are connected in any case.

Character Formation Through Subject Teaching. Let us look first at character training and personality development through academic subject teaching. Any reader can probably work out for himself how the Soviet teaching profession might be expected to use history, social studies or literature to convey values, but teachers of mathematics and science do not escape the same responsibility - far from it. The introduction to a recently published chemistry syllabus gives pride of place to the beneficial moral and ideological effect of studying chemistry: the subject is said to arm pupils with the knowledge and skills necessary for active participation in communist construction, and to contribute to the formation of a dialectical-materialist world-view and atheistic convictions (9). The case of biology teaching may be taken as a representative (and vivid) example. A chapter on biology in a recent book on the content of the curriculum (10) devotes a good seven pages out of 17 to an argument for the subject as 'realizing the principle of unity of education, cognitive and character development'. It is instructive to see how the Soviet pedagogue conceives of biology conveying the desired values. Biology 'convinces the pupils' of the material basis of the functioning of human and animal bodies and of all their activities, including intellectual ones. Scientific materialism is therefore firmly established in the children's minds. Understanding of the processes of evolution and the work of Charles Darwin instils in children a conception of evolution in historical development too, which leads to 'correct' understanding of social issues. The logical arrangement of the course persuades children that the laws of the natural world can be discovered, and it creates in their minds a scientific picture of the world. This establishes a firm basis for atheistic education by 'exposing the antiscientific character' of religious belief. The author stresses that biology teaching cannot be neutral: systematic atheistic education must be carried on and 'modern

5

religious dogma' must be confronted with scientific
interpretations of biological processes.

Patriotic education is to be carried on by
pointing out the achievements of Soviet biologists
and agriculturalists and by stating that the first
conservation laws were instituted by Lenin. The
enormous role of the Party and government in
furthering biological science and its applications
in agriculture and industry are to be taught.
(Certain well-known setbacks to this in the 1930s and
1940s are not mentioned.) The Soviet system of health
care is to be praised, and it should be pointed out
that in capitalist countries workers and employees
have little access to medical services. Also the work
of Darwin, Linnaeus, Pasteur, Mendel and other
scientists is used in order to reveal the
international nature of the science.

Biology is very important, it is argued, for
both ecological and aesthetic education. Nature is 'a
source of beauty' and teachers should use it to
arouse pupils' feeling for beauty. Biology helps
children to understand the need for physical fitness
and sports, and supplies the scientific basis also
for 'hygienic, labour and sex education'. The content
of the biology syllabus relates partly to industrial
and agricultural processes and so contributes both to
polytechnical education (in the sense of general
knowledge of industry and the economy and of
industrial and agricultural skills) and to careers
guidance. The ways of thinking taught in biology
lessons (listed as analysis, synthesis, comparison,
the establishment of connections and causal links,
abstraction and concretisation, and generalisation)
and skills of observation, experiment and
description all contribute strongly to children's
mental development. However slack and lacking in
rigour some of these arguments may be - and however
much they may apply to subjects other than biology -
the purpose of repeating them here is to demonstrate
the way in which Soviet educationists use one subject
to convey moral, philosophical and political values.
The points claimed for biology cover at least nine of
the eleven components of vospitanie noted above.

Extra-curricular Upbringing. Vospitanie is carried
on outside the classroom both by teachers operating
in a pastoral context (as class tutors), and by
leaders of the youth organisations - who may or may
not be adults. It is the duty of the class tutor to
instil desired values into the children by, for

example, developing a collective spirit in the
organisation and carrying out of the more domestic
classroom duties, by preparing for the celebration of
Soviet festivals such as Lenin's birthday, by
organising debates, talks entertainments and the
production of a class newspaper. The children are to
be guided to take initiative for themselves and to
socialise each other, ideally without the tutor being
involved in the long run. The tutor is supposed to
work in the background, checking over-dominant
characters, chivvying the passive, and instilling
awareness of the qualities necessary for successful
operation of the system: trust, reliability and
initiative. Class tutors are expected to cooperate
with the leaders of youth organisations - Octobrists,
Pioneers and Komsomol - the activities of which are
of the greatest importance for moral and ideological
education. These organisations cover almost every
conceivable sporting, cultural and political
pursuit, and attach importance to helping younger
children with their work and hobbies and to engaging
in 'socially-useful labour'. The political context
is highly important, and children in the youth
organisations are taught about the flags, symbols and
anthems of the state and of their republic, and they
take part in awe-inspiring ceremonies, often with
marching, drumming, bugling and banner-bearing.

Recent Books on Moral Education. In contrast with
many Western countries it can confidently be stated
that the values propagated by the media do not
conflict with those taught in the schools. Study of
the popular and serious press - books and periodicals
for teachers, children and parents - provides useful
evidence to the non-Soviet observer on two matters in
particular. Firstly, the contents of these books and
magazines fill out our perceptions of exactly how
Soviet educators interpret the values they seek to
instil. (They also, it must be said, contain evidence
about the not always very rational prejudices held by
leaders of society.) Secondly, publications indicate
current preoccupations and show whether or not any
issues stand out as being of special concern. It is
well known that likely public demand plays little
part in the plans of Soviet book publishers. If a
book appears, then that is an indication that some
moral overlord - or committee of such - not merely
permitted it, but probably actively planned its
appearance. The print run is decided on a basis of
what the planners think it ought to sell, not what it

7

would be likely to sell if market forces had their way (11). Some publications are for teachers and are written in formal academic style; others are for parents and the general public, and these are more popular - though no less serious in intent. Many of them can be read by children, and there are books too which are specifically intended for children and adolescents. Closer examination of a representative sample of these books will indicate many of the current concerns of Soviet moral educators (12).

Among those for teachers, a particularly interesting example is a little paperback on the educational value of folklore. Actually this book (13), with a print run of 30,000, contains several interesting examples of what we are discussing. The argument is that folklore is good, because it springs from the masses of the people; it is of great educational importance because it develops children's language, thinking, ethical sense and historical awareness, and because - being an art form in itself - it acquaints children with culture. A chapter on lullabies underlines the fact that such songs, apart from introducing children to poetry, song, language, etc., instil interest in the world of work, love of homeland, knowledge of historical facts, and - being often intended for a child of one particular sex - the qualities expected of members of that sex. 'The general subject matter (of lullabies) is the concern of adults, past and present, for the new man, for his good, many-sided development' (p. 31). Fairy tales require more intellectual involvement from children; if parents make a practice of telling children a story before bedtime, this creates a routine, and therefore shapes 'discipline - which is very important for future good citizens' (p. 45). (Extraordinary statements such as this in Soviet books on upbringing are almost as common as statements of the obvious, which sometimes, by creating an impression of naivety, obscure the good sense of the general argument). Fairy tales inspire children to creativity, develop 'profound moral ideas', create moderation in desires and foster a sense of humour. They are imbued with the great respect which the masses have for knowledge and the desire to overcome difficulty; they instil hatred of the exploiting classes and solidarity with the toiling masses. Tales of wicked stepmothers, rich and cruel adults and the like encourage social awareness (though, of course, nowadays there are no wicked stepmothers in the Soviet Union). Afternoon stories in the kindergarten or bedtime tales at home, then,

8

are no cosy exercise in fantasy, but a serious
venture in moral education - and we are not to forget
it!

Turning to books with a higher content of
theory, it is possible to discover several by N.I.
Boldyrev, an experienced exponent of upbringing
(14). His <u>Nravstvennoe vospitanie shkol'nikov</u> (Moral
education of schoolchildren) begins with an
exposition of Marxist-Leninist theory and some
philosophy and psychology, and it sets the scene for
the next few years of research in the field by
indicating that there is a very great deal to be done
in supplying answers as to the ages at which children
can benefit from training in specific moral
qualities, and to the effectiveness and practical
application of moral teaching. The same author has
published a guide to class tutors in putting these
ideas into practice, and a textbook for teachers on
the methodology of upbringing work in schools. (15)
Some of the same ground is gone over in a sensitive
book by O.S. Bogdanova and others (16) on the moral
education of adolescents. It has a chapter on the
'personality of the modern adolescent' which
contains much good sense, and one on the 'activation
of the role of parents in moral education', but is
probably of most interest for ten pages of teaching
material, stories for discussion in class by
different age-groups, which are intended to raise
questions mainly about honour, truthfulness,
sympathy and understanding for others.

Of particular interest in relation to the
fostering of the collective spirit is another book
for teachers by N.S. Dezhnikova and I.B. Pervin (17),
<u>Tovarishcheskaya vzaimopomoshch'shkol'nikov</u> (Com-
radely mutual assistance between schoolchildren).
The authors say that an undesirable feature of
bourgeois and Russian pre-revolutionary education
was the active discouragement of cooperation between
children at school. The book gives many examples of
how teachers can organise and encourage cooperative
working both in academic subjects and in labour
training. On the academic side, Dezhnikova urges
constructive commenting in younger classes on other
pupils' efforts, pair work for adolescents, and for
senior classes group work. Group work consists of
problem-solving after an introduction by the
teacher, followed by reporting back. A system of
'consultants' is suggested, that is six to eight
pupils per class, all of whom score high marks
regularly, and who are appointed formally, after
agreement with the 'class collective' and the

teacher, by the school branch of the Young Communist League. Their work is thus dignified as social and political duty. Dezhnikova also outlines how a 'public inspection of knowledge' may be organised, when a jury consisting of pupils from other classes, a deputy head and other teachers tests the knowledge of a class in an academic subject. The class has to pull together to impress the jury, but in a solemn ceremony afterwards <u>individual</u> marks are read out.

A common category of recent book seeks to acquaint young people and their parents with the demands of the law and with the rights, duties and privileges of citizens. It was believed that a significant amount of juvenile delinquency was attributable to ignorance of the law on the part of adolescents and their parents, and 'legal (<u>pravovoe</u>) education' is enshrined both within <u>vospitanie</u> and as a separate subject within the curriculum: The Basis of Soviet Government and Law, taught for one lesson a week in grade 8. It also figures to some extent in Social Studies (two periods a week in grade 10). Under the new dispensation (1984 School Reform changes - <u>Ed</u>.) both subjects will again figure with slight adjustments to the timetable in the last three years of compulsory education. One reason why people are unaware of their obligations under the law could be that the press is most reluctant to publish full accounts of crime and the prosecution of offenders. M.A. Ivanov's book, <u>Roditeli, podrostok, zakon</u> (Parents, the adolescent and the law) (Moscow, 1980), places the responsibility on parents, schools and society to do all they can to 'guard the adolescent from disaster' (p. 8). It is clear from Ivanov's introduction that the parents of delinquents have often been astounded to discover what a tough line courts take with what they imagined to be the childish pranks of their offspring. The moral message of the book is very serious: 'Self-discipline, collectivism and a high level of legal culture will help the adolescent of today to become a member of our society with full legal rights' (p. 6).

The real preoccupations of orthodox Soviet moralists are betrayed by less academic publications. One in particular can scarcely have been intended for consumption outside the Soviet Union, though 105,000 copies were printed for home sales (18). The sentiment expressed by the author is clearly anticapitalist: we in the West are attacked for weighing down our children with back-breaking labour, caring more for our dogs than for children, whom we beat and maim — as anyone can read 'in the

<u>Sunday Times</u>'. We also let them deliver newspapers for money - which, apparently is not, as it seems to us, socially - useful work, but encouragement of unscrupulous moneymaking. If anyone wishes to understand how much better life is under socialism, he should just think of the 'Israeli pilot who drops a doll full of napalm to Palestinian children, or the American doctor (sic) who runs a Vietnamese child through with a bayonet' (p. 47). The reason for our barbarism is the economic basis of our society, and if we lived under socialism we should become wise, humane and disinterested - or so it is assumed.

A typical book for children deals with etiquette and polite and considerate behaviour in public places (19). It contains numerous anecdotes and teasing problems of polite and considerate behaviour for the young readers to sort out; answers are given in the back. The book interestingly and unconsciously illustrates Soviet everyday life. It is sometimes intelligently critical of contemporary customs, for example meaningless present-giving on 'Women's Day'. The authoress holds up various well-known people as setters of good moral standards; as would be expected they include Lenin (but not too frequently). To find Lord Chesterfield, Lev Tolstoy and Stanislavsky among their number is a little more unexpected. Topics covered include tidiness, cleanliness, correct behaviour in theatres, dress, and so on. A section on shops clearly indicates that the poor service one so often receives there in the Soviet Union is due to a cultural difference; the customer is not always right, and should cause as little inconvenience to the shop assistant as possible! The book is not solely concerned with such minor matters: serious ethical discussion is carried on over the question, 'What would you do if your friend asked to copy from you in a test?' The authoress expects that very few children would tell the teacher; she explains why this would be the right thing to do, but admits she would not have done it herself, so deeply ingrained is the school tradition of 'honour among thieves'.

A most interesting collection of newspaper articles on moral and ethical issues by the well-known children's author Sergei Mikhalkov, provides much inside information to anyone who wishes to know about live issues in Soviet life today (20). Mikhalkov criticises lack of respect for the nation's cultural heritage, the discouragement of children's imaginative powers, crazes for 'imported' goods, lack of respect for older people and parents, neglect of politeness, and gratitude, the breakdown of family relationships, poor cultural levels of conversation between friends and reliance on tittle-tattle, superstition, hypocrisy, egotism (while praising self-knowledge), bad artistic taste, racial hatred, lack of patriotism and marriage with foreigners.

From what has been said already in this chapter most of the topics covered by Mikhalkov will cause no surprise, but four of them deserve some comment. Family breakdown is a major cause of public anxiety at present and great efforts are being made to lessen the problem. Raising the cultural level of discourse is not a hobbyhorse of Mikhalkov's alone, but is becoming a major point in attempts to improve family life. We shall see both of these points illustrated when we consider the school syllabus on ethics and psychology of family life later. The argument is that if people, especially in families, discussed books and films more and did less gossiping about trivial personal matters there would be less divorce. The criticism of racial hatred is possibly coded: it begins with a violent attack on South Africa and America, but finishes by asking whether the Russian who grumbles about the Armenians in the flat above while his children are taught to recite poems about the brotherhood of man has the right to feel superior. Finally, the patriotism commended is far from the communist ideal of love for the first socialist state, but is very largely an expression of fondness for Russia. There might appear to be no harm in that, except that in one anecdote a woman who had married a Frenchman left him to return to Russia, not because of any disagreement in the marriage, but because she could not live without 'the pure Russian sky'. It must therefore be assumed either that if two values - stable marriage and patriotism - conflict, the second should win; or it may be that marriage with a foreigner does not count so strongly.

Moral Issues in the Educational and Popular Press. A scan of the subject matter of articles in the most serious educational press for 1985/6 - <u>Sovetskaya pedagogika</u> (Soviet pedagogics) and <u>Narodnoe obrazovanie</u> - indicates that these topics are by no means dead. Every issue of the latter has a clutch of articles on <u>vospitanie</u>, and in the last twelve or fifteen months that heading has thrown up the following topics: family matters (frequently), political education, Lenin as an example to all, work habits, internationalist, environmental, legal,

ideological, political and aesthetic education and
alcohol abuse. Labour education is listed
separately, and it scores highly in frequency of
appearance. <u>Sovetskaya pedagogika</u> in the last few
months has contained articles on alcohol abuse,
labour education, social involvement of children,
numerous pieces on moral and patriotic education,
aesthetic, atheistic and environmental education,
the law, the cultural heritage, the family and social
education, careers counselling and ideological
education. A recent issue of the <u>Byulleten'</u>
<u>normativnykh aktov ministerstva prosveshcheniya SSSR</u>
(Bulletin of normative documents from the USSR
Ministry of Education) publishes instructions about
Pioneer ceremonies recalling revolution and war,
anti-alcohol education, and explaining the Twenty-
Seventh Congress of the Communist Party to children.

The more popular press is equally taken up by
issues of communist morality. What has appeared from
that citadel of middle-aged complaint, the satirical
journal <u>Krokodil</u>, in 1986? Poor workmanship, poor
standards of public service and the poor quality of
manufactured goods head the list. (Woman: 'We've just
received a commendation for a face-lift on this block
of flats.' Man: 'Six months ago I got a commendation
for finishing it ahead of schedule!' Another cartoon
shows some people unpacking a new computer: 'They've
sent it with a full set of notices!' - the notices
say 'Under repair', 'Out of order', etc. One cook is
tasting a liquid, while the other asks, 'What shall I
put on the menu - soup or tea?') Poor education in
attitudes to work might be thought to be at the root
of this. Backward attitudes to new technology are
frequently mocked. Corruption, waste and drunkenness
are all criticised. (Children are shown in one
cartoon receiving a lesson 'Bread - one of our
valuable commodities' while a worker from the canteen
next door is throwing out heaps of it.) A telling
cartoon on standards of integrity in industry shows
an angry boss yelling down the telephone, 'If you
don't report at once that you've completed the work,
I'll make you complete it!' If any particular
emphasis can be traced it is on the family and on
labour training. There is a good deal of satire of
scientific research institutes (not specifically in
education) for undertaking timewasting and
impractical research. Defective attitudes to
marriage come in for their share. (Man: 'I've a
Mercedes in its own garage and a Japanese video ...'
Woman: 'Carry on, darling, I can talk of love for
ever.' In another cartoon, a cupid with rubber-tipped

13

arrows is 'servicing non-serious friendships'.)

A glance at <u>Sem'ya i shkola</u> (Family and school) for the last six months shows that several of the same matters recur. This is, of course, a particularly good source, since it is a popular magazine for the parents of children at school. Authors and correspondents in recent issues have written about peace, the family as the nucleus of society, patriotism, love of work, the glorification of agricultural labour, drunkenness as a destroyer of the family, corporal punishment by parents and the qualities of masculinity and femininity and how they can be developed. A child writes about her parents' unwillingness to have the grandmother to live with them; there is a story about a boy who experienced what we in the West call 'school rejection' because of bullying, and a teacher writes to deplore parents' preventing children from attending after-school club meetings. In an issue for mid-1986 topics from letters printed included the siege of Leningrad and the need to inspire children with heroic memories, helping people in the street, teaching children songs with a sound moral message, protests at careless treatment of communal property and at parents who bring up children with inflexible discipline.

Moral Education in the School Curriculum. Anyone who was to study the press for the last twenty or even fifty years would expect to find many of the same issues recurring, and it would have been very surprising if the collection of books described above had showed a marked difference of emphasis in the values they were purveying in the early 1980s as opposed to now. If there is a difference it is in the increased importance now attached to the family as the basic unit of society. Nothing could be clearer than that the leaders of society are concerned about lack of preparation for marriage among young people, the light-hearted way they enter into it and the bad effects upon the children of unsuccessful marriages. If socialist society ever did regard marriage as a bourgeois institution, worthy of the scorn of emancipated men and women, it does not take this view in 1986. This leads us on to the question of moral and civic education in the curriculum of schools. As indicated above, it figures in two ways: the ninth-grade (by the post-Reform numbering) course in Soviet government and law (and to some extent the social studies course in grades 10 and 11), both of which are part of legal education, and the course entitled

'Ethics and Psychology of Family Life' which begins in the second half of year nine and continues for the first half of year 10.

A course simply entitled 'Ethics' appeared in the Belorussian Republic in 1975, first as an option and then as an experimental series of 35 lessons for all pupils in grade 8. In 1980 I had an opportunity to discuss this course with teachers in Minsk. (21) It was presented as a <u>mirovozzrencheskii kurs</u>' (a course in outlook) which would 'teach the pupils to think'. The lessons were taken by literature and history teachers. I was unable to examine the syllabus for 1979/80 at length, but noted the following topics which the teachers were to cover: our Soviet way of life, ethics - the science of morality, communist morality - the highest achievement in the moral development of humanity, respect for fellow human beings, and the 'culture of language'. It was a course in ethical behaviour in the most general sense. However, the impression in Belorussia at that time was that the course had proved so successful that the Union was going to take it over, so the title of the new Union syllabus seemed to indicate that it would be at least in part an adaptation of the Belorussian experiment. If this is so, then none of the topics mentioned above have survived and the whole spirit of the new course is different. The official printed version of the syllabus (22) makes no acknowledgement to the Belorussian Ministry of Education and attributes authorship to employees of two research institutes of the Academy of Pedagogical Sciences of the USSR.

The content of this syllabus is of the greatest interest, but it would be quite impossible to do full justice to it here without translating it in its entirety. The following survey should give an impression of its contents. It begins with four lessons entitled 'Personality, society, family', which consists mainly of straight social psychology mixed with some moral instruction on what we might call 'the dynamics of family relationships and their relationship with society'. This is followed by eight lessons on inter-personal relationships in youth: two on the psychology of it, two on the moral basis of boy-girl friendships and the nature of young male and female personality, two on friendships in general and two on 'love as the highest human emotion' between the sexes and within families. All of this is placed in the context of society and its demands upon smaller groups such as the family. There are then five lessons on marriage and the family: what is

15

readiness for marriage? (two lessons) - here social, physical, economic and psychological readiness is discussed, as are roles within the family. Two more lessons in. this section deal with the Soviet family and its functions, and a very sociological approach is adopted; the last lesson in the year goes on characteristics of the young family - mainly practical problems of embarking upon a new way of life and coping with likely difficulties.

The seventeen lessons in the following year are grouped under two headings: the first is 'Fundamentals of family relationships' and covers eleven lessons. One of these goes on the ideological basis of the family and contains a great deal of what might be termed socio-politics. The next two deal with the moral basis: equality, duty, responsibility, conscientiousness, respect, frankness, etc. Two more are entitled 'The collectivism of the Soviet family', a difficult and abstract topic, which reads like a mishmash of psychological and sociological concepts not all of which appear closely related to the subject. Consider this paragraph:

> The specifics of intra-family intercourse. Its dependence on multifaceted family relationships (economic, ideological, emotional and moral, sexual, parental), on naturalness, permanence, mutual interest, and on the purpose of ensuring all sides of the vital activity of the members of the family, etc. The new content of the concept 'head of the family'. Mutual help by spouses in family matters. The family council.

It would be difficult to make that accessible to a mixed-ability group, and so it would with the next two lessons on 'the psychological climate of the family', which is about compatibility - temperamental, psychological, ideological and so on. One note reads: 'exaggeration of the role of sexual compatibility in the creation of a good psychological climate'.

Three more single lessons, still under the heading of the basis of family relationships, cover the family's working atmosphere and household budgeting, and 'estetika byta' (a difficult phrase to translate - literally, 'aesthetics of everyday life', a topic which embraces such matters as turning the home into a cosy, inviting and intellectually stimulating environment) and leisure (here we return to matters of culture and the arts, the struggle against bourgeois concepts of beauty and comfort, and

16

fashion - the psychological need both to follow it and to adapt it to the individual). The last lesson of the eleven goes on the consequences of infringing family relationships, and is, in fact, about family break-up and divorce.

The last section is entitled 'Family and children' and it deals with parents as educators and upbringers of their offspring, and with their obligations in this respect both to the children and to society (three lessons), the upbringing of children within the family - how and how not to do it (two lessons), and finally one lesson on 'the child in the young family', - feeding, daily routines, the child's emotional and physical treatment.

The sheer mass of the content of this course must surely mean that it can only be conveyed by a straight didactic lecturing style of teaching - if the whole content is to be covered. Six-and-a-half pages of content in indigestible telegram-style Russian is followed by a mere quarter-page containing four subjects for discussions, six for lecturettes, three for 'readers' conferences' - obviously special events with a theme like 'the image of father and mother in literature', four topics for case-study discussion (or possibly, although the technique is not widely practised in the Soviet Union, role-playing) - e.g. 'the young family and parents', and a list of six films. The titles of 26 books are appended, 13 of them party or other political documents, and the remainder mainly very serious academic treatments with the odd popular work thrown in. A textbook has not at the time of writing appeared, but a hefty 'experimental' handbook for teachers with the same title as that of the course: <u>Etika i psikhologiya semeinoi zhizni</u>, edited by I.V. Grebennikov (Moscow, 1984) is available in a print run of 263,000 copies. We must await evidence of the progress and success of the course, but it looks very much as if most teachers will feel that they are being forced to do what they usually do: stand up and talk hard at the children for almost all the lesson.

Sex Education in the Soviet School. There is a fairly obviously omission from this account of the ethics course. There is little if any sex education in it. It has already been criticised on this account. This matter of sex education is an important one, or in the words of a Soviet teacher, 'intricate and delicate' (23). Soviet teachers are amazingly coy on the subject, and most of them see it as no business

17

of the school to become involved. I have been rebuked by a Soviet teacher for allowing a relatively senior pupil in England to refer to Nicholas I's 'mistress', and the cuts which Soviet children's publishers think necessary in standard classics of Russian literature in order to make them decent for young eyes to read can often be surprising. In this whole course of ethics and psychology of family life the word 'sexual' is used no more than four times, always in passing and, as we have seen, in one case specifically with the purpose of deprecating the importance of sex. Surely someone in the Soviet Union must believe that in the late twentieth century schoolchildren ought to be told something more than this about the subject?

A teacher called K.A. Khadzhinov, writing in <u>Biology in School</u> under the promising title 'Experience of working on the moral and sexual education of schoolchildren' typifies the priorities of the profession. (24) One is often told that sex education is given in grade 8 biology lessons during the course on human anatomy, physiology and hygiene. Examination of syllabuses and textbooks makes it clear that the children are indeed taught a little about the scientific side of human reproduction, that it is confined to a very few lessons, and that the emotional and moral aspects of human sexuality are not included. The more naive child may, in fact, receive a very unbalanced impression of the subject from the teacher who sticks rigidly to the book (25). Khadzhinov tacitly admits this failing, by stressing the importance of the moral side to sex education. Nevertheless, much of his article is concerned with how to lay the foundation for scientific understanding of procreation through botany and zoology lessons before grade 8. When we look more closely at the 'moral' content of his teaching, it includes an attack on bourgeois capitalist 'norms of behaviour' (which are 'incompatible with communist morality'), persuading girls not to wear high heels because it may harm their ability to bear children safely, warning both sexes of the dangers of smoking and drinking alcohol, and promoting sport as an aid to healthy procreation. Only in one short paragraph is there an acknowledgement of the emotional power of sexual instincts. It is to be hoped that the teacher concerned can help adolescents to cope with this. He has not a little to say about self-control, manly concern for the female and maidenly modesty and honour.

There have been local experiments in sex

education. In a journal article for December 1985
(26) an official from the Stavropol area writes under
an innocuous title ('Concern for moral and ethical
upbringing') about an experimental course designed
to strengthen the family and improve preparation for
marriage. The standard syllabus summarised above is
not mentioned at all. Sexual issues are covered among
many of the other matters included in the official
ethics course, but the local notabilities who planned
the experiment were led by a professor who is a
doctor of medicine, and though full details of the
course are not given, it clearly has a strong health
education side - on alcohol and tobacco as well as
sex. Among visitors who come into schools to teach
are psychiatrists, doctors and even a consultant
venerologist. The paper is nothing if not tactfully
written - what these people lecture <u>about</u> is not
stated. Again, it is clear we must wait for further
developments in this area before we can assess
whether or not the emotional side of sexuality is
adequately dealt with.

Conclusion. It is time to draw to a conclusion by
listing the principal qualities of the new Soviet man
or woman which the child will eventually become. That
person is

    a patriot
    an internationalist
    sober
    incorruptible
    conscientious at work and study
    respectful of the environment, of state
    property and resources
    an atheist
    able to find fulfilment working in a team
    courageous and adventurous
    supportive of Soviet industry
    disinclined to seek material wealth
    in favour of stable marriage and respectful of
    his elders
    respectful of manual labour and the craft of the
    artisan
    mindful of war dead
    forward-looking and technologically minded
    understanding in treatment of the opposite sex
    well-behaved in public and considerate of other
    people in general
    conventional by Soviet norms.

It is one purpose of the study of comparative education to use the study of an overseas system in order better to understand one's own. 'Bourgeois' onlookers may feel inclined to consider the nature of Soviet character training and personality development and ask whether or not they approve of the values teachers convey or whether they approve of the methods used to convey them. It would not be easy for a Soviet observer of education in the capitalist world to produce an equivalent list of characteristics of the person which our education seeks to create. Liberal democratic Western teachers, when challenged to produce some values they thought should be taught, might well be inclined to object to the 'indoctrination' or 'brainwashing' of schoolchildren. It is certain that to take this attitude excuses teachers from the really hard business of thinking what values they might consciously instil.

Some years ago, in the days before heterodox multiculturalism took our schools in its grasp, an Anglican bishop said that the aim of religious education should not be to convert children to Christianity, but so to instruct them in it that if they chose to accept or reject it, at least they would know what it was they were accepting or rejecting. This shows an attitude to religious education (which may be regarded in some ways as a close relation to vospitanie) based on knowledge. However, some British teachers are now speaking of and arguing for 'anti-racist' education - in other words, they wish actively to change the attitudes of school children by combating the values held in those children's homes or by their circle of friends. This is much nearer to the Soviet concept of vospitanie. We have to ask ourselves, do we approve of schools instilling moral values, whatever those values are?

To answer yes to this question is not to be illiberal or inconsistent. It is not wrong in principle for teachers in any country, including the Soviet Union, to place a moral and ideological point of view before pupils. One can dispute the values actually conveyed, one can be sceptical of the ways in which teachers try to instil them, one can even be fearful of the power of those views. But the notion that schools exist to pass on the best values in a society is sound, and if it is sound, it is the duty of teachers to do so. The fear of ideological bias and of brainwashing which occasionally arises in public discussion is often greatly exaggerated. Children are healthily resistant to teachers who

20

purvey propaganda, and there is plenty of reason to believe that is true in the Soviet Union. The virtue of the Soviet system is that the values - whether you share them or not - are explicit and for the most part unconcealed. Many take them, but there are those who leave them too.

Notes

1. V. Mitina, 'Znachenie opyta sovetskoi shkoly i popytki ego fal'sifikatsii', Narodnoe obrazovanie, no. 11, 1985, pp. 83-5.

2. Private information given at a meeting in the Ministry of Education of the USSR, Moscow, September 1984.

3. A useful introductory section appears in J. Dunstan, 'Soviet Moral Education in Theory and Practice', Journal of Moral Education, vol. 10, no. 3 (May 1981), pp. 192-202. Another useful and short article in English is D.H. Long, 'Soviet Education and the Development of Communist Ethics', Phi Delta Kappan, vol. 65 (1984), pp. 469-72.

4. N.I. Boldyrev, Metodika vospitatel'noi raboty v shkole (Moscow, 1981).

5. Ibid., p. 4.

6. Ibid., p. 30.

7. Quoted by S.M. Rosen, Education and Modernisation in the USSR (Addison-Wesley, London, 1971), pp. 137-8. (Shortened and adapted.)

8. 'Constitution (Fundamental Law) of the Union of Soviet Socialist Republics, Adopted at the Seventh (Special) Session of the Supreme Soviet of the USSR, Ninth Convocation, on 7 October 1977' in Institute of Marxism-Leninism, CPSU Central Committee, Leonid Il'ich Brezhnev: A Short Biography (Pergamon Press, Oxford, 1977), pp. 191-240, especially pp. 207-11. The original can be consulted in Konstitutsiya (Osnovonoi zakon) SSSR (Izdatel'-stvo politicheskoi literatury, Moscow, 1977), pp. 23-5.

9. Programmy vos' miletnei i srednei shkoly: Khimiya. (Prosveshchenie, Moscow, 1983), p. 1.

10. I.D. Zverev, and M.P. Kashin, Sovershenst-vovanie soderzhaniya obrazovaniya v shkole (Moscow, 1985), pp. 191-208.

11. G. Walker, Soviet Book Publishing Policy (Cambridge, 1978), especially p. 9.

12. For this part of the discussion I have relied heavily on this review article: J. Muckle, 'Questions of Moral Upbringing and Character Training in Some Recent Soviet Educational

Publications', Journal of Russian Studies, no. 45 (1983), pp. 41-9.

13. N.M. Beeshu, Vospitatel'nogo znacheniya detskogo fol'klora (The educational significance of children's folklore) (Kishinev, 1980).

14. One of Boldyrev's works is detailed above, note 4. I refer also here to his Nravstvennoe vospitanie shkol'nikov (The moral upbringing of schoolchildren) (Moscow, 1979).

15. The first of these books is entitled Klassnyi rukovoditel' (Moscow, 1978). (The title means 'The class tutor'.) The second is referred to in note 4 above.

16. O nravstvennom vospitanii podrostkov (On the moral education of adolescents) (Moscow, 1979).

17. Tovarishcheskaya vzaimopomoshch' shkol'-nikov (Moscow, 1981).

18. V.K. Kotyrlo, Rastet grazhdanin (The citizen grows) (Kiev, 1980).

19. B.V. Busheleva, Pogovorim o vospitannosti (Let's talk about civilized behaviour) (Moscow, 1980).

20. S. Mikhalkov, Vse nachinaetsya s detstva (It all begins in childhood) (Moscow, 1980).

21. J. Muckle, 'Classroom interactions in some Soviet and English schools', Comparative Education, vol. 20, no. 2 (1984), pp. 237-51 (especially 238-42).

22. 'Etika i psikhologiya semeinoi zhizni', Vospitanie shkol'nikov, no. 6 (1984), pp. 42-9.

23. K.A. Khadzhinov, 'Iz opyta raboty po polovomu prosveshcheniyu i vospitaniyu shkol'nikov', Biologiya v shkole, no. 5 (1986), pp. 45-9.

24. Ibid., p.49.

25. Ann Feltham, 'Education for Family Life in the USSR', Soviet Education Study Bulletin, vol. 4, no. 1 (1986), pp. 1-11, contains a valuable account of attitudes to sex education.

26. A. Akhverdov, 'Zabota o nravstvenno-eticheskom vospitanii', Narodnoe obrazovanie, no. 12 (1985), pp. 11-13.

Chapter Two

RECENT DEVELOPMENTS IN POLITICAL EDUCATION IN THE
SOVIET UNION

John Morison

I have discussed the development of political
education in the USSR to 1981 and its impact in an
earlier article. (1) The present essay continues the
story to May 1986. Since 1981, Brezhnev has died,
Andropov and Chernenko have come and gone, and
Gorbachev has arrived with an obvious determination
to effect major changes. Fundamental educational
reforms have been initiated in 1984. None of these
events has diminished the importance to the
leadership of political education, defined both in
specific terms within the school and higher-
education curricula and in general as a wide-ranging
programme of endeavours and activities designed to
enlist the population at large as conscious and
dedicated builders of Communism. Rather, the
increased stress on political education, which was
noticeable in the 1970s and culminated in the decree
of 26 April 1979 'On the Further Improvement of
Ideological and Political-Educational Work', has
been maintained and if anything developed still
further.

Pronouncements by the Leadership. On 15 June 1983,
the Central Committee of the Soviet Communist Party
approved a new decree entitled 'Essential Questions
of the Ideological and Mass-Political Work of the
Party'. This accepted that progress had been made
since 1979, but noted that some serious deficiencies
remained and that not all party committees were
giving due attention to this area. It was emphasised
that 'the further improvement of ideological
activity and the raising of its effectiveness is one
of the most important tasks of the Party'. Addressing
the Central Committee on the same day, the General
Secretary Yu. V. Andropov said:

23

> It is necessary decisively to raise all our
> ideological, upbringing and propaganda work to
> the level of those large and complex tasks which
> the party is undertaking successfully in the
> process of perfecting developed socialism.
> Party committees at all levels and each party
> organisation must understand that ideological
> work has all the more moved to the forefront
> notwithstanding the importance of other
> questions with which they have to concern
> themselves (economic, organisational and
> other).

The press, radio and television, oral propaganda and
the huge network of academic establishments of all
types were to be used as weapons in raising the level
of political consciousness of the masses and of their
productivity at work. (2)

It was at this plenum that the decision to
undertake a major reform of the school system was
announced. The final guidelines for this reform were
approved by the Supreme Soviet on 12 April 1984. The
most notable features of these measures are
structural changes and the great emphasis given to
labour training and work experience. Nevertheless,
when Deputy Chairman and Politburo member G.A. Aliev
presented the reforms to the Council of Ministers he
insisted:

> The formation of a scientific Marxist-Leninist
> world view in boys and girls must be paramount
> in all this work. The school is called upon to
> lay a firm foundation of communist convictions
> in its pupils, to bring them up in a spirit of
> internationalism and brotherly friendship among
> peoples, and to rear patriots of our
> multinational motherland who will always be
> ready to come to its defence. By the time they
> have finished their secondary education our
> youth must fully understand the salient
> features of the present stage of social
> development, must possess class self-
> consciousness, and must know how to defend our
> ideals and to repulse hostile ideologies
> firmly. The reform creates the prerequisites
> necessary to raise the level of all work on the
> communist education of the younger generation
> to that of the high demands made on us by life,
> and to prepare active and courageous citizens
> who will be supremely loyal to the party and to
> the people. (3)

M.S. Gorbachev devoted a large section of his address to the 27th Congress of the Communist Party of the Soviet Union on 25 February 1986 to ideological matters. His general theme was the need for greater dynamism and creativity in this area in order to secure genuine mass involvement in building the new society.

> Any of our plans will hang in the air if people remain indifferent to them and if we do not manage to arouse the working and public activity of the masses, their energy and initiative. The foremost condition of accelerating the socio-economic development of the country is to turn society to new tasks and to engage the creative potential of the people and of each work collective in carrying them out. (4)

An authoritative definition of political education was given in the new Programme of the Communist Party of the Soviet Union which was approved by the 27th Congress on 6 March 1986 and replaced the Third Programme, which had been adopted under Khrushchev in 1961. Eight main objectives were identified. (1) All the Soviet people should have a deep understanding of Marxist-Leninist teaching and a world outlook which will raise their political culture, and will consciously involve them in working out the Party's policies and in actively implementing them. Marxism-Leninism is seen not as a static theory but as one that is creatively developing in the light of new discoveries and of the experiences of the worldwide communist, working class, national-liberation and democratic movements.
2. A deep respect for and readiness to undertake conscientious work for the common good should be formed in each Soviet citizen, whether that work be intellectual or physical. Work is defined as a sacred duty and as the foundation of the communist training of the personality.
3. Communist morality should be strengthened as progress is gradually made towards Communism. Communist morality is defined as having three essential characteristics. It is collective. Its basic principle is 'one for all and all for one' and it is incompatible with egoism, self-love and self-seeking. It is humanistic. It thereby inculcates a respect for work and promotes comradely collaboration and mutual help, goodwill, honesty, simplicity and modesty in both personal and public life. It is active and energetic. This means that it rouses

citizens to new work and creative achievements, to enthusiastic participation in the life of the collective and of the whole country, to active rejection of all that contradicts the socialist way of life, and to pertinacious struggle for communist ideals.

4.   Patriotic and internationalistic education will imbue Soviet man with love for the motherland of the October Revolution and with pride for the historical achievements of the first socialist state in the world. This will be combined with proletarian and socialist internationalism, and with a feeling of class solidarity with the workers of brotherly countries and with all who fight against imperialism for social progress and peace. Under this heading, the multinational composition of the USSR is acknowledged and the commitment of the Party to ensure friendly and brotherly relations between the Soviet nationalities is reaffirmed. Manifestations of nationalism and chauvinism, of nationalistic narrow-mindedness and egoism are not to be tolerated. Additionally, military and patriotic education is seen as remaining an important aspect of ideological work. Citizens must be made ready to defend their socialist homeland, if needs be at the cost of their lives.

5.   The need to educate people to respect Soviet laws and the rules of a socialist society is stressed. More than that, intolerance of any breaches of socialist legality and a readiness to participate actively in the preservation of law and order must be developed.

6.   Atheistic education is promoted in a manner which shows a surprising sensitivity to the rights of believers. Thus, a scientific-materialist world view must be widely disseminated in order to overcome religious prejudices, but in a manner 'which does not offend the feelings of believers'. The constitutional guarantees of freedom of conscience will, it is said, be strictly observed, although the Party condemns attempts to use religion to damage the interests of society and the individual. It is interesting to note that the most important component part of atheistic education is now considered to be 'the raising of the work and public activity of people, their enlightenment and the wide distribution of new Soviet rites and customs'.

7.   All manifestations of alien ideology and morality must be combated, together with all negative phenomena connected with survivals from the past in the consciousness and conduct of the people. Under

this heading comes the campaign to improve work
discipline, to root out embezzlement and bribery,
speculation and sloth, drunkenness and hooliganism,
private property psychology and money-grubbing
greed, servile flattery and sycophancy.
8.   Stress is laid upon the battle against bourgeois
ideology in a period of sharp ideological conflict
between the two conflicting world views of socialism
and capitalism. In this context, the task of
political education is to take to the people the
truth about real socialism and the domestic and
foreign policies of the Soviet Union. The inhumane
character and the exploitative essence of
imperialism must be exposed. The Soviet way of life
should be extolled and high political consciousness
and watchfulness be formed in the Soviet people. (5)

Motivation. There can thus be no doubting the extreme
importance given by the present Soviet leadership to
political education, both within the educational
system and in society at large. All educationalists,
party agitators and members, and workers in the media
are exhorted to commit themselves wholeheartedly and
fully to this struggle. Even though the Brezhnev era
may itself be under a cloud and many of Brezhnev's
associates retired, dismissed or in some cases
disgraced, the same imperatives with regard to
political education continue to apply.
     In considering the motivation of the Soviet
leaders in this area, four main themes stand out in
their pronouncements. Firstly, they continue to
believe in the existence of a dangerous threat of the
ideological subversion of the population through a
wide-ranging and powerful campaign of propaganda,
blandishments and misinformation by the United
States and her imperialist allies. In his speech of
14 June 1983 on the ideological and mass-political
work of the Party, K.U. Chernenko emphasised that:

     The class enemy has openly announced its
     intention to liquidate the socialist order.
     President Reagan has issued a summons to a new
     "holy crusade" against Communism. And
     imperialism sees "psychological warfare" as one
     of the main means of achieving its aims. This is
     being conducted by the West on the most extreme
     and, one might say, hysterical anti-Soviet and
     anti-communist note. The enemy has embarked on
     downright piracy on the ether. We are now
     confronting an attempt to organise a real

informational and propaganda incursion against
us and to turn the radio and television channels
into weapons used to interfere in the domestic
affairs of other states and to carry out
subversive activities.

This is why we must develop offensive
counter-propaganda work on a wide scale not only
in the international arena but also at home. (6)

Since his succession to political power M.S
Gorbachev has reiterated this theme on a number of
occasions. His lengthy speech to the 27th Party
Congress on 25 February 1986 gave considerable
attention to the misdeeds of United States
imperialism, and to its increasingly aggressive
egoism. The USA was depicted by him as a skilled
class enemy with an enormous and sophisticated
machine for mass propaganda which was engaged in a
campaign of psychological warfare to win people's
minds. (7) In his television address to the nation on
14 May 1986, devoted to the accident at the Chernobyl
nuclear power station, Gorbachev appeared to speak
with genuine passion and conviction in accusing the
USA and some of its allies of spreading misinformation about the incident as part of this
campaign to discredit the Soviet Union internation-
ally and 'to sow new seeds of distrust and suspicion
of the socialist countries'. (8)

Secondly, political education continues to be
seen as vitally important in helping to bind together
a multinational state. The new Communist Party
Programme puts as one of its aims 'the development of
a unified culture for the Soviet people which is
socialist in content, diverse in its national forms
and internationalist in spirit. This culture is based
on the best achievements and original progressive
traditions of the people of the USSR.' (9) Whereas in
the late tsarist period the Orthodox faith was widely
regarded in official circles as the cement which
would bind together the component parts of the
Russian Empire, socialism is now regarded as
fulfilling a similar function. A good command of
Russian in addition to the native language is held to
be essential to the development of this common
socialist culture. It also provides access to
scientific and technological information and serves
as the means of internal communication within the
USSR. In his report on the 1984 School Reform G.A
Aliev, himself a non-Russian, stressed that deepened
study of the Russian language had been discussed with
great interest. Russian had been voluntarily

accepted by the Soviet peoples as the means of communication between the nationalities:

> The Russian language, the language of friendship and brotherhood, has organically entered the lives of millions and millions of our compatriots of all nationalities, has given them access to the riches of world civilisation and has become a factor of exceptional socio-political and cultural significance. (10)

All secondary-school graduates should be fluent in Russian. Even if one discounts the speculation of some Western scholars that nationalism is a force about to tear the Soviet Union asunder, the leadership has to take account of national differences as a potential basis for internal discord and therefore to make strenuous efforts to achieve a common political culture.

The third and fourth themes are closely interrelated. Economic growth is now seen as largely depending on increased productivity by the workforce. This has to be achieved not solely by better training and a higher level of skill but also by improved attitudes and a greater commitment to the goals of society. Political education has a key role to play in this improvement in attitudes. Economic success will, however, be achieved at the risk of backsliding in political consciousness. Greater individual initiative and material incentives to stimulate increased effort could lead to the 'bourgeois' vices of consumerism and individualism or, in other words, of putting individual goals before those of society as a whole. In a society officially classified as having entered the stage of 'advanced socialism' and as proceeding towards full Communism such ideological degeneration cannot be permitted. Moreover, there must be a flood of eager volunteers to serve in local soviets and other such bodies if 'socialist democracy' is to become an effective reality.

In their quest for continued economic growth, Soviet planners are facing genuine problems. Traditionally, Soviet leaders have been able to achieve economic growth by pouring in increased manpower from the natural increase in population and the surplus millions living in the countryside. Now the surpluses in the countryside have been largely exhausted, and in most areas agriculture itself is facing a labour shortage. The exception is in Central Asia and parts of the Caucasus where fertility

29

remains high, but the increased population is reluctant to move to other areas of labour shortage. Elsewhere declining fertility rates have generally threatened to lead to a decline in the population with a consequent reduction in the size of the labour force of working age. A recent slight recovery gives only the prospect of stability but not of growth. (11) Increased labour productivity is therefore vital.

Whilst strong central direction of the economy will remain, Gorbachev has been strongly committed through his career to the removal of the excessive bureaucratic supervision at the factory and shopfloor level which has traditionally made the Soviet worker a passive instrument in the industrial process. Workers should be free to organise their own work, with material rewards for displays of initiative and increased effort which lead to genuine improvements in results, but financial penalties for those who fail to fulfil their contracts with the state. It should be noted, though, that these incentives will be offered to small groups rather than to individuals. Collectivism has thus been a recurring theme of Gorbachev's economic measures and speeches. Economic and ideological imperatives demand that political education should implant this collectivism deep in the Soviet citizens' consciousness. (12)

Measures
The School Curriculum.
The main thrust of the 1984 School Reform was to make the Soviet school system more responsive to the needs of the economy. (13) By mounting a new course in computing, by strengthening the labour and vocational training element and by introducing compulsory 'socially-useful productive labour' and actual work practice it is hoped to produce a work force that will be more alert to the demands of a modern economy and more flexible in outlook and better trained to use new technology to the best advantage. By reducing the number of those entering the final two years of the secondary general school for a more academic training and by increasing the proportion of those completing their education at a secondary vocational-technical school it is hoped to solve the problem of shortages of skilled labour in key areas of the economy. (14) By introducing a course on career choice into the curriculum and by preparing teachers to give more effective career guidance it is planned to reduce the present

30

.astefully high labour turnover and to correct the ailure of many schoolleavers to enter the job for which they have received specific training. The ntroduction of these new elements into the timetable combined with the explosion of knowledge in the raditional subjects has necessitated the adding of a .ear to the period of compulsory education by owering the starting age to six.

The main purpose of the school reform is herefore not to promote political education. .owever, a comparison of the new model curriculum ith that for 1981-1982 (see Appendices 2.1 and 2.2) hows that the concern of the leadership in this area s not empty phrase-mongering. At a time when competition for space on the timetable is intense, hose subjects which are most specifically connected ith political education, namely history, social .tudies and the principles of the Soviet state and aw, maintain the total number of hours devoted to hem unchanged. The emphasis on an adequate command .f Russian as a prime means of the political .ducation of the non-Russian nationalities is eflected in the provision of an additional three .ours per week of language study in their schools .ver all years of the course save the first. In .ussian schools, Russian language and literature has mproved its privileged position, now receiving a .otal of 80 hours per year spread over 11 years as .pposed to the previous total of 72 hours per year .ver ten years. This is largely accounted for by .even hours per week in the new first year, although .here is some readjustment in subsequent years. The .ourse material in this subject is deliberately .eared to serve the ends of political education. .ptional courses in the seventh to eleventh years .nclude such subjects as 'the contemporary .deological struggle and youth', 'bourgeois .ationalism in the service of imperialism' and 'learn .rom Lenin the art of argument and counter-propaganda'. These courses vary from school to .chool. (15)

Reforms in Higher Education. Higher education has .ecently become the object of considerable attention .y the Soviet leadership. In his speech to the 27th .arty Congress on 25 February 1986, Gorbachev .emanded that the research potential of higher .ducational establishments should be utilised more .ffectively. They contained over 35 per cent of the .oviet Union's research and educational personnel

31

but carried out no more than 10 per cent of the research projects. Links between industry and the universities should be strengthened, both in research and teaching. (16) In response to this urging, the Party's Central Committee published a draft plan for the reform of higher and secondary specialised education on 1 June 1986. This will be widely discussed and, following usual procedures, will no doubt be confirmed within a few months with minor modifications. The main purpose of these measures is to improve the contribution of higher education to the economic development of the country. The key is seen to be closer collaboration between universities and industry, agriculture and research institutes. Standards of university staff must be raised, their research become more relevant to the real needs of the economy, and their students display more initiative and be wider in outlook, with direct production work experience in their specialism. Continuing education must be built into the career pattern of specialists in industry in order to keep them abreast of technological innovations. Investment in equipment, facilities and salaries in higher education must be significantly increased. The authority of the Ministry of Higher Education must be strengthened in order to combat the lack of coordination, inefficiency and dissipation of effort caused by the subordination of the specialised secondary and 894 higher educational establishments to a total of 74 all-Union and republic ministries and departments.

It would be very misleading to assert that political education is a prime concern in this reform. Nevertheless, it is not ignored, and one of the objectives is stated to be 'to make fuller use of the great possibilities offered by educational establishments in improving the communist training of the youth and of all workers'. In addition to references throughout the text to the need to raise the level of political knowledge and ideological commitment of staff and students, one of the ten sections of the draft plan is devoted exclusively to political education. This makes explicit the need to strengthen work on the ideological-political, work and moral training of students and pupils. The main practical means of achieving this goal in political education is seen to be a unified academic programme in social sciences for all types of higher educational establishments, the publication of new textbooks and the setting up of a state examination in Marxism-Leninism. The need for state examinations was a favourite theme of conservatives in the late tsarist period who thereby hoped to control the syllabus and curb freethinking by staff and students. In the contemporary context, the purpose must surely be to ensure that students are forced to take their political studies seriously and to prevent leniency in internal examinations in a subject for which it is notoriously difficult to arouse the enthusiasm of students, particularly in the science and technical faculties. (17)

Textbooks. Soviet education theorists have for many years seen the rewriting and improvement of textbooks as a prime way of improving standards. The 1984 school and 1986 higher educational reform plans have yet again demanded new textbooks. One important objective is to combat overloading of the curriculum by eliminating superfluous detail. Livelier books, avoiding the 'formalism and dogmatism' which is now so roundly condemned, are expected to improve standards of learning. The new teaching programmes 'should be at a high level but accessible to all pupils', (18) a high ideal which it will be difficult to achieve. The new textbooks in all subjects are also supposed to be yet further impregnated by ideological content, thus making political education effective and all-pervasive throughout the curriculum. The geography course is, for instance, to be subjected to particularly radical overhaul. It is intended that the new programme should expose pupils more fully to key concepts in developing their world outlook and in particular 'to the idea of the advantages of the socialist order'. (19) In higher education, new textbooks are also promised for the unified programme in social sciences which will operate everywhere. (20)

Teaching Methods. A conscious policy decision was taken in the late 1970s to dispense with Stalinist teaching methods in the Soviet schools whereby pupils sat in disciplined rows uncritically imbibing masses of information which they were then required subserviently to repeat without alteration as proof that they had mastered the contents of the syllabus. The process of learning had to become an active one, pupils had to work things out for themselves, and were to be encouraged to relate their own experiences to the theoretical material which they were studying. (21) The campaign against 'formalism' and

'dogmatism' and for effective political indoctrination has reached a new level of intensity under
Gorbachev. In his speech to the 27th Party Congress
he demanded 'maximum concreteness in ideological
work'. (22) The new Party Programme states that:

> Ideological activity must be distinguished by a
> close union with social practice, by its depth
> of ideological and theoretical content, by a
> full and exact account of the realities of
> internal and international life and of the
> enhanced intellectual needs of the working
> population, by its closeness to people, by its
> truth and by its reasoned and concrete nature.
> (23)

Practical steps are being taken to ensure that
these exhortations do not fall on deaf ears in the
educational system. The 1984 school reforms retain
the lesson as the basic means of instruction, but
stress that there must also be lectures, seminars,
colloquia, practicals and consultations in the
senior grades. The 1986 proposals for the reform of
higher education make similar demands. Specifically
discussing the political education programme in the
shape of the compulsory social sciences course, the
importance of removing the last traces of dogmatism,
scholastic theorising and uncritical approaches is
emphasised. 'The quality of lectures must be raised.
Key questions of theory must be made clear in them,
as must the practical tasks of social development and
the domestic and foreign policies of the CPSU. There
must be an increase in the time devoted to seminars
and to individual work with the students.' It is
hoped that this will implant in students the need and
habit of systematic and thorough study of the works
of Marx, Engels and Lenin and the documents of the
CPSU. To help the transformation of knowledge into
communist convictions students should be involved
much more widely in propagandising the Party's
policies among workers and in ideological work with
children and adolescents. To make an individual
approach to learning possible, it is promised that
there should be no more than 15 students in groups
for seminars, practicals and laboratory work. A
gradual reduction of class size in the secondary
school is also intended, to a maximum of 30 pupils in
grades one to nine, and of 25 in the top two years.
For foreign-language classes and work training class
sizes will be five fewer. Laboratories, equipment and
student hostels will be improved. (24)

The new teaching methods are probably most easy
to adopt in subjects such as labour training and
modern languages. Many of the success stories
published as models for others to follow have
concentrated on these two areas. Concrete examples,
analysis of real-life situations and role-playing in
a workshop situation fit naturally into place in work
training classes. Pupils can produce their own
answers to problems of increasing productivity, of
improving the layout of workshops and so on. Results
can be compared. An atmosphere of creative,
collective endeavour can be created. The teacher's
role is to stimulate discussion and new ideas, to
encourage a 'nonstandard approach' to the solution of
problems and to sum up the results of the exercise
and provide a general evaluation. In modern
languages, intensive methods are being widely used,
with a large volume of material being covered in a
short space of time. Dialogues, conversations,
playing situations and technical aids are in wide
use. (25)

In work training, modern languages and the like,
individual work and the pupils' own ideas and input
can lead to a variety of results and conclusions,
provided that they are within the general framework
of the objectives of the course. In the social
sciences, history and other more specifically
political subjects, the results must be uniform, even
if the material and methods used in achieving them
may be diverse. Seminars, projects, debates and
discussions have to lead to the ideologically correct
conclusions, which gives little ground for
manoeuvre. Active teaching methods are very well-
suited to political education in a pluralistic
society, but are much more problematic in the Soviet
Union where a monopoly of political wisdom is still
claimed by the sole ruling party which moreover
possesses an ideology which it considers to be
uniquely and exclusively correct. Nevertheless,
teachers are admonished to enliven their classes by
the introduction of debates and disputes, using
material drawn from the pupils' own experience which
illustrates the negative as well as positive aspects
of Soviet life. Lip-service and passive acceptance of
the received truth is not enough. Pupils and students
must become convinced and engaged supporters of the
Party's policies.

A recent development in Party policy has made it
easier to enliven political education by drawing on a
wider range of material. References to glasnost',
('openness' or 'publicity'), have recently become

35

ritual in speeches by political leaders. Addressing a conference on the ideological work of the Party on 10 December 1984, Gorbachev himself identified this as a vital component in raising the level of activity of the work force. 'Broad, timely and frank information is proof of trust in the people and of respect for their intellect and feelings, and for their capacity to evaluate events for themselves'. It is a real means of struggle against bureaucratic distortions in Party and state organs, and leads to a more considered approach to the taking of decisions. It improves control over their implementation and helps to eradicate faults and negligence. Gorbachev returned to this theme in his speech to the 27th Party Congress on 25 February 1986. Greater openness (glasnost') was a matter of principle for the leadership. It was a political question. There could not be democracy, political creativity by the masses or their participation in administration without it. It was necessary for the psychological readjustment of party officials and as a guarantee of a responsible attitude to the common cause by millions of workers, collective farmers and intellectuals. The truth was needed about decisions taken both at a national and a local level. Caution should be rejected in discussion of failings, omissions and difficulties. Such publicity would expose the slipshod and dishonest and help to uphold legal and moral standards. (26) Peter Frank has pointed out that this does not mean that there will be openness as conventionally understood in Western countries. Rather, it involves a selective increase in the flow of information to the public. Control over information and its release will remain vested in the Party and the public will not have the right to claim independent access to it. (27)

Whatever the limitations may be in the implementation of this policy, it has definitely resulted in a significant increase in the amount of information available to the public. This provides new opportunities for the political educator, but also faces him with a challenge. In his efforts to stimulate debate and achieve a lively and fresh approach to his subject he has at his disposal a greater range of raw material about the realities of the Soviet Union at a national and local level, both of a positive and a negative character. However, the officially approved ideological conclusions still have to be unanimously reached, no matter how diverse, wide-ranging and even contradictory class discussions may be. This is far more difficult to achieve than the previous ritual imparting of information about Marxist theory and party policies and history to be formally repeated by the recipient in examinations. One can see the possibility of deficiencies illustrated by examples from local life getting out of hand, particularly at the senior secondary and tertiary level. Teachers of political education are bound to be very cautious in experimenting with a more active methodology.

The Teacher. The continued but increased emphasis on political education, the demand that it be conducted in all areas of the curriculum and the call for new and more active teaching methods have increased the importance of the role of the teacher, and also the stress to which he is subjected. To quote an authoritative source, 'a real teacher not only transmits knowledge, but also preaches progressive ideas and passionately believes in the significance and strength of his words'. Each teacher must be a propagandist of the ideas of the Party, and should have deep ideological convictions, political maturity and class feeling. (28) The Soviet teacher is 'an active warrior on the ideological front'. (29) As such, teachers are expected to be involved not just in the classroom but also in the out-of-school activities with the youth and with parents, and with the population at large. Social-political clubs and clubs of legal knowledge have to be organised, political information disseminated and discussions and 'schools for the young lecturer' organised. (30) Round-table discussions, question-and-answer sessions, political debates and conferences are other activities singled out for encouragement. Strong pressure is exerted on teachers to join the ranks of the society _Znanie_ (Knowledge), which is active in propagandistic work. (31)

In an effort to raise the status of the school teacher, large pay rises were promised in the 1984 school reforms. These turn out to be of the order of 30 to 35 per cent, with a wide variety of extra payments for qualifications and responsibilities. (32) Pay rises, improved pensions and better living conditions have been promised to staff in higher education in the draft plan of 1 June 1986. (33) It still remains to be seen whether this additional money will in the long run attract more male recruits to the teaching profession and decrease the significant numbers of those leaving the profession for other employment.

37

The reforms announce a determined effort to raise the qualifications of teachers at all levels, with specific reference being made to the level of political preparation. Teaching programmes in pedagogical institutes are being reorganised to take account of this with many special seminars on ideological themes. Courses in Marxism-Leninism are being put on for subsequent in-service training every four or five years. Pedagogical instruction of university students destined to become teachers is to be improved. 'Greater attention will be paid to the political education of lecturers in higher education. They will study relevant problems of Marxist-Leninist theory and the policies of the CPSU and the work of methodological seminars will be activised'. (34) Teachers are being pressed to enrol in schools of scientific communism, of which over 128,000 existed in 1984, and in evening universities of Marxism-Leninism organised by local Party committees. (35) None of these measures may be new, but the scale of operations and their intensity has been increased.

Political Education Outside the Educational System. From its early days the Soviet Communist Party has insisted on the implementation of an all-embracing programme of political education in society at large. Youth organisations, trade unions, party agitators, clubs for the dissemination of knowledge, the arts, the press and the mass media in general have traditionally always been mobilised in this campaign. The general profile of work in this area remains unchanged, although the Komsomol has received admonishments to improve its effectiveness and Party officials have been sharply reminded that inflated figures of lectures delivered do not necessarily mean that the desired effect has been achieved. Two changes in emphasis are of significance. One, the demand for glasnost' or more openness and information in the press and on radio and television has already been noted. This has already had a significant effect, and recent commentaries in Pravda suggest that some progress is to be expected. (36) The second development is the increased emphasis being given by the school reform to political work in the place of residence by ideological groups composed of Party and soviet officials, elected deputies, Komsomol workers, agitators, teachers and others. Meetings on political themes, work on organising their own museums, involvement as 'young friends of the militia' or 'young Dzerzhintsy' and the like are intended to reinforce the work being done elsewhere. (37)

Conclusions

Gorbachev has continued the enhanced emphasis given to political education by his three immediate predecessors since the late 1970s. Indeed, he has given added urgency to the campaign to raise the political consciousness of the population as a vital precondition of economic gowth and improved living standards. Changes in the organisation of political education have tended to be ones of emphasis rather than of substance. Nevertheless, there is a note of real immediacy and determination in his repeated pronouncements on the subject.

It is easy to equate words and intentions with deeds and achievements. The gap between theory and reality has been evident in the Party as well as in the population. Stephen White has recently pointed out that successive Party resolutions tend to recapitulate failings listed in their predecessors. Promises to ensure speedy reform are followed by criticisms of particular Party committees for their failure to take effective action. (38) This cyclical process shows no sign of ending. The latest ideological exhortations have been followed by widespread press criticism of 'formalism', and by specific attacks on identified Party committees. For instance, complacency and worse in Armenia was assailed in Pravda on 21 October 1984. The survival of religious ceremonies and other such 'negative phenomena' in Uzbekistan was cited in Pravda Vostoka on 30 July 1985 as evidence of the need to improve political education among the masses, and young people in particular. More recently, the Gorkii regional committee was publicly admonished by the Central Committee for its failure effectively to implement the 1984 school reforms. (39) There has been much criticism of the Komsomol for relative inactivity.

If the Party itself cannot be relied upon to perform its supervisory role adequately, it is not surprising that there should be backsliding among the population at large. It is relatively easy to measure the impact of the Soviet political education process in terms of the school curriculum and the formal process of dissemination of propaganda among the population. What is difficult or indeed impossible to assess with confidence is the impact of this on the political consciousness of the Soviet people as 'conscious creators of history', mobilised and displaying 'creative initiative' in constructing a new life. It is now legitimate for Soviet writers and political figures to criticise the late Brezhnev period for failings in this area and for serious deficiences in 'socialist discipline'. (40) A number of studies by Soviet sociologists have given substance to the view that political education has been deficient in its impact. (41) The 1984 and 1986 educational reforms are intended to improve this situation. However, there are significant obstacles to be overcome.

Overloading of the curriculum remains a problem and seems to have been made worse by the reforms. Despite the introduction of an extra year of study, the number of compulsory hours per week at school remain virtually unaltered, and the addition of a demanding new course on computer technology adds to the burden of the final two years. What really adds weight, though, are the 23 hours of socially-useful productive labour and the 82 days of labour practice (see Appendix 2.2). Even if the new textbooks do succeed in eliminating some details, this seems unlikely to compensate children adequately for the extra hours thrust upon them. The problem will be especially acute in the non-Russian national secondary schools, with their extra 30 hours of language study. In the competition for the time and attention of pupils, the pressure to improve technical skills and competence seems likely to prevail over that to increase the attention given to political education throughout the syllabus. To expect teachers of natural science, mathematics and technology to devote considerable attention to the formation of the materialistic world outlook of their charges is unrealistic at a time when they have to impart the basics of their own subjects in a limited number of hours in a crowded timetable.

Although the activisation of teaching methods may succeed in modern languages and some of the technical subjects, political education is more problematic. The activisation of social science and history teaching, which has traditionally been noted for the dry recitation of factual information, may be most desirable but imposes a high degree of responsibility on the teacher. Lessons which are enlivened by debates referring to inadequacies in Soviet society may easily provoke fundamental criticisms of the regime and of the Soviet political

40

system. It is not surprising that the stress in recent issues of educational journals has tended to be on counter-propaganda work. It is much easier and safer to score points off the opposing bourgeois world of capitalist societies of which the pupils have no first-hand experience or knowledge than to conduct serious discussion of the problems of the Soviet Union. But even here the continued desire to wean Soviet youth from its devotion to the 'bourgeois deviations' of Western fashions and pop music seems unrealistic. The problem of inculcating Soviet patriotism in a younger generation that has not experienced revolution or war is recognised as a real one. The emphasis on school museums and on ceremonies to commemorate the war and revolutionary events may spread knowledge but is divorced from the experiences of real life on which the new teaching methods are supposed to be based.

The improved status of the teaching profession which is fundamental to the successful implement-ation of the reforms will depend on the realisation in practice of the ambitious plans for improved initial training, subsequent regular in-service courses and improved teacher-pupil ratios. The large pay rises should improve morale and help to develop wholehearted involvement both inside and outside the school. However, the average monthly salary in education was 138.2 rubles in 1983, significantly less than the national average wage of 182 rubles. (42) Thus, even the present large rise will bring teachers as a whole only up to the national average, and regular subsequent increments will be needed to raise the relative status of the teaching profession significantly.

The main purpose of political education for the present leadership, to obtain active involvement and hence increased productivity by the masses, will be difficult to achieve. References to Russia's past might lead one to expect the appeal to collective endeavour to strike a responsive chord. Certainly there is a genuine collectivist tradition in Russian history. Some aspects of the peasant commune, the artel', the consumer cooperatives and the zemlyachestva (worker or student associations of those who had migrated to the city from the same region) were genuinely popular in origin and deep-rooted in popular affection. The peasant commune, however, had another side to it, as an institution imposed by the state for its own purposes, to ensure collective responsibility for the payment of taxes and dues. There is a similar dualism in the leadership's present enthusiasm for collectivism. On the one hand, Gorbachev's enthusiasm for the small work brigade paid according to its collective results and allowed a degree of initiative corresponds to the genuine popular tradition. On the other hand, retention by the state of strong central planning controls in matters such as resource allocation and prices may well lead in many instances to unfairness to the work brigades who may not earn as much as comrades in other geographical areas or industrial sectors as the result of decisions taken at the centre in the interests of the larger national collective rather than the local one.

Much will depend on the degree of credibility which Gorbachev succeeds in developing and maintaining. He will have to prove himself different in deed as well as word from former political associates whose complacency and venality is now at least openly hinted at. Tangible economic results will be needed, otherwise Gorbachev's recent promise at the 27th Congress to raise real wages by 60 to 80 per cent in 15 years and to double resources available to improve living standards will haunt him just as Khruschev was haunted by his ill-advised pledge to achieve full Communism by 1980. For political education there is a real dilemma. The exhortations of the educators are designed to produce extra popular effort which will achieve economic results, but the results themselves are needed before genuine and enduring increased effort and political commitment can be obtained.

Notes

1. John Morison, 'The Political Content of Education in the USSR' in J.J. Tomiak (ed.), <u>Soviet Education in the 1980s</u> (Croom Helm, London and Canberra, 1983), pp. 143-172.
2. <u>Pravda</u>, 16 June 1983, p.2.
3. <u>Uchitel'skaya gazeta</u>, 13 April 1984, p.1.
4. <u>Pravda</u>, 26 February 1986, p.9.
5. <u>Pravda</u>, 7 March 1986, p.6.
6. <u>Pravda</u>, 15 June 1983, pp.2-3.
7. <u>Pravda</u>, 26 February 1986, pp.2-3, 10.
8. Text printed in <u>Pravda</u>, 15 May 1986, p.1.
9. <u>Pravda</u>, 7 March 1986, p.6.
10. <u>Uchitel'skaya gazeta</u>, 13 April 1984, p.2.
11. Warren Eason, 'Demographic Trends and Soviet Foreign Policy: The Underlying Imperatives of Labor Supply' in S. Bialer (ed.), <u>The Domestic Context of Soviet Foreign Policy</u> (Westview Press,

Boulder, Colorado and Croom Helm, London, 1981), pp. 203-26.

12. For a discussion of Gorbachev's record in this area, see George G. Weickhardt, 'Gorbachev's Record on Economic Reform', Soviet Union, vol. 12, no. 3 (1985), pp. 251-76.

13. For a discussion of the 1984 school reforms see John Dunstan, 'Soviet Education Beyond 1984: A Commentary on the Reform Guidelines', Compare, vol. 15, no. 2 (1985), pp. 161-187 and John Dunstan, 'Soviet Schools and the Road to Reform', Journal of Russian Studies, no. 49 (1985), pp. 27-37.

14. John Dunstan in his article in Compare, cited in note 13, reported a conversation with Mr Yu. Yu. Ivanov, head of the Chief Department of Schools at the USSR Ministry of Education, in which the latter stated that the proportion of middle-stage completers entering the new tenth grade (old ninth grade) of the general school must decrease to 30%. This conflicts with a recent published statement by the President of the Academy of Pedagogical Sciences of the USSR that 45% of middle-stage completers will continue at secondary schools, that 40% will enter secondary vocational-technical schools, as opposed to the 60% posited by Dunstan, and that 15% will enter technicums, as opposed to Dunstan's projection of 10%. See M.I. Kondakov. 'Pedagogicheskaya nauka i reforma shkoly', Sovetskaya pedagogika, no. 4 (1986), p. 10. If Kondakov is correct, the more radical of the reformers have suffered a setback.

15. V.E. Taranenko, 'Kontrpropaganda v sisteme ideino-politicheskogo vospitaniya', Sovetskaya pedagogika, no. 4 (1986), pp. 38-9; Pravda, 29 April 1984, pp. 1 and 3.

16. Pravda, 26 February 1986, p.4.

17. Pravda, 1 June 1986, pp.1-3.

18. Kondakov, 'Pedagogicheskaya nauka', p.12.

19. I. Mel'nikov, 'Soyuz znaniya i truda', Sovetskaya pedagogika, no. 4 (1986), p.19; V.P. Maksakovskii, 'Puti sovershenstvovaniya shkol'nogo uchebnika', Sovetskaya pedagogika, no. 3 (1985), pp. 58-62.

20. Pravda, 1 June 1986, p. 2.

21. Morison, 'The Political Content', pp. 153-4.

22. Pravda, 26 February 1986, p.10.

23. Pravda, 7 March 1986, p.6.

24. Uchitel'skaya gazeta, 17 April 1984, p.2; Pravda, 1 June 1986, pp.2-3; Pravda 29 April 1984, p.3.

25. For instance, A.I. Novikov, 'Metody

povysheniya poznavatel'noi aktivnosti uchashchikh-sya', <u>Sovetskaya pedagogika</u>, no. 2 (1986), pp. 87-91.

26. <u>Pravda</u>, 11 December 1984, p. 2; <u>Pravda</u>, 26 February 1986, p.7.

27. Peter Frank, 'Conspiracy of Silence a Setback for Gorbachev,' <u>Times Higher Educational Supplement</u>, 16 May 1986, p. 15.

28. 'Sovetskii uchitel', leading article in <u>Sovetskaya pedagogika</u>, no. 9 (1985), p.3.

29. D.S. Yagofarova, 'Podgotovka uchitelya k ideologicheskoi rabote', <u>Sovetskaya pedagogika</u>, no. 7 (1985), p. 66.

30. Ya. V. Sokolov, 'Kontrpropaganda v protsesse pravovogo vospitaniya', <u>Sovetskaya pedagogika</u>, no. 6 (1985), p.27; Taranenko, 'Kontrpropaganda', p. 39.

31. L.-S. Lomize, 'Vsesoyuznoe obshchestvo "Znanie" i reforma shkoly', <u>Sovetskaya pedagogika</u>, no. 5 (1985), pp. 42-6.

32. <u>O reforme obshcheobrazovatel'noi i professional'noi shkoly</u> (Politizdat, Moscow, 1984), pp. 106-11.

33. <u>Pravda</u>, 1 June 1986, p. 3.

34. <u>Uchitel'skaya gazeta</u>, 3 June 1986, p. 3 and 17 April 1984, p. 3; Taranenko, 'Kontrpropaganda', p. 37.

35. 'Sovetskii uchitel'', p.5; L.D. Gireva, 'Uchitel' v sovetskom obshchestve, ego rol' v formirovanii lichnosti uchashchegosya', <u>Sovetskaya pedagogika</u>, no. 2 (1985), pp.73-4.

36. See, for instance, Dmitrii Lyubosvetov, 'Vremya na ekrane', <u>Pravda</u>, 19 May 1986, p.3.

37. V.A. Protopopov and F.K. Kondrat'eva, 'Mikroraion - vazhnyi faktor vospitaniya', <u>Sovetskaya pedagogika</u>, no. 9 (1985), pp.38-42; V.G. Bocharova, 'Edinstvo semeinogo i obshchestvennogo vospitaniya shkol'nikov', <u>Sovetskaya pedagogika</u>, no. 7 (1985), p.13; V.O. Kut'ev, 'Razvitie vospitatel' nykh funktsii shkoly', <u>Sovetskaya pedagogika</u>, no. 1, (1985), p.48. Dzerzhinsky was the first head of the Soviet secret police.

38. Stephen White, 'Propagating Communist Values in the USSR', <u>Problems of Communism</u>, vol. 34 (November-December 1985), pp. 10-11.

39. <u>Pravda</u>, 10 August 1985, pp.1-2.

40. R. Yanovskii, 'O vozrastayushchem znachenii politicheskogo soznaniya', <u>Kommunist</u>, no. 1 January 1986, pp.21-2.

41. White, 'Propagating Communist Values', pp. 3-7.

42. <u>Narodnoe khozyaistvo SSSR v 1983 g</u>

(Finansy i statistika, Moscow 1984), pp. 394 and 411.

Appendix 2.1: Model Curriculum for Soviet Primary, Eight-Year and Secondary Schools, 1981/2 (1977/8 in parentheses, where different (d))

Subjects		Periods per week by grade (year)									
	I	II	III	IV	V	VI	VII	VIII	IX	X	Total
1. Russian Language	12	11	10	6	6	4	3	2	–	–	54
2. Literature	–	–	–	2	2	2	2	3	4	3	18
3. Mathematics	6	6	6	6	6	6	6	6	5	5/4 (5)	57.5 (58)
4. History	–	–	–	2	2	2	2	3	4	3	18
5. Soviet State & Law	–	–	–	–	–	–	–	1	–	–	1
6. Social Studies	–	–	–	–	–	–	–	–	–	2	2
7. Nature Study	–	1	2	1 (2)	–	–	–	–	–	–	4 (5)
8. Geography	–	–	–	–	2	3	2	2	2	–	11
9. Biology	–	–	–	–	2	2	2	2	1	2	11
10. Physics	–	–	–	–	–	2	2	3	4	4/5 (5)	15.5 (16)
11. Astronomy	–	–	–	–	–	–	–	–	–	1	1

Appendix 2.1: continued

	1	2	3	4	5	6	7	8	9	10	Total
12. Technical Drawing	–	–	–	–	–	–	–	1	1	– (1)	2 (3)
13. Chemistry	–	–	–	–	–	2	2	2	2	2	10
14. Foreign Language	–	–	4 (–)	3 (4)	2 (3)	2 (3)	1 (2)	1 (2)	1 (2)	–	14 (16)
15. Art	1	1	1	1	1	–	–	–	–	–	6
16. Music & Singing	1	1	1	1	1	1	1	–	–	–	7
17. Physical Education	2	2	2	2	2	2	2	2	2	2	20
18. Labour Training	2	2	2	2	2	2	4 (2)	4 (2)	4 (2)	–	24 (20)
19. Elementary Military Training	–	–	–	–	–	–	–	–	2	2	4
Total Compulsory Periods	24	24	27 (24)	29 (30)	29 (30)	29 (30)	30 (31)	32	32	32	280 (281)
20. Options	–	–	–	–	–	–	2	3	4	4	13

Notes: a The 1977/8 periods are for the RSFSR (from Sbornik prikazov i instruktsii Ministerstva prosveshcheniya RSFSR, no. 7, 1977, p. 27).

Source: Byulleten' normativnykh aktov Ministerstva prosveshcheniya SSSR, no. 12, 1980, pp. 27-30.

Appendix 2.2: Model Curriculum for the Secondary General School (a) (1984 Reform)

Subjects	I	II	III	IV	V	VI	VII	VIII	IX	X	XI	Total
							Periods per week by grade (year)					
First Language and Literature	7	9	11	11	11	9	6	5	5	3	3	80
Mathematics	4	6	6	6	6	6	6	6	6	4/5	4	60.5
Principles of Information Science and Computer Technology	–	–	–	–	–	–	–	–	–	1	2	3
History	–	–	–	–	2	2	2	2	3	4	3	18
Principles of Soviet State and Law	–	–	–	–	–	–	–	–	1	–	–	1
Social Studies	–	–	–	–	–	–	–	–	–	0/2	2/1	2.5
Ethics and Psychology of Family Life	–	–	–	–	–	–	–	–	0/1	1/0	–	1
The World Around Us	1	1	–	–	–	–	–	–	–	–	–	2
Nature Study	–	–	1	1	1	–	–	–	–	–	–	3
Geography	–	–	–	–	–	2	3	2	2	2/1	–	10.5
Biology	–	–	–	–	–	2	2	2	2	1	1/2	10.5
Physics	–	–	–	–	–	–	2	2	3	4/3	4	14.5
Astronomy	–	–	–	–	–	–	–	–	–	–	1	1
Chemistry	–	–	–	–	–	–	–	3	3/2	2	2	9.5
Technical Drawing	–	–	–	–	–	–	1	1	–	–	–	2
Foreign Language	–	–	–	–	4	3	2	2	1	1	1	14
Art	2	1	1	1	1	1	1	–	–	–	–	8
Music and Singing	2	1	1	1	1	1	1	–	–	–	–	8
Physical Education	2	2	2	2	2	2	2	2	2	2	2	22
Elementary Military Training	–	–	–	–	–	–	–	–	–	2	2	4
Labour and Vocational Training (b)	2	2	2	2	2	2	2	3	3	4	4	28
Total	20	22	24	24	30	30	30	30	31	31	31	303

Appendix 2.2: continued

Subjects	Periods per week by grade (year)											
	I	II	III	IV	V	VI	VII	VIII	IX	X	XI	Total
Socially-useful Productive Labour (compulsory) (c)	-	1	1	1	2	2	2	3	3	4	4	23
Options	-	-	-	-	-	-	2	2	2	4	4	14
Labour Practice (in days) (d)	-	-	-	-	10	10	10	16	16	20	-	-

Notes:

(a) The Model Curriculum for the 11-Year National Secondary General School is exactly the same as the above, except that the first entry and Total read as follows:

	I	II	III	IV	V	VI	VII	VIII	IX	X	XI	Total
First and Russian Language and Literature	7	12	14	14	14	12	9	8	8	6	6	110
Total	20	25	27	27	33	33	33	33	34	34	34	333

(b) Vocational training takes place in grades VII-XI. One period a week in each of these grades is devoted to the course 'Principles of Production. Choosing a Career'.

(c) The time allocated to compulsory socially-useful productive labour may be concentrated.

(d) 3 hours a day in grades V to VII, 4 in grades VIII to IX, 6 in grade X.

Source: Byulleten' normativnykh aktov Ministerstva prosveshcheniya SSSR, no. 6, 1985, pp. 24, 25.

Chapter Three

ATHEISTIC EDUCATION IN THE USSR

John Dunstan

Introduction

The USSR's constitution of 1977 affirmed the equality
of citizens before the law 'without distinction ...
of attitude to religion' (article 34), and guaranteed
its citizens 'freedom of conscience, that is the
right to profess or not to profess any religion'. It
went on to say, however, that citizens had the right
'to conduct religious worship or atheist propaganda'
(article 52). The latter alternatives are not
equivalent in the scope for action that they provide,
and they indicate the thrust of the Soviet
educational effort in this sphere. The proceedings of
the June 1983 Plenum of the Central Committee of the
Communist Party of the Soviet Union offer a more
explicit policy statement. Having noted that 'a
section of the people still remain under the
influence of religion, and, to be blunt, not all that
small a section either', the Plenum resolved 'more
actively to conduct the propagation of scientific-
materialist views among the population and to devote
more attention to atheistic education'. (1)

In general, the 1977 constitution said nothing
new about religion and atheism. It restated a legal
position going back to 1929, or in some respects to
1918. Let us briefly trace this. A decree of 20
January 1918 separated the church from the state and
the school from the church. It gave every citizen the
right to profess any religion or none and abolished
all existing restrictions on these freedoms. It
guaranteed the freedom to perform religious
ceremonies as long as there were no infringements of
public order. But it also deprived religious bodies
of the right to own property; all such property was
nationalised, and buildings and objects for use in
worship were to be made available to such bodies free
of charge. Religious instruction was banned as a

50

school subject and restricted to the private domain. (2) The former state church, the Orthodox Church, saw this as disastrous, while other denominations which had suffered under the old regime largely welcomed it. To take a little-known example, the small Methodist Church increased its membership from some 200 on the eve of the Revolution to nearly 2,300 by 1928. (3)

The Stalinist crackdown on religion during the First Five-Year Plan brought changes in legislation. In April 1929 youth work on the part of religious associations was prohibited, as indeed were meetings, events and facilities of any kind except for worship. In May the phrase 'freedom of religious propaganda' in the then constitution was replaced by 'freedom of worship'. The Soviet Union's entry into the Second World War effected a sort of concordat between the state and the churches, but soon restrictions were reasserted. On 10 November 1954 with the issue of the decree 'On Errors in Conducting Scientific Atheistic Propaganda among the Population' the tone was set for a prolonged antireligious campaign, which after a false start began in earnest five years later. In the early 1960s it became illegal to involve young people in any religious group which caused their health to be harmed or led them to reject social activity or civic duties. (4) In 1959 an optional course in scientific atheism had been launched on a modest scale in higher education. In January 1964 the Party issued a decree 'On Measures to Improve the Atheistic Education of the Population', making this course compulsory at all universities and at those higher educational establishments training teachers, doctors and agronomists, introducing the specialism of scientific atheism on higher education courses in history and philosophy faculties, increasing the antireligious content of school work, and calling for the wide use of extracurricular and out-of-school activities in atheistic upbringing and for the organisation of atheistic work among parents and in the community. (5) Khrushchev's downfall followed in October, but his hard line can still be detected in the Pioneer Leader's Handbook published in 1968, (6) as we shall see below. The extensively rewritten Handbook issued in 1982 is significantly less strident and more sophisticated in its approach, but makes it clear that the atheistic education of the young Soviet citizen is still squarely on the agenda, (7) as the June 1983 Plenum has since confirmed.

In the present overview of atheistic education

in the USSR, with particular reference to the school,
four questions will be addressed. Why is atheistic
education important? Who are involved in the teaching
and learning of atheism? How is it taught and learned
(in what settings and by what means)? And difficult
though it is to evaluate, how well is this done?

Why is Atheistic Education Important?

Atheism is taught, just as religion is opposed, for
doctrinal reasons, social reasons, and reasons of
practical politics; all three could be called
ideological. According to Marx and Engels, religion
is both invalid and deluding. According to Lenin, it
is not only deluding, it is loathsome and dangerous.
A quick scan of the doctrinal sources is in order,
starting with the most celebrated one. 'Religion',
Marx wrote, 'is the sob of the oppressed creature,
the heart of a heartless world, the spirit of
conditions utterly unspiritual. It is the opium of
the people ... The removal of religion as the
illusory happiness of the people means the demand of
the people for their real happiness' (Introduction to
Critique of Hegel's Philosophy of Right, 1844). (8)
Thus religion, for Marx, is a perverted consciousness
of the world, arising because society itself is
perverted, and invented by men and women to help them
to cope. Two years later in The German Ideology Marx
and Engels presented their famous statement of the
materialist view of history. By materialism is meant
the doctrine that matter or the material world alone
possesses reality, and that the products of mind are
simply reflexes of this material world. In the
classic phrase, 'Life (being) is not determined by
consciousness, but consciousness by life.' Thus God
and other wholly spiritual entities can exist only in
man's imagination. (9) In A Contribution to the
Critique of Political Economy (1859) Marx expressed
this in terms of the base and superstructure:
material production and production relations are the
basic determining forces of history and the
foundation of society, and on this base arises the
superstructure of ideas and institutions, including
religious ones. (10) Engels returned to the subject
in Anti-Dühring (1877) and Ludwig Feuerbach and the
End of Classical German Philosophy (1886). He
maintained that morality, like religion, is derived,
as part of the superstructure, from class relations,
so there are no eternal moral laws; and since
primitive man personified natural forces as God,
there was no creation or primacy of spirit over

nature. (11)

This is not the place for a critique of these teachings, but a point should be added that is often forgotten. Marx and Engels were atheists, but regarded attacks on religion as misconceived, 'because the real enemy (was) the perverted social order'. (12) They considered that, as history advanced, religion was in any case withering away. In fact, some would argue for the humanity of the statement about the opium of the people; they would say that Marx saw religion as a need, a humane response to an inhumane world. By contrast, Lenin was vehemently opposed to religion, using much stronger language than Marx. He called it 'one of the most vile things existing in the world' (articles on Tolstoy, 1908-11); and the word translated as 'vile' is gnusnyi, meaning 'verminous'. A religion of pure moral conviction and love would present a dangerous alternative to Bolshevism. (13) Lenin altered Marx's 'opium of the people' to 'opium for the people'; religion was no longer essentially something that wretched humanity had invented to make its suffering bearable, but something that the ruling class doled out to keep the people quiet. In 1917 the Orthodox Church, conservative, cosseted and chained as part of the tsarist power structure, was seen to stand in the way of Soviet progress, and when the Revolution came, action against it was quick to follow. Doctrinal reasons thus provided Lenin with support for social and political ones.

But, it may be objected, that was a long time ago. Surely, with all those years of Soviet power, the Orthodox Church and other religious bodies can no longer be an obstacle, let alone pose a threat? So why do believers still suffer, as our media are constantly telling us? Agreed that atheistic education must have been necessary from the official point of view at one time, why is it so necessary now? Indeed, the first and third questions are sometimes publicly asked by the Russians themselves. If they listen to foreign radio stations, they may privately ponder the second too.

To some extent these questions answer each other. If there are still religious people against whom action has to be taken, then atheistic education must still be necessary. If atheistic education still exists, then there must be some perceived threat or other need for it. It does not seem enough to regard it as one of various ways of stimulating Party activism, and thus to explain it as a self-generating and self-justifying activity, even though it does

perform this function. (14) The fact must be that
religion still exists on a sufficient scale to be
regarded as doctrinally, socially and politically
dangerous.

There have been a number of sociological studies
on attitudes to atheism and religion in the USSR. A
five-(sometimes seven-) point scale of classification is often used: convinced atheists (sometimes
subdivided with natural (<u>stikhiinye</u>) atheists); non-
believers; indifferent; waverers; and believers
(sometimes divided into believers by tradition and
convinced believers). A 1971 survey of the adult (18-
plus) population of the city and region of Kaluga,
located some 150 kilometres south-west of Moscow and
chosen as typical of a wide area of the European
USSR, elicited the following broad results, which
also offer an urban-rural comparison: convinced
atheists, city 20.6 per cent, region 11.5 per cent;
non-believers, 54.3 per cent and 51.0 per cent;
indifferent, 12.5 per cent and 12.9 per cent.
Summing these three categories as a broad index of
non-belief, we have a figure of 87.4 per cent for
town and 75.4 per cent for country. Waverers
constituted 5.3 per cent in the city and 9.3 per cent
in the region, and believers 6.2 per cent and 14.6
per cent, yielding a broad index of belief as 11.5
per cent urban and 23.9 per cent rural. No answer was
given by 1.1 per cent of urban respondents and 0.7
per cent of rural, but the anonymity of respondents
was stated to have been preserved. (15) Other
conclusions reached in this investigation were that
convinced atheism was strongest in those aged from 21
to 40, rose with levels of education, training and
occupational status, and occurred with significantly
higher frequency in men than women. The researcher
saw a connection between the lower representation of
highly- and medium-skilled workers in the rural
population (9.7 per cent, compared to 33.2 per cent
urban) and the greater incidence of religiousness
there. (16) These conclusions are scarcely
startling, but it should perhaps be added that, if
anything, the figures for religious belief somewhat
understate - and inevitably over-simplify - the wider
picture as presented in the classic study by Lane,
(17) which must be consulted for a detailed analysis.
In strongly Catholic areas religiousness is much more
widespread, whereas in new towns it is non-existent
or virtually so. Its extent among young people will
be considered in our evaluative section below.

Now let us consider a cautionary tale from the
<u>Pioneer Leader's Handbook</u> that was in use until

recently.

At a school, the older pupils were getting ready to join the Komsomol. They were all excited and the school was unusually animated. Just one girl remained apart, indifferent to the general exhilaration. 'Lida, are you going to join the Komsomol?', the other youngsters asked. 'No', Lida replied, 'I can't.'

'I can't.' And nobody was disturbed by these words. Nobody even remembered that Lida had spoken them once before. That was when she had been invited to join the Pioneers, some years previously. Only then Lida had answered, 'I can't, Mummy won't let me', but now she said, 'I can't, I believe in God.' Five years of indifference and unconcern from her classmates and the Pioneer leaders and teachers had turned this little girl, scared of her parents, into a teenager with a crippled mind. With her parents' help, Lida was lured away by members of a sect. They acted much more cleverly and energetically than the school. They organised a music group and choir for the young people, they sent their preachers around the local villages, and settlements to fish for weak souls.

And they found them, where the Pioneer brigades and Komsomol organisations were slack, where there was no friendship and respect for one's comrades in the detachments, where church people were not resisted, and where children's minds had not been toughened. (81)

Although this story has been excised from the new Handbook, presumably because its emotive language was felt to be out of keeping with the more sensitive and sophisticated approach now in favour, it exemplifies a number of reasons why religion is considered dangerous. Religion causes people to withdraw from collective life, or rather from officially approved forms of it. It is believed to warp people's minds and personalities, and to be especially damaging when they are at a formative stage. It presents an alternative and alien ideology, and may do so both attractively and aggressively. Another factor, absent from the Lida case, is that it may reinforce nationalistic tendencies. Let us explore those points a little further, supplementing the traditional objections with some current emphases.

The conventional picture of religious believers

55

being preoccupied with gloom and doom, and inflicting unhealthy introspection upon their young recruits, is still encountered in popular atheistic propaganda, but writers on atheistic education sometimes give the impression that this stereotype reduces the real challenge of their task. The truth is that 'youngsters from believing families usually enjoy taking part in religious ceremonies'. This particular authority links such participatory enthusiasm with adolescent strivings for autonomy and the wish to seem adult. (19) With all this sense of communality and music groups too, it cannot be taken for granted that the state-sponsored collectives, if only they put their houses in order, will automatically prove more appealing to young people. Atheistic education has to operate on a much broader front than this.

Some writers, however, still stress a negative, otherworldly image of religion. (20) To be sure, certain faiths practised in the USSR may encourage the development of personality traits very different from the outgoing public-spirited activism that is meant to be displayed by New Soviet Man. Islam, for example, is criticised for its teachings of total submissiveness to the will of one's parents and of Allah, and of predestination which encourages passivity. (21) Some Christian sects have an outlook vying with pure Islam in its unworldliness; some religious parents regard the communist youth organisations as of the devil and refuse to let their children participate; some communities run clandestine religious schools and youth clubs. Most often, it appears, the young, whether Muslim or Christian, learn to keep their religious beliefs secret. (22) Religion, functioning within the parameters imposed upon it, then incurs the charge of turning young Soviet citizens into hypocrites. (23)

Particularly in more recent atheistic literature, the tendency of some priests and theologians to operate, as it were, within the world rather than outside it is regarded as equally, if not more, insidious. Modern churchmen, it is claimed, try to undermine the typical understanding of the scientific-atheistic world-view as inalienably opposed to and firmly refutatory of religion, by attempts to reconcile science and religion, while postulating God as the prime mover. (24) What atheistic educators find particularly dangerous, given young people's search for heroes, is the presentation of Jesus Christ as the ideal moral pattern. Here too they see modernisation at work, with stress not on the traditional Jesus of gentleness and forgiveness, but on the man who sacrificed his life for the people's good and happiness. (25) Lenin, in other words, has a rival, and it would be difficult to invent a greater heresy than that.

In general, however, the moral alternative offered by religion is presented by educationists in less dramatic terms, though as no less inimical to the Soviet world-view. The Orthodox Church, they report, tries to exploit people's deeply-held ideals of patriotism and intolerance of social injustice, and has lately espoused national liberation struggles as a manifestation of divine creative activity. (26) The fondness of Baptist and Reform Baptist (initsiativniki) preachers for sermons on public and private morality, established in the 1960s as comprising up to a third of all sermons, (27) has evidently been sustained in more recent times, if their activities in the Chuvash Autonomous Republic may be taken as typical. Such themes comprised between 30 per cent and 35 per cent of Baptist and Reform Baptist preaching (though in some respects the two groups differed widely, as in the latter's well-known defiance of Soviet power). (28) Churches and sects alike are said to capitalise on young people's natural interest in moral ideas and the meaning and purpose of life. (29) Numerous Western radio stations also get in on the act, while Reform Baptists (30) and Lithuanian Catholics actually assert that atheism and true morality are incompatible. (31)

Religion is also dangerous because it may reinforce nationalistic tendencies within the USSR. In Soviet parlance, clergy and sectarians propagate the notion of unity of national and religious affiliation: every true Lithuanian must be a Catholic, every Uzbek a Muslim. (32) Catholicism, in Lithuania and elsewhere, is additionally suspect since it is beholden to a leadership in the West. Attempts 'by present-day clerical extremists ... to use religion to achieve reactionary political objectives, undermining the friendship of peoples and reviving bourgeois-nationalist sentiments' were denounced by the Lithuanian Communist Party in the spring of 1982 and made the occasion of an atheistic education campaign. (33)

Particularly, however, one thinks of Islam. The Soviet policy of dismantling the religious and cultural unity which pertained to Russian Islam before the Revolution and of developing separate nations with their own languages, cultures and traditions was successful only up to a point. The emergence of a degree of national consciousness has not obliterated the common heritage. (34) The tenacious linkage beteween the national and the religious does not appear to have been weakened either by the official Islamic leadership's policy of going along with Communism - justified by a fatalistic outlook combined with a belief in the eventual inevitable triumph of Islam - or by the constant campaign of antireligious activities to which it has nevertheless been subjected. The quietism of the Islamic authorities has not led to rank-and-file apostasy, as might have been expected, partly because Muslims do not depend upon a priesthood and partly because of the existence of a popular unofficial movement which is particularly vigorous in rural areas. This also maintains a network of secret Koranic schools, teaching elementary Arabic and religious knowledge. (35) Further problems for the Soviet authorities are the difficulty of prompting the local intelligentsia and officials into action against what they regard as the national religion, (36) and the propagandistic activities of 'reactionary foreign Islamic centres' in the wake of events in Iran and Afghanistan. (37) These various factors provide no guarantee that the average Muslim citizen of the USSR has very deep religious belief, but he does have a strong sense of custom and community that crosses geographical boundaries.

To sum up, atheistic education is important in the USSR because religion is considered to have no rightful place in Soviet society, being irrational, illusory and dangerous. It is thought dangerous because it impedes progress in a militantly secular society, it impairs the desired spirit of collectivism, it allegedly cripples the personality development of the individual, and it encourages alternative and thus anti-Soviet loyalties. The Party, by definition the determining and directive force, is not in the business of power-sharing, nor can it be expected to abnegate its unique responsibilities in any area of life. It is therefore bound to oppose religion and religious institutions. Religion, regarded as a survival of the past in people's consciousness, is doomed to disappear but is slow in going because of the lag of consciousness behind reality. As the nineteenth-century revolutionary Zhelyabov said of history, it needs a push. Atheistic education ought to be the most enlightened impellent.

Who Are Involved in the Teaching and Learning of Atheism?

Atheistic education is officially held to be an essential component of the upbringing of Soviet citizens. For maximum success it should start as soon as possible, while they are at their most formative stage, especially since it is then that they are particularly vulnerable to any religious influences present in their own families. Since the study of atheism is conceptually difficult, however, more formal teaching - except by way of illustration through other subjects - must wait until the age of 16 and after. So both children and students are on the receiving end. But parents need educating as well; only a relatively small minority pass on religious beliefs to their children, but a lot more have their children baptised, and more still observe religious holidays. (38) Many of the sects are on the lookout for converts. It is a truism nowadays that responsibility for education cannot be restricted to the family and the school and that every adult needs to be a teacher; such 'teachers' themselves have to be taught, so atheism has also to be part of lifelong adult education.

Atheistically missionary-minded adults are, one suspects, much thinner on the ground than the authorities would like. So atheism has to be inculcated by more conventional agents: adult education lecturers, higher education lecturers, schoolteachers, youth leaders, and Party and Komsomol activists. Less conventional, from our point of view, is the involvement of the children's collectives themselves. To make a comparison of opposites, we in British education are used to religious study groups and to evangelistic students; evangelistic children, however, are not so common. But in the USSR, as it may be remembered from the Lida episode, the children themselves are expected to have a role in the atheistic teaching and exhortation of their religious or backsliding fellows, and even, as will be seen, in showing their old grandmothers the error of their ways.

Before the effective teaching of atheism can begin, the person in charge must have some knowledge of the individuals involved. We have the impression that this has been increasingly emphasised with the more sophisticated requirements of recent years. A series of preliminary appraisals should be carried out. Which pupils may be under religious influence? Oblique questions and observation can be of service here. Responding to the question why there has been a

good harvest this year, a child may reply that it was
due to help from God. Drawings done at home or on
free-choice subjects may yield pointers. A child not
joining in games may be acting on the instructions of
religious parents. (39) Then, what sort of religious
influence are they under? It is thought to be easier
to deal with children and teenagers believing vaguely
in the existence of some supernatural power than
those affected by traditional religion, because the
former are more open to conviction by rational
argument. (40) On the other hand, reasoned argument
is a waste of time with the children of Reform
Baptists, who may well have trained them to resist it
anyway; it is better to concentrate on involving such
children in interesting activity with their
classmates, who should be well disposed to them.
(41) Children from Orthodox families are thought to
fall somewhere in the middle; they are more concerned
with liturgy and tradition than with doctrine, and
parents are less likely to be rigid in the event of
disagreement. Here a more fruitful approach will be
to demonstrate the negative and backward in the
historical role and practices of Orthodoxy.

Atheistic education involves all children, not
merely those exposed to religious influence, as
teachers sometimes seem to think. It is necessary to
identify the position of each child on the gamut of
belief and non-belief, in categories such as those
mentioned earlier. Natural atheists, for example,
whose attitude to religion has been formed mainly
under environmental conditions, can usually be
turned quite soon into convinced atheists when given
a scientific basis for their views. Those who are
indifferent to both religion and atheism also require
such teaching, but in addition need to be shielded
against any possibility of religious influence. (42)
Waverers merit particularly tactful handling; they
are in a conflict situation - between faith and
doubt, family and school - and shrink from talking
about such matters with their peers, but are
interested in organised debates and literature on the
subject. Here the teacher should come to the aid of
the child individually, co-ordinating activities
with club leaders and librarians and also visiting
the parents. (43) Thus the corollary of the universal
remit of atheistic education should be an awareness
that the group consists of individuals potentially in
differing situations and with varying needs.
Educators nevertheless have to follow a general line
and operate most of the time in collective settings
with global methods, and it is to these that we now

turn.

How is Atheism Taught and Learned?

It is appropriate to begin this section by first
considering approaches to atheistic education
generally, and then referring to some statements on
the aims and objectives of atheistic education in the
school. Atheistic education in general has two sides,
two approaches, and the problem is choosing the right
one or achieving the right mix. There is the 'pro-
atheistic' approach and the 'antireligious'
approach. (44) The pro-atheistic approach is
essentially positive and exhortatory; the antireligious approach, rather, is negative and admonitory.
The pro-atheistic approach involves creating an
optimistic and progressive environment, bringing
about social change that will make people better
educated and healthier and happier, so that they will
not want a substitute ideology. It also entails
setting up holidays and rituals for people to enjoy
in place of religious ones. The antireligious
approach stresses criticism of religious beliefs and
practices, exposing believers as fools or
hypocrites, and going sometimes as far as harassment.
The two approaches are combined in an enormous
propaganda campaign, devised and supervised by the
Propaganda Department of the Central Committee of the
CPSU and implemented at the usual administrative
levels, usually with the assistance of 'councils of
scientific atheism'. (45) There is disagreement as to
which approach is more fruitful, as to whether
activists should concentrate on strengthening
atheists or on converting believers and agnostics to
atheism, and as to the use of coercion. (46) In
general, the Propaganda Department prefers the image
of conducting a positive struggle for atheism. For
'struggle against religion', then, read 'liberation
of people's consciousness and behaviour from
religious survivals'. (47) In theory, blunt coercive
measures to this end are now frowned upon, but local
practice may present a very different picture.

Returning now to the atheistic education of the
younger generation, we shall take two recent
statements of aim and objectives, supplementing a
more terse set with a more elaborate one in
parentheses. (48) The aim of atheistic education in
the school is to bring up convinced atheists (to form
the pupils' materialist world-view and corresponding
life-purposes). Its objectives are (1) the re-
education of religious children (overcoming the

61

influence of religion in pupils under the sway of religious ideas); (2) the formation of atheistic conviction in non-religious pupils (developing in them a conviction, based on knowledge of the social and natural sciences, of the worthlessness of the religious-idealistic world-view, and an irreconcilable attitude to it); and (3) the education of militant atheists (teaching them to assert their atheistic convictions, backed by argument; developing in them the desire to conduct atheistic propaganda and simultaneously forming a positive attitude to scientific atheism and an understanding of its value). Thus the final goal is no mere intellectual assent, but an internalised conviction that must also find purposeful expression.

In the 1950s, student teachers were told: 'Scientific-atheistic education is effected first and foremost in the process of subject-teaching, in lessons.' (49) This is still important, as we shall see, but since then the emphasis has shifted to extracurricular activities and parent education, matching the general trend, characteristic of the 1970s and continuing into the 1980s, of increased concern about upbringing. The Pioneer Leader's Handbook in use over this period set out a short syllabus of atheistic education. The youngest Pioneers, aged 10-11, were to be told about the origin of religious beliefs and festivals and the harmfulness of religion and belief in God. Suitable literary and artistic works were to be used, and the children were to prepare and mount 'atheist's corners' (small displays) at school and at home. In the next year the youngsters, while continuing certain of these endeavours, should be taught to 'understand the antiscientific essence of religion' and organise anti-religious evenings for their juniors, parents and local people, with talks and visual aids. The 13-to 15-year-olds were to develop 'conscious atheistic views and a militant antireligious stance', and, in addition to some of the activities already noted, were to carry on active work with children from religious families. (50) There is some progression here, from talk to action. We note that by the age of twelve the children are regarded as potential propagandists of atheism generally, and that by 13 or 14 they are thought capable of atheistic evangelism of their religious fellows.

The 1982 Pioneer Leader's Handbook goes into much more detail on forms of atheistic education, but without relating them to age groups. It lists, for

62

example, 'discussions, interesting science and technology evenings, questions and answers on atheistic subjects, observations of nature and explanations of natural phenomena, thematic film festivals, debates, quizzes on natural science subjects, young atheists' clubs, excursions to museums and planetariums, reading and dicussion of books on leading scientists and naturalists, and atheistic exhibitions'. (51) The young atheists' club has the role of a ginger group, catering for activists and encouraging the other Pioneers. Starting as an informal study circle, it should develop into a number of teams organising talks and other events for the school, compiling resource banks for its young speakers, issuing news bulletins and a monthly wall newspaper, (52) and possibly also spreading the atheistic word in the local community.

Recent materials of the how-to-do-it variety provide further evidence of the desire to use tact and avoid confrontation, thus contrasting markedly with the aggressive style of the Khrushchev era and its aftermath. Here is another anecdote from the 1968 Handbook.

> It was decided that every Pioneer would set up an atheist's corner at home ... Grandma's icons were hanging in one corner, and on the opposite wall her grandson Seryozha hung a sheet of paper with anti-religious pictures, poems and sayings by scientists and writers. It was headed: 'I am godless'. No sooner had he hung it up than Grandma tore it down and destroyed it. Seryozha hung up another sheet. Again Grandma sailed into action for religion ... Seryozha then went to extremes. He threatened Grandma that he would do the same to her icon. Being a religious person, Grandma feared the divine wrath, and left Seryozha in peace.

The author concludes that although the boy will hardly re-educate an ignorant old woman, his victory is very important because now he will not yield in more difficult situations. (53)

That story has also disappeared from the 1982 Handbook. Threats are officially out. Educators and their youthful helpers must tread carefully in their dealings with the believing child at school and with the family. Under no circumstances must such a child be openly required to renounce his or her faith. (54) The term 'militant atheist' may indeed have counterproductive implications. The battle is

63

against religious ideas, not against the believer as a person. What is needed is patient explanation, (55) most effectively on a one-to-one basis. The slightest lack of tact with a young believer may turn public opinion against him or her, causing withdrawal and alienation; it is essential for such a child to be an active member of a warm and friendly collective at school. (56) On no account should debates take the form of rival presentations from believers and non-believers; rather should the theme be understanding the meaning of life, with criticism of religion receiving less limelight, and the setting should be a fairly intimate one. (57) Here the methodologist is presumably seeking to avoid a situation where the young believer gets into an emotional and embattled state (and/or even outdoes the opposition, as may occasionally happen with a sectarian child (58)).

The 1982 <u>Handbook</u> takes pains to point out that neither the school nor any other public body has the legal right to order parents not to take their children to a registered church, unless physical violence is used. (59) In a locality where religion is strong, it may be essential to avoid atheistic confrontations with parents and bring up the subject obliquely when chatting to them about their children's life in the school collective and the pressures arising. (60) The important thing is to show them kindness and concern for the youngsters' health and moral welfare. (61) Why are parents religious anyway? The teachers' newspaper records an incident which adds a dimension to atheistic education. 'Near a Baptist prayer house the author saw a woman in black, with a girl of about twelve. "Why are you taking <u>her</u>?" the author cautiously asked. "What's wrong in that?" the woman answered defiantly. "Here they don't just talk about helping, they do help ... They bought her a little coat."' The author intervenes, the school is energised, and the widow and her daughter are saved - from the sect. (62) The phenomenon of religiousness may spring from hardship, grief, sickness, or loneliness, and the cause must be tackled first. (63) Thus, it would seem, the atheist appropriates the charismatic gift of caring.

As far as class teaching is concerned, atheistic education is meant to take place through all subjects, although some lend themselves more to it than others. The major subjects most often cited include nature study and biology, physics, chemistry, history and literature. Science lessons, for example, can be used to confute the accounts of

he creation of the world in Genesis. History can
ighlight the church's antiscientific, reactionary
nd cruel role in persecuting people like Copernicus
nd Galileo. As well as the use of prescribed texts,
ttention can be drawn to modern Soviet children's
iction on antireligious themes. One such novel is
ev Ovalov's <u>Remember Me</u>, re-issued in 1976 in an
dition of 100,000 copies. (64) This is a dramatic
story of a schoolboy detective searching for a girl
ho has fallen into the clutches, not of conventional
riminals, but of members of an underground religious
ect (one that actually exists, the True Orthodox
andering Christians). The boy's encounters with an
rthodox priest are of particular interest.

The final year of the senior stage of general
education includes a compulsory course on social
studies (obshchestvovedenie). At the time of
writing, this course was being revised in connection
with the 1984 education reform, so reference will be
ade instead to the materials previously in use. The
syllabus contained two relevant topics. The first,
headed 'Materialist conception of history', referred
to the 'irreconcilability of materialism and
idealism', and this was the main link with the
textbook. The second, entitled 'Spiritual culture of
developed socialism', mentioned 'ways of forming a
scientific world-view; opposition of the scientific
and religious world-view; scientific atheism'. (65)
If one may judge from the teacher's handbooks, these
topics were each intended to occupy one 50-minute
period in a 70-period course. (66) Given that matters
other than religion and atheism had to be included,
the small extent of coverage seems a little
surprising. An alternative handbook for teachers was
still more succinct about it. (67) The textbook
itself devoted little more than two pages in a total
of over 300 to religion and atheism, mainly
antireligious rather than pro-atheistic in approach.
(68) Perhaps this reflects the view that at the age
of 16-17 extracurricular work and illustration
through school subjects continue to be more useful
than straight academic teaching. Certainly, the then
textbook looks heavy going, and a Western
educationist who sat in on a social studies lesson
(not on atheism but the Soviet state) reported that
no attempt was made to render the difficult material
digestible, or to check that the concepts explained
were understood. (69) Though I speak with the tongues
of Marx and Engels, and have not clarity, I am
nothing ... Apparently a few schools run an option
(elective) on atheism, (70) but we have not been able

65

to identify any of the materials used.

At universities and pedagogical, medical and agricultural institutes, 'scientific atheism' is still a compulsory subject, though a minor one. At the Lenin State Pedagogical Institute in Moscow in the late 1970s, 18 hours of lectures and six of seminars were devoted to it, comprising 0.5 per cent of the total workload. (71) In contrast to the school social studies component, it appears to lay more stress on the commendation of atheism than on the criticism of religion. Following a general introduction, the five sections of the textbook are headed 'Religion as a Social Phenomenon' (the essence, principal elements and social functions of religion; historical forms of religion; world religions; national religions; the crisis of religion in present-day conditions); 'Atheism and Social Progress' (the development of atheism in accordance with the laws of humanity's spiritual progress; atheism before Marx; Marxist-Leninist atheism as the highest form of atheism; atheism and the present-day ideological struggle); 'Principles of the Atheistic World-View' (the opposition of the religious and scientific world-view; the natural-science basis of atheism; the materialist conception of history and atheism; the moral content of scientific atheism); 'Atheism and Religion in Socialist Society' (the development of mass atheism in socialist society; specific features of the manifestation, and reasons for the persistence, of religiousness under socialism; Marxism and Leninism on freedom of conscience); and 'Scientific-Atheistic Education' (the scientific principles of Communist Party policy in regard to religion and the church; the system of scientific atheistic education). (72) The students are also required to do some practical work in the form of lectures and talks to the public, perhaps under Komsomol auspices. (73) In faculties of philosophy and history, as mentioned earlier, whole programmes of atheism-oriented courses may be taken, such as the set of four courses leading to a specialism in the history of religion and atheism at the Chuvash State University, comprising 270 hours of lectures, 100 of seminars and 100 of practicals, and including 34 hours on the theory and practice of atheistic education. (74) Elsewhere in higher education, courses on scientific atheism are entirely voluntary and unassessed. (75)

As well as teacher education, in-service training pays a certain amount of attention to atheistic education and the formation of a scientific

66

world-view. One way of illustrating this is to
examine the USSR's standard educational bibliogra-
phy. The four issues for 1984 each contain about 15
such items, though unidentified others may also be
partly relevant. The typical distribution would
perhaps be four general articles or pamphlets on
atheistic education plus two on the scientific world-
view, two on atheistic education in particular
schools or areas, three on atheistic education or
forming the scientific world-view through teaching
(geography and mathematics figuring prominently in
addition to the more usual subjects), one on extracurricular activities, one referring to vocational-
technical schools, and two to teacher education. (76)

Finally mention must be made of two other means
of atheistic education which, while not always
intended exclusively for young people, may have a
special bearing upon them. One is ritual. The purpose
of ritual in revolutionary societies, according to
Lane, is 'to change deep-seated moral orientations'
and '"educate their citizens to this newly chosen way
of life and mobilise them in support of deliberately
cultivated values" and modes of social behaviour'.
(77) As an example of ritual that is specifically
directed at older teenagers, we may cite the Estonian
'Summer Days of Youth' held as coming-of-age rites at
18. They were originally designed as a counter-
attraction to the Lutheran confirmation rite, but
they have developed wider significance as civic
initiation ceremonies. The six-day programme usually
begins with a ball and continues with a series of
social and educational events, with topics ranging
from militant atheism to beauty care! It culminates
in the Day of Maturity with a procession - featuring
white dresses, dark suits, candles and flowers - and
congratulatory speeches, presentations and a grand
concert. (78) This is apparently being imitated in
some of the other republics, but in the RSFSR the
conferment of the internal passport at 16 is the
nearest parallel ceremony, though on a smaller scale.
(79)

There are other secular rituals meant to replace
religious festivals. The well-known New Year
holiday, with a decorated tree, Grandfather Frost and
the Snow Maiden in attendance, supplanted the 'Holy
Days' of the Orthodox Church. A Holiday of Spring has
been instituted in competition with the Orthodox
Easter. (80) Although the Party leadership now
disapproves of interruptions to lawful religious
ceremonies, counter-demonstrations are still on. The
former <u>Pioneer Leader's Handbook</u> recorded one such

67

with approval: 'On May Day morning the whole (Pioneer) brigade paraded round the village to the sound of drums and bugles, demonstrating not only their solidarity with the workers of the world but also their open rejection of the religious customs of their forefathers.' (81) This action was apparently too aggressive to suit the more sophisticated style of the new Handbook.

And then, of course, young people will notice antireligious messages in the mass media which may or may not be specifically targeted on them. Powell has made a fascinating study of a particular case of this: cartoons. (82) Broadly speaking, these either ridicule and try to undermine religion directly, by presenting believers as cynical, stupid or antiquated (or a combination thereof), or they do so indirectly, using religious symbols to make a political point. An example of the former features a rather angry little boy, his grandmother and a toy robot. The boy is wearing overalls and carrying a wrench, thus representing the advanced Soviet worker, who is invariably an atheist. The robot is kneeling before an icon. The boy is saying to the old lady, 'Grandma, what have you been doing with my robot?' (83) While the main aim is to make religious Grandmas look foolish, there may well be the secondary notion that believers are mindless automatons.

As an example of indirect subversion of religion, we have a Brueghelesque picture of Paradise. Angels are picking apples and emptying their containers over the wall into the bags and baskets of devils, who are paying them with cash and the odd bottle. Meanwhile St. Peter snoozes at the gates. Pointing to the angels, one devil is saying to another, 'Nothing that is human is alien to them! (84) This scene, somewhat mystifying to the Western viewer, is satirising collective farm workers who steal the common produce, presumably for private speculation. At the same time, the Book of Genesis takes yet another knock. Yet the resilience of holy writ, religious ceremony and faith is in no way to be underestimated. It is time to consider what effect the enormous input of atheistic effort has achieved and to assess its continuing problems.

How Well is Atheistic Education Carried Out?

One might well suppose that if all the atheistic measures described were implemented widely and efficiently, the secularisation of Soviet society

would be almost complete. Overall there is no doubt
that religious belief has greatly declined since
1917. It also needs to be remembered, however, that
such a decline is usually characteristic of
industrialising, urbanising and generally advancing
societies, whether communist or not. A further factor
over the history of the Soviet period has been
coercion. The decline cannot possibly be ascribed to
atheistic education alone, (85) and it seems
impossible to tell how far it is due to it. There
are, naturally, a goodly number of positive
assertions about it in the mass media.

On the other hand, press reports also show that
officialdom is deeply dissatisfied with the level of
atheistic consciousness among young people. A survey
reported in 1970 showed that only just over 40 per
cent of tenth-graders (then aged 16-17) were
convinced atheists. (86) Even so, it is quite
possible that this figure was artificially inflated
by those who felt it advisable to give the approved
response. The Kaluga inquiry elicited a similar
figure of 39 per cent convinced atheists for students
aged 18-25, though a further 52 per cent were
recorded as non-believers. The shares of the entire
local population aged 18-20 were slightly less
satisfactory: convinced atheists (urban and rural)
32 per cent; non-believers - urban 59 per cent, rural
62 per cent. (87)

What is the proportion at the other end of the
atheism-belief scale? In the same study, waverers
comprised 2 per cent of the students and 1 per cent
of all 18-20-year-olds, and there were no believers
whatsoever among either group. (88) Lane cites
several Soviet estimates published between 1967 and
1975 to conclude that the proportion of believers
among young people ranges around 3 per cent; the
tendency is for it to be higher among sectarians and
in rural areas, lower among Orthodox and in towns.
(89) A detailed survey of atheism and religiousness
covering over 14,000 young men and women in the
Chuvash Autonomous Republic - 600 kilometres east of
Moscow, predominantly rural and traditionally
Orthodox - is sufficiently interesting to reproduce
in full (see Table 3.1). The term 'young people' is
not defined, but most often in such studies signifies
those aged under 30. Salient features of the table
are the much higher incidence of belief among rural
youth, its very low level among students in higher
education, the rather unimpressive degree of
convinced atheism among senior pupils in comparison
with the surveys quoted above, and the considerable

extent of indifference across the socio-occupational spectrum.

Table 3.1: Chuvash ASSR: Young People's Attitudes to Atheism and Religion by Socio-occupational Group, 1976 to 1980, %

	School students (grades 9 and 10)	VUZ students	Young workers	Collective- and state-farm youth
1 Convinced atheists	25.7	40.6	31.2	17.7
2 Natural atheists	28.4	37.9	33.0	26.7
3 Indifferent non-believers	42.7	19.4	31.3	44.3
4 Waverers	2.0	1.5	3.1	6.1
5 Believers	0.8	0.6	1.2	2.7
6 Convinced believers	0.4	-	0.2	2.5
Total entries 1-3 (a)	96.8	97.9	95.5	88.7
Total entries 4-6 (a)	3.2	2.1	4.5	11.3

Note: (a) Not in original table.

Source: Yu. S. Gurov, 'Sotsialisticheskii obraz zhizni i problemy ateisticheskogo vospitaniya molodezhi' in <u>Problemy istorii religii i ateizma</u> (Chuvashskii gosudarstvennyi universitet, Cheboksary, 1981), p.90.

Given that religiousness among young people in the USSR must have generally declined since the early Soviet period as part of the broad social picture, it is interesting to ponder whether the process has latterly been sustained, halted or reversed. Western claims that belief among young Soviet citizens is growing are, not surprisingly, denounced in the USSR as bourgeois falsification. Yet references in Soviet writings suggest concern, firstly about growth of belief at least in certain sections of Soviet youth, and secondly about increasing indifference among them to atheistic principle. The scantiness of relevant statistical material and longitudinal studies on this sector of the population means that the evidence constitutes an unusually mixed bag.

On the first question, A.V. Belov, a leading ideologist, has stated that the average age of members of the Protestant sects is actually declining. (90) This point is confirmed by the Soviet scholar V.A. Saprykin, who implies that the change came about in the 1970s, and emphasises the prominence of the Baptists here. Atheistic education has to contend with a '"new type of believer: a relatively young person who has, as a rule, good vocational training and an education to match"'. Such believers are of an intellectual disposition, interested in 'the atheistic and philosophical aspects' of their creed, and, in Saprykin's judgement, requiring a new kind of antireligious propaganda. (91) So far the evidence adduced has not been specifically about youngsters at school, although there is a clear inference that the 'relatively young' people were not duly immunised against religion in their earlier youth. An authority on atheistic education, however, recently stated, rather unobtrusively in an appendix to an interesting article cited above, that the percentage of young people in religious communities has increased; (92) and other writers have alluded to young people's current interest in the history of religion and to the need for the youth organisations radically to improve their work among the young intelligentsia. (93) Atheistic work among the young in some parts of Uzbekistan is evidently not furthered by the tendency of local officialdom to permit the erection of buildings for religious purposes, including hotels for pilgrims. (94) Overall, the evidence suggests, despite certain counter-evidence about unbelieving students, that it is the more thoughtful and educated young people who tend to be attracted to religion in the USSR.

As to the second question, that of increasing indifference to atheism, there is some direct evidence of this, and it is also implicit in the degree of concern expressed. When young workers were questioned on their reaction to a comrade being involved in infant baptism, in 1969 and again in 1978, it transpired that they had become less willing to condemn him either publicly or tacitly, and the proportion of those indifferent to the matter had risen from 60.5 to 66.3 per cent. (95) Leading writers on atheistic education are certainly alarmed by the number of young people indifferent to religion, (96) and by the tendency of upbringers to regard indifference as a manifestation of atheism. (97) A lecturer in Marxism-Leninism deplores the rather large quantity of young people 'who have adopted a conciliatory attitude to religion'. They are not believers, but regard atheistic and antireligious propaganda as unnecessary. Even some of the Komsomol members among them think it in order to have baptisms and church weddings, celebrate religious holidays and wear crosses. (98) Rogova rightly points out that the indifferent may turn either into atheists or believers. (99) Logic would add to this that 'indifferent' is also the category most likely to subsume secret believers.

Why, in conclusion, is atheistic education the cause of dissatisfaction in the USSR? The question is complex, but we may boil it down to three main reasons: shortcomings of content and method, popular perceptions, and the nature of a secular belief system. The chief shortcomings can be briefly summarised from what has been said. They may include a tendency either to direct atheistic teaching indiscriminately at all children and young people without regard to their level of belief or unbelief, or else to concentrate on young believers without heed to the character of their religious background. There may even be a failure, due to insufficient vigilance and care, to identify believing children at all. There may be a lack of tact and concern to avoid confrontation at school and at home, to secure the young believer a warm place in the collective, and to become aware of unhappy family circumstances which might induce religious profession. In short, a more sensitive approach is required.

Problems of content and method also spring from the conceptual difficulty of the scientific world-view. Consider the following statements from what is generally, believe it or not, a sensible and practical manual on atheistic education. The author is relating it here to science studies. 'A high intellectual and theoretical level of instruction is combined with the development of pupil capacity for an independent understanding of basic scientific concepts, theories and ideas ... Lectures demonstrate to pupils the logical structure of scientific theory and its world-view, atheistic and practical significance.' (100) How are the majority of pupils to respond to that? Coping means learning the right answers. In recent times there has been an added dilemma in the comparatively undifferentiated nature of the senior-stage general school, where, it seems, the conventional approach to atheistic education is insufficiently sophisticated for the intellectual minority. It may be, however, that the doubling of the intake into the vocational-technical sector at the age of 15-plus will somewhat ease the

tensions here by raising the average academic level
of the pupils who remain in the general school.

Popular perceptions of atheistic education,
tenaciously held, though deplored by the
authorities, are basically threefold. The first is
that the church's influence has been overcome and the
vast majority of children are unaffected by religion,
therefore atheistic education is unnecessary. (101)
The second is that atheistic education may actually
draw attention to religion and thus be counterproductive. (102) The third is that it is too
complicated for the average teacher. (103) Thus,
according to reports, teachers tend to leave
religious children alone, provided that they are not
neglecting their work, and atheistic efforts are
likely to be patchy, occurring only at the time of
'Holy Days'. (104) Research has shown that a very
large number even of convinced atheists feel that the
'struggle against religion' is best left to
specialists; in the Kaluga survey, only 43 per cent
of them were actively engaged in it. (105) Professing
atheists among senior school students also evince
varying degrees of commitment. (106) In higher
education, scientific atheism seems to be generally
regarded as uninteresting. It is of limited appeal
for postgraduate research, and the staff often lack
enthusiasm. (107) Perhaps it is in recognition of the
paradoxicality of enthusing about an essentially
negative concept and criticising the allegedly non-
existent that the stress is now on positive promotion
of a materialist world-view.

Yet in a materialist and secular belief system
there remain inherent problems. One is that atheism
does not in itself convincingly address personal
crises such as suffering and bereavement; religion
may or may not provide an acceptable explanation, but
it can certainly comfort. Interestingly, some
atheistic educationists see the need for the broadest
pastoral dimension to their work, but this can be
effective only to the extent that personal
difficulties are of such a kind as to be remediable
by human agency. Another problem is that when such a
belief system is monistic as well, it still has to
reckon with adolescent strivings for autonomy. The
more reflective young people may turn to religion as
one of the very few alternative ideologies available
to them, since it may well offer not only a
purposeful stance for living and a sense of community
but also a way to positive self-understanding – three
vital needs of youth. True, quietism is part of
certain religious traditions, and it has also been

brought upon believers by Soviet reality; but
nowadays, except perhaps in cases of hardship, the
old stereotype of the ignorant, self-absorbed and
submissive wretch is likely to be more of a liability
than an asset to atheistic educators.

A third problem is that the atheist cause
depends on reason, yet it is very difficult to
destroy faith – which, as distinct from belief, is
based upon trust – by rational argument, and
impossible so to do if the believer is very committed
or very young. Some Soviet writers on atheistic
education concede this and in effect say that such
people have to be loved into apostasy and not argued
into it. We will end with a graphic illustration of
the dilemma from a Soviet journal cited by David
Powell. A teacher was telling her eight-year-olds
that Soviet cosmonauts had travelled 300 kilometres
up into the sky without seeing God; so God did not
exist. She asked a religious child what she thought
about this. 'I don't know if 300 kilometres is very
much', the little girl said, 'but I do know that only
the pure in heart shall see God.' (108)

Notes
1.   P. Shcherban', 'Iz opyta ateisticheskogo
vospitaniya   v   shkolakh   Ukrainy',   Vospitanie
shkol'nikov, no. 1 (1984), p.7.
2.   Narodnoe obrazovanie v SSSR. Obshcheobrazovatel'naya shkola. Sbornik dokumentov 1971-1973
gg. (Pedagogika, Moscow, 1974), pp.12-13.
3.   John Dunstan, 'George A. Simons and the
Khristianski Pobornik', Methodist History, vol. 19,
no. 1 (1980), pp.38, 40.
4.   Andrew Blane, 'Protestant Sectarians and
Modernization in the Soviet Union', in Dennis J. Dunn
(ed.), Religion and Modernization in the Soviet Union
(Westview Press, Boulder, 1977), p.399.
5.   Narodnoe obrazovanie v SSSR, p.70.
6.   Kniga   vozhatogo   (Molodaya   gvardiya,
Moscow, 1968), pp.197-200.
7.   Kniga   vozhatogo   (Molodaya   gvardiya,
Moscow, 1982), pp.121-2.
8.   Cited in Richard T. De George, Patterns of
Soviet Thought (University of Michigan Press, Ann
Arbor, 1966), p.39. Our emphasis.
9.   Ibid., pp.46, 48, 53.
10.   Ibid., p.64.
11.   Ibid., pp.87, 95.
12.   Cited in David E. Powell, Antireligious
Propaganda in the Soviet Union (MIT Press, Cambridge,

Mass. and London, 1975), p.5.

13. Bohdan R. Bociurkiw, 'The Ukrainian Autocephalous Orthodox Church, 1920-1930', in Dunn, Religion and Modernization, p.339.

14. Powell, Antireligious Propaganda, p.158.

15. A.A. Lebedev, Konkretnye issledovaniya v ateisticheskoi rabote (Politizdat, Moscow, 1976), pp.4, 19, 41, 58.

16. Ibid., pp. 27-9, 36-7, 47-9. We shall avoid the sociological term 'religiosity' because of its highly pejorative connotation in non-specialist use.

17. Christel Lane, Christian Religion in the Soviet Union (Allen & Unwin, London, 1978), especially pp.222-8.

18. Kniga vozhatogo (1968), p.198.

19. I. Galitskaya, 'Ateisticheskoe vospitanie shkol'nikov', Politicheskoe samoobrazovanie, no. 1 (1984), pp.93-4.

20. A. Okulov, 'Ateisticheskoe vospitanie. Opyt, problemy', Politicheskoe samoobrazovanie, no. 12 (1984), p.47.

21. R.M. Rogova (ed.), 'Atheistic Education in the School: Theoretical and Practical Issues', Soviet Education, vol. 24, no. 8/9 (1981/2), pp.193, 196. (Original: Ateisticheskoe vospitanie v shkole (Pedagogika, Moscow, 1979).)

22. Yaacov Ro'i, 'The Task of Creating the New Soviet Man', Soviet Studies, vol. 36, no. 1 (1984), p.39, citing an article by David K. Shipler on the Soviet Muslims, New York Times, 7 January 1979; Rogova, 'Atheistic Education', p.208.

23. As in Rogova, 'Atheistic Education', p.208.

24. Ibid., p.7; A.V. Druzhkova (ed.), Izuchenie obshchestvovedeniya v srednei shkole (Prosveshchenie, Moscow, 1975), p.99; I.A. Galitskaya and N.T. Abramova, 'Ateisticheskoe vospitanie shkol'nikov', Sovetskaya pedagogika, no. 1 (1984), p.93.

25. Galitskaya and Abramova, 'Ateisticheskoe vospitanie', p.93.

26. Rogova, 'Atheistic Education', pp.176, 181.

27. Lane, Christian Religion, pp.161-2.

28. L. Yu. Braslavsky, 'Evolyutsiya sotsial'-no-eticheskikh pouchenii v staroobryadchestve i khristianskom sektantstve', in Problemy istorii religii i ateizma (Chuvashskii gosudarstvennyi universitet, Cheboksary, 1981), p.118.

29. Rogova, 'Atheistic Education', pp.167-8.

30. Galitskaya and Abramova, 'Ateisticheskoe

vospitanie', pp.94-5.

31. L. Serpetis, 'The Schools' Lofty Duty is to Instill in Pupils the Best Qualities of Builders of Communism', Current Digest of the Soviet Press, vol. 34, no. 15 (1982), p.4. (Original: Sovetskaya Litva, 17 April 1982.)

32. Rogova, 'Atheistic Education', p.169.

33. P. Griskavicius, 'Greater Exactingness and Responsibility in Upbringing and Educational Work', Current Digest of the Soviet Press, vol. 34, no. 15 (1982), p.5. (Original: Sovetskaya Litva, 18 April 1982.)

34. Alexandre Bennigsen, 'Modernization and Conservatism in Soviet Islam', in Dunn, Religion and Modernization, pp.265-7.

35. Ibid., pp. 259, 263-5; Alexandre Bennigsen and S. Enders Wimbush, 'Muslim Religious Dissent in the USSR', in Richard T. De George and James P. Scanlan (eds), Marxism and Religion in Eastern Europe (D. Reidel, Dordrecht and Boston, 1976), pp.139-41.

36. Bennigsen and Wimbush, 'Muslim Religious Dissent', p.145; Ro'i, 'The Task', p.40.

37. Okulov, 'Ateisticheskoe vospitanie', p.51.

38. Lane, Christian Religion, p.63, speaking here of Orthodoxy.

39. Rogova, 'Atheistic Education', pp.69-70.

40. Galitskaya, 'Ateisticheskoe vospitanie', pp.94-5.

41. Rogova, 'Atheistic Education', pp.202-3.

42. Ibid., pp.137-8; Galitskaya, 'Ateisticheskoe vospitanie', p.94.

43. Rogova, 'Atheistic Education', p.138.

44. I do not recall meeting these terms elsewhere, but if credit should be given I must apologise. According to a Soviet colleague, they are not used in the USSR. For an interesting discussion of the problem, see Powell, Antireligious Propaganda, pp.16-20.

45. Ibid., p.47. To discuss the structures for this would exceed our brief and our space. For essential data on the Knowledge Society, atheism clubs, museums etc., see ibid., pp.48-51, 57-62, 65.

46. Ibid., pp.18-20.

47. Lebedev, Konkretnye issledovaniya, p.10.

48. D.I. Penner and R.G. Krotova, Nauchno-ateisticheskoe vospitanie pri obuchenii fizike, 2nd edn (Prosveshchenie, Moscow, 1982), p.22; Galitskaya, 'Ateisticheskoe vospitanie', pp.91-2 (in that order).

49. I.A. Kairov (ed.), Pedagogika (Uchpedgiz, Moscow, 1956), p.257.

50. Kniga vozhatogo (1968), pp.115, 125, 135.
51. Kniga vozhatogo (1982), p.121.
52. Ibid., p.122.
53. Kniga vozhatogo (1968), p.199.
54. Kniga vozhatogo (1982), p.121.
55. Galitskaya and Abramova, 'Ateisticheskoe vospitanie', pp.94-5. In this authoritative article the point is made twice.
56. Ibid., p.99; Rogova, 'Atheistic Education', p.203; Kniga vozhatogo (1982), p.121.
57. Rogova, 'Atheistic Education' pp.146-7.
58. Ibid., p.140.
59. Kniga vozhatogo (1982), p.121.
60. Rogova, 'Atheistic Education', pp.149-51.
61. Galitskaya and Abramova, 'Ateisticheskoe vospitanie', p.99.
62. Yu. Plotnikov, 'Poka khot' odin ...', Uchitel'skaya gazeta, 11 September 1980.
63. Rogova, 'Atheistic Education', p.155.
64. Lev Ovalov, Pomni obo mne (Detskaya Literatura, Moscow, 1976).
65. Obshchestvovedenie (Politizdat, Moscow, 1978), pp.9, 14.
66. Druzhkova, Izuchenie obshchestvovedeniya (1975), pp.95-100, 102, 267-9. The 1983 edition is slightly different.
67. A.P. Sheptulin (ed.), Izuchenie obshchestvovedeniya v srednei shkole (Prosveshchenie, Moscow, 1980), p.269.
68. Obshchestvovedenie. Uchebnik dlya vypusknogo klassa srednei shkoly i srednikh spetsial'nykh uchebnykh zavedenii, 13th edn (Politizdat, Moscow, 1975), pp.38-9, 271.
69. James Muckle, 'Classroom Interactions in Some Soviet and English Schools', Comparative Education, vol. 20, no. 2 (1984), p.242.
70. Powell, Antireligious Propaganda, p.53.
71. Mervyn Matthews, Education in the Soviet Union (Allen & Unwin, London, 1982), p.120.
72. Nauchnyi ateizm, 2nd edn (Politizdat, Moscow, 1974).
73. Powell, Antireligious Propaganda, p.56.
74. G.E. Kudryashov, 'Nauchnye osnovy spetsializatsii studentov vuza po istorii religii i ateizma', in Problemy istorii religii i ateizma, pp.58-62.
75. V. Nosovich, 'At Odds with Logic', Current Digest of the Soviet Press, vol. 24, no. 15 (1982), p.6. (Original: Sovetskaya Estoniya, 14 March 1982.)
76. Literatura po pedagogicheskim naukam, nos. 1, 2, 3 and 4 (1984); published 1985.

77. Christel Lane, <u>The Rites of Rulers</u> (Cambridge University Press, Cambridge etc., 1981), p.2, also quoting McK. Marriott, 'Cultural Policy in the New States', in C. Geertz (ed.), <u>Old Societies and New States</u> (New York and London, 1963), p.29.

78. Lane, <u>The Rites of Rulers</u>, pp.103-5; Powell, <u>Antireligious Propaganda</u>, p.74.

79. Lane, <u>The Rites of Rulers</u>, pp.99-102.

80. Ibid., pp.131, 137.

81. <u>Kniga vozhatogo</u> (1968), p.200.

82. David E. Powell, 'Religion and Secularization in the Soviet Union: The Role of Antireligious Cartoons', in Dunn, <u>Religion and Modernization</u>, pp.136-201.

83. Ibid., pp.149-50.

84. Ibid., pp.150-2. This remark is a variant of a famous Marxist slogan.

85. Powell, <u>Antireligious Propaganda</u>, p.132.

86. Felicity Ann O'Dell, <u>Socialisation through Children's Literature: The Soviet Example</u> (Cambridge University Press, Cambridge etc., 1978), pp.246-7, also citing I.I. Ogryzko, <u>Deti i religiya</u> (Leningrad, 1970), p.67.

87. Lebedev, <u>Konkretnye issledovaniya</u>, pp.33-4, 43.

88. Ibid.

89. Lane, <u>Christian Religion</u>, pp.224-5.

90. <u>Komsomol'skaya pravda</u>, 4 April 1981, cited in Paul A. Lucey, 'The Soviet Press on Religion and Youth', <u>Religion in Communist Lands</u>, vol. 10, no. 2 (1982), p.207.

91. V.A. Saprykin, <u>Sotsialisticheskii kollektiv i ateisticheskoe vospitanie</u> (Politizdat, Moscow, 1983), pp.67, 350, cited in a review by Sherman Garnett, <u>Religion in Communist Lands</u>, vol. 13, no. 1 (1985), pp.108-11. See also D. Pospielovsky, 'Intelligentsia and Religion: Aspects of Religious Revival in the Contemporary Soviet Union', in Dennis J. Dunn (ed.), <u>Religion and Communist Society</u> (Berkeley Slavic Specialties, Berkeley, 1983), pp.12-13, 31.

92. Galitskaya, 'Ateisticheskoe vospitanie', p.100.

93. Okulov, 'Ateisticheskoe vospitanie', p.50.

94. 'Vospityvat' ateistov', <u>Pravda Vostoka</u>, 1 Aug. 1986 (editorial).

95. Yu. S. Gurov, <u>Ot bezrazlichiya k ubezhdennosti</u> (Cheboksary, 1982), p.33.

96. Rogova, 'Atheistic Education', p.6.

97. Galitskaya and Abramova, 'Ateisticheskoe vospitanie', p.96.

98. A. Chertkov, 'The Price of a Lack of Principle', <u>Current Digest of the Soviet Press</u>, vol. 35, no. 25 (1983), p.26. (Original: <u>Komsomol'skaya pravda</u>, 23 June 1983.)

99. Rogova, 'Atheistic Education', p.137.

100. Ibid., pp.80-1.

101. For example, see Plotnikov, 'Poka khot' odin ...'; Shcherban', 'Iz opyta', p.6.

102. For example, see Chertkov, 'The Price', p.26, and criticism by Rogova, 'Atheistic Education', p.73; Galitskaya, 'Ateisticheskoe vospitanie', p.93.

103. Powell, <u>Antireligious Propaganda</u>, pp.52, 54.

104. Ibid.; <u>Kniga vozhatogo</u> (1982), p.121.

105. Lebedev, <u>Konkretnye issledovaniya</u>, pp.21-2.

106. Galitskaya, 'Ateisticheskoe vospitanie', p.94.

107. Powell, <u>Antireligious Propaganda</u>, p.57.

108. Powell, <u>Antireligious Propaganda</u>, p.54, citing E. Aleshko, 'Tletvornye zerna', <u>Nauka i religiya</u>, no. 3 (1967), p.64. Direct quotation re-translated.

Chapter Four

FORMING SOCIALIST ATTITUDES TOWARDS WORK AMONG SOVIET
SCHOOLCHILDREN

Felicity O'Dell

Introduction

Socialisation, as all of the essays in this book
demonstrate, is at the heart of the entire education
process in the Soviet Union. There are many values
and behaviour patterns for the child to be socialised
into accepting. Similarly, there are many methods
used to encourage socialisation both inside and
outside the school. This chapter concentrates on the
values and behaviour patterns which relate to work
and it analyses how they are taught to the Soviet
schoolchild. It looks first at the place of work in
the socialisation process as a whole. It then
considers both the nature of the desired work values
and behaviour patterns and the ways in which these
values and behaviour patterns are taught. Finally, it
discusses the extent to which socialisation into work
values is successful and attempts to analyse reasons
for a certain lack of success which can be seen in
some areas.

What is the Place of Work in the Overall Socialisation Process?

When looking at the nature of socialisation in Soviet
schools as a whole the value which stands out as
being most prominently inculcated is that of
patriotism. Why is this the case when feelings of
patriotism were condemned rather than praised by Marx
and Lenin? It can be partly explained by the fact
that patriotism is a value which has been found among
many nationalities and in many periods; it was
certainly a value very familiar to the inhabitants of
the Russian Empire. In other words, patriotism was
not a new Soviet value - its roots were already
present in the pre-revolutionary system, some might
even argue in human nature itself. Accordingly, it

was a fairly straightforward matter for the Soviet
socialisation system to take the existing value of
patriotism and to endow it with some specific
characteristics of its own.

It is clear from any Soviet literature that
Soviet patriotism is not just a geographical love for
the place where one was born; it is a political
loyalty to the social system of the Soviet
motherland. It can thus be seen as uniting people of
very different geographical backgrounds within the
one Soviet state. It is a patriotism which is
concerned more with red flags and Lenin than with
birch trees and Mother Volga although people's
natural love for the physical beauties of their
homeland is certainly one of the major bases on which
Soviet patriotism is built.

From the political loyalty which Soviet
patriotism encourages stem two other major sets of
values which the Soviet state is anxious to
inculcate; the first of these is military and
encompasses a preparedness to fight and to lay down
one's life for the motherland in the event of war;
the second is economic and covers the various aspects
of socialisation for work with which this chapter is
concerned. The Soviet schoolchild is taught in
different ways, explicitly and implicitly,
throughout his or her school career that the main way
in peacetime to demonstrate one's patriotism and to
serve the Soviet Union is through work. Only by the
dedicated labour of all its citizens can the USSR
progress towards its ultimate goal of Communism.
Unlike patriotism love of work does not have such
firm roots in the Russian tradition.

Also unlike patriotism, work has an important
place in the Marxist-Leninist philosophy which
underpins the Soviet system. The phrase 'From each
according to his abilities, to each according to his
work' is the well-known and significant definition of
socialism. Marxist-Leninist philosophy analyses
history from a class point of view and attributes
particular importance to the role of the working
class in the development of society. The USSR is held
to be a workers' state and the nobility of work and,
accordingly, workers is revered by all adherents to
Marx's and Lenin's ideas.

In view of this important philosophical
position of work and the working class in Soviet
society, it was easy to legitimise the campaign for
the hard work that would be necessary to build up the
economic base of the Soviet Union after the ravages
of the Civil War. It was - and still is - used as an

important element in motivating people to discipline themselves to greater efforts to work hard for the good of the future society. The personal contentment to be found in work is sometimes presented in a way reminiscent of the manner in which joy was previously claimed to be found in leading a religiously pure life.

A major goal of the USSR is to build up its economic strength. To this end people not only have to be motivated to work hard, they also have to learn the practical skills necessary for the construction of socialism. Some of the practical skills required are simply physical, others have more of a moral dimension. Self-discipline and on occasion self-sacrifice are as necessary as the ability to manipulate tools. Early Soviet educators of necessity gave the development of work skills and attitudes pride of place in the education process. This significance has not been diminished even though the practicalities and details of instruction have been modified by various educational reforms throughout the Soviet period.

How do Soviet Educators Today See their Work Values?

There are a number of strands to the work values which the Soviet education authorities explicitly wish to inculcate. These intertwine in many ways but it will clarify our discussion to separate them here. The points made here are those identified by the writers of the book, The Foundations of Communist Morality, which is a basic textbook for young people. (1)

The first point made is that <u>it is through work that the individual can find his own happiness and purpose in life</u>. It is pointed out that people who do not work lose their way in life and end up either in despair or in depravity. In other words, labour is 'as necessary for the spiritual development of mankind as fresh air is for physical development.' (2) It is significant that labour is thus presented first and foremost not in terms of the good of society but in terms of the wellbeing of the individual.

Social aspects of the value of work are included in the next point when it is argued that <u>socialism has radically improved the relationship between people and their work</u>. An example of this is the <u>subbotniki</u> which regularly take place in Soviet life. These are days when people give their labour to society without expecting any payment. The satisfaction, it is claimed, comes from knowing that, in the words of Lenin, each worker is 'part of the great army of liberated labour, able to build his or her own life without landowners or capitalists, able to build a communist order'. (3) Schoolchildren also take a part in these subbotniki from an early age – by doing some extra work tidying up their school garden or their local courtyard, for example.

A third tenet of the communist attitude to work is that all kinds of work deserve respect. This point is given especial stress because it is noted that, even today, some people hold some jobs in lower esteem than others. It is acknowledged that jobs are not equal – some are more difficult than others, some are more creative than others, some require a higher degree of skill and training than others, some are even relatively better paid than others. (4) What is, however, important is that each job has its own significant role to play in the building of society and none must in any way be looked down upon. In earlier Soviet writing the equality of all jobs was claimed; it is evident that this is not acceptable to contemporary youth in current Soviet conditions. The philosophy has, therefore, been slightly modified.

A further element in the Soviet citizen's arsenal of attitudes towards work is that work must be carried out conscientiously. Only thus can the individual experience full self-respect. Working conscientiously involves not only a desire to work well but also the ability to do so. It is each person's responsibility to learn to work in the most efficient way. This means knowing how one's own work fits in with that of others and doing one's best to coordinate as efficiently as possible – even if on occasion this causes one as an individual some inconvenience. Working conscientiously can mean putting the state before one's individual interests. It requires a strict discipline in one's work but it is emphasised that this discipline is very different from 'the discipline of the stick'; it is a voluntary discipline imposed from within not by any outside authority. (5) It also implies a serious concern about the quality of one's work. It is far from enough merely to fulfil the norms set for one, one must ensure that tasks are done to the highest possible standard. (6) It is through the inculcation of this value that the Soviet authorities seek to improve the quality of work, a pressing concern in recent years.

Socialist competition – the system whereby groups of people compete with one another in order to

83

increase the quantity or quality of production - is held to be another significant element in the moral code relating to work in the Soviet Union. It is argued that socialist competition is a powerful motive force in the development of production. It is said to be based on co-operation and mutual help and to be particularly instructive in bringing the less efficient up to the level of the best. (7) The system of socialist competition is said to encourage people to do their best for the good of their group rather than for any petty individual benefit. The system of socialist competition is employed in schools too. Classes or rows of children compete to see who can get the best marks; rewards are given to the Octobrist or Pioneer links with the best behaviour record; rewards are withheld from a whole group if one of their members incurs the disapproval of his teachers.

In conclusion, the place of work in Soviet society is summed up in The Foundations of Communist Morality in the following way:

> Soviet people see their high patriotic duty in terms of labour for the good of society. Whatever position a person occupies, whatever job he does, he plays his part in the social transformation of society ... Through his labour man does not only change the nature of the world, he also changes himself, bringing out in himself the best characteristics of the New Man - goal-directedness, nobility of thought, feelings of collectivism and comradely co-operation, determination in the face of difficulties and a demand for constant spiritual improvement. Labour was, and has remained the basis of the development of humanity and is a decisive factor in the blossoming of people's moral and spiritual qualities. (8)

In other words, the significance of work can at times be seen to have a semireligious aura in its Soviet presentation. This is no doubt created partly in order to inspire youngsters to dedicate themselves to the cause of socialist construction. In addition, a number of very practical work values - discipline and conscientiousness - are also given prominence to encourage young people not only to feel positively about their work but also to apply themselves to the work they do in the most efficient way possible.

How Are Soviet Work Values Taught to Schoolchildren?

In this section the intention is to look at the basic Soviet attitudes to work and to see how they are illustrated in a number of current textbooks. We shall draw examples from the following subjects showing how they each in their way help to promote the desired work values - from reading to zoology, from history to the labour lesson. Examples are drawn from programmes and textbooks for different grades of the Soviet school in order to try to get an overview of the socialisation process.

It must be remembered that what is described in detail below is only one part of the formation of attitudes towards work among Soviet children. As well as having their attitudes formed in school, children are subject to other agencies of socialisation. The youth organisations, children's television and young people's magazines, for example, can all be influential. They all, however, put across the same attitudes to work that are fostered in the schoolroom. Comics never glamorise idleness, for example, nor do television programmes show undisciplined children going unpunished. Moreover, there are many facilities for children to pursue work-connected interests in their spare time. Young Technicians' Clubs exist in many areas and they are well-equipped to help children develop their skills. Pioneer Palaces and regional and factory-based Palaces of Culture similarly have clubs for young people where they can learn more about technology, the theatre, languages, sport and other subjects which often have a work-related application. In many towns there are Children's Railways which are almost entirely staffed and run by schoolchildren. Through this rich provision of facilities the idea of the importance and the enjoyability of work is reinforced for Soviet youngsters and, in addition, their skills and interests are developed for the future benefit of the Soviet state. Outside school, then, the attitudes taught in the school are backed up by a range of media and institutions all adhering to the same values. Indeed the only agency of socialisation which may not necessarily put across the work ideas desired by the state is the agency which is accepted as being of prime importance, the family.

The Labour Lesson. One of the major classes in the school curriculum in which attitudes to work are formed is the labour lesson. From the very first year at school this is a compulsory part of any child's

85

schooling. In labour lessons pupils are trained in practical work skills but they are also an important means of forming disciplined work habits and other desired attitudes. This is done partly by teacher exhortation and example but also by establishing links between schools and local factories and farms. It is felt that right from the very beginning of their school career children should be involved in producing things that are actually useful to society (simple sewn or crocheted objects, for example). (9) The 1984 Educational Reform seeks to strengthen these links and to make them more effective. Benefits are held to be mutual. Work places will provide equipment and often instruction to help train schoolchildren and the children will play their part in the life of the workplace by, for example, tending plants there or giving their paintings to decorate factory or farm buildings. The aim of such measures is moral as much as it is practical. It is hoped to imbue children with a sense of respect for and belonging to their local industry as well as to give them a feeling of early participation in the Soviet collective.

Reading. Reading lessons in primary classes are a time when much moral education work is carried out. It is significant that one primary school teacher, whose work is very highly considered and whose approach is described at length in a teachers' journal, is said to use reading lessons in this way:

> Raisa Nikolaevna constantly draws the children's attention to the fact that socially-useful work and its results define a person's role in the life of society and that our state is a workers' state. She tries to impress on her pupils the awareness that labour for the good of the Motherland is the very basis of morality and that only his work makes a person both necessary to others and happy in himself. (10)

In reading books for the junior grades there are many texts which help to form the correct Soviet attitudes to labour. Certain themes emerge again and again. There are many stories, for example, which honour the working class by illustrating their role in the October Revolution and by showing their suffering and bravery in pre-revolutionary times. Working people today are shown as carrying on the heroic tradition started by these working-class revolutionaries. An extra historical dimension is added by the frequency of stories about people who fought for the Motherland in the Great Patriotic War – it is implied that the military dedication of Soviet citizens in the past is paralleled by the dedication of contemporary citizens in their working lives. Then there are numerous stories in which Lenin is used as a role model; among his other positive characteristics, diligence is given pride of place – it is shown how he loved to study when he was a child and how he never wasted time when he was adult; Lenin's respect for ordinary workers is also frequently illustrated.

Texts and poems illustrate how even small children can play a useful part in the work of the home. The importance of working hard at school in order to be a good worker later on is also stressed in many examples. Another common theme is that which points out the need to respect common objects because of the work which they represent. Proverbs which praise work are quoted, the equally traditional Russian proverbs disparaging work are ignored. The need to work primarily for the collective good is regularly emphasised. Children are shown ordinary people at work and it is pointed out that ordinary work on a farm or at a factory is both important and enjoyable. The more typically glamorous job of being an astronaut is also commonly depicted in the textbooks. (11)

A little story in the reading book for children in their first year at school illustrates the duties that must be carried out by even the youngest Soviet citizen, especially those (almost all in fact) who belong to the youngest youth organisation, the Octobrists. It also suggests that joy is experienced in doing one's duty.

> 'Look', Vovka opened his coat. On his chest shone a red star. 'I'm an Octobrist now! I'm going to live in the Octobrist way!'
> Vovka was glowing with happiness.
> 'What do you mean live in an Octobrist way?'
> 'Well, you have to know the Octobrist rules. Because I'll be a Pioneer one day. That means I have to live cheerfully, to work hard, to help older people. To be honest.'
> 'What else?'
> 'To study well, to love school, to be friendly ...'
> 'What else?'
> 'To sing, to draw.'
> 'What if I don't want to sing?'
> 'If you don't want to, then don't sing, of

87

course. How funny you are!'
'Could I live in the Octobrist way?'
'Well', said Vovka, 'what can I say ... I think
that you could, of course. Today, for example, I
cleaned the floor. You can do that too.'
'Certainly, I can.'
'Well', Vovka went quietly on, 'You can do it.
But you don't have to do it. But I don't have
any choice. I'm an Octobrist!'
How I envied Vovka!
He is so lucky. Even more than lucky. He's got a
red star. He's an Octobrist! He's a real pupil.
He's got duties, obligations. And I don't have
to do anything ... I was very sad!
'Well, I must go', Vovka said, 'I've got things
to do.' He's become quite a different person!
(12)

This story also serves to illustrate the way the
youth organisations support the values of the school
and the other official Soviet agencies of
socialisation. It makes it quite clear that
industriousness is a virtue of prime importance in
the moral code of the ideal young Octobrist.

Literature. For older children, the literature lesson
takes over from the reading lesson. Literature is
well known as being expected to serve socio-political
as well as artistic ends in the USSR. How is this
illustrated in practice in schools? As far as the
formation of work attitudes are concerned, a main
method is by selecting Soviet works for children to
read where there is a strong 'positive hero', a man
or woman who shows the desired attitudes to work and
with whom pupils are encouraged to identify. Pre-
revolutionary classics of Russian literature are
also fully covered by the syllabus; the ideological
approach there is to use these works as illustrations
of the class struggles they learn about in a more
abstract way in the history lesson. Moreover, the
literature lesson is expected to foster reading
habits which will not merely provide the child with a
joyful leisure activity but will give him or her the
knowledge to develop their own work skills. This is
expressed in terms accessible to the eleven-year-old
in the introduction to the Literature textbook for
the fourth grade. The following text is part of a
slightly longer passage eulogising books and
libraries.

From books you'll learn how people from
different countries live and how they fight for
freedom, you'll learn about the great
discoveries of science and technology, about
the stars and planets, about plants and animals.
  With a book you can fly round all of our
enormous country and the whole world, you can go
to the distant planets, you can travel from the
present to the past and the future, you can
learn to understand and to love people and their
constructive labour.
  You, children, are lucky enough to have
been born in our remarkable country which is
building Communism. Humanity's dream will take
place before our very eyes. You will live and
work under Communism.
  Prepare yourselves to go to these great
heights. Get as broad knowledge as you can.
Read widely and persistently. (13)

his text stresses the practical value of reading for
he pupils' future work and it emphasises how reading
ill enable children to learn about other people's
ork. It does not refer to the more artistic or
sychological lessons that can be learnt from
iterature.

anguage Studies. Russian language textbooks for
upils in non-Russian schools seem to be a
articularly rich source of socialising material.
hile much of this has a primarily patriotic theme,
here is plenty also that relates to the formation of
ttitudes towards work. Typical is this story which
mphasises the respect due to anything that
epresents other people's labour.

Grisha took a large piece of bread and went
outdoors. The bread was good. Grisha ate all he
wanted but there was still some bread left. Some
other children called to Grisha to come and play
ball with them. What could he do with the bread?
Grisha threw the bread away and ran to play.
  Uncle Matthew was going past. He stopped
and asked, 'Who threw away that bread?' The
children answered, 'It was Grisha who didn't
finish his bread and threw it away.' Uncle
Matthew picked up the bread and said, 'In this
piece of bread is my work, the work of my father
and mother and the whole collective farm. You
must love bread and take care of it.' (14)

The connection between the patriotic theme and the concept of finding one's own fulfilment through work is illustrated by a story:

Conversation round the Campfire
Once at a Pioneer camp, some children were sitting round a campfire and dreaming of what they would be.
'I'm going to be a driver and drive cars all round our country', said Volodya.
'And I'm going to cure people. I'll invent a medicine so that people live for two hundred years', said Raya.
'And I'm going to grow a huge orchard in our collective farm. In it I'll have raspberries and currants, apples and cherries', said Misha happily.
'What about you, Kolya? Why haven't you said anything?'
'I'm going to be a cosmonaut and fly to the Moon.'
In our country you can be anything you like. (15)

It is not uncommon for children to be informed even at an early age about quite specialist aspects of work. The following text illustrates the implications of one government decision that directly affects schoolchildren, i.e. the decision not to sell textbooks to each class of children for them to keep indefinitely but to loan them to each class for a year asking for them back at the end of the year to pass them on to the next group.

You receive your textbooks free. At the end of the school year you hand them on to pupils who are younger than you and they also pay nothing. This is economy, so to speak, on a family scale. But what about the state?
Schools now do not order new textbooks. Two schools, three schools, thousands of schools. The government economises tons of paper.
The long life of the textbook lengthens the life of our forests.
There is less need for machines to turn trees into paper. Metal is economised - this can be used for new cranes, fridges, pipes. And the trucks which carried the timber are freed. They can carry other important goods to all four corners of our country. (16)

The Russian course described above is only followed by children of non-Russian nationalities. Russian children are subjected to plenty of other moral instruction to compensate for what they miss here. Language courses for non-Soviet languages, for instance, also have an educative role to play. Foreign language textbooks in Western countries usually take children into the culture of the country where the particular language is spoken. Stories in French textbooks for English-speaking children, for example, are set in Parisian homes and on Mediterranean beaches. A rather different picture emerges if we look at Soviet foreign language coursebooks. The English textbook for pupils in the third grade is set firmly in Soviet reality even if some of the characters mentioned have anglicised names. This is an example of a typical presentation from the third lesson.

> This is your new friend. Her name is Nina. She is not a little girl. She is a pupil. Her family lives in Lenin Street.
> Nina's mother is a teacher. She works at school. Nina's father is a worker. He works in a plant. He is a very good worker.
> Her grandfather is an old man. But he works in a hospital. He is a doctor. Nina's grandmother doesn't work. Her aunt and uncle are engineers. They work in an office. They come to see Nina's family every Sunday and they all go for a walk. (17)

From this short text several things are immediately noticeable. Firstly, the family described lives on Lenin Street rather than Sycamore Avenue. Secondly, each character is defined in terms of their work. Thirdly, the learner is introduced at a very early linguistic stage to words like 'worker' and 'plant' (meaning factory). There is no stereotyping of women into more menial jobs than men. And it is worthy of note that the grandmother - who like many Soviet grandmothers doubtless spends a lot of time doing housework for the extended family - is defined as 'not working'. Finally, school itself is implicitly honoured in the statement that Nina is no little girl now but a pupil. Further examples of the attitudes suggested by these points could be found throughout any Soviet foreign language coursebook and they lose no opportunity to reinforce attitudes presented elsewhere throughout the Soviet education process.

The English textbook for students in the eighth grade of the general secondary school can naturally include texts of a much more linguistically advanced nature. It has a text on Lenin and the First Workers' University, an article on the atomic icebreaker called The Lenin, an interview with Valentina Tereshkova describing how she combines being an astronaut with 'all the usual duties of a housewife' and a number of texts on the difficulties encountered in their work by such foreigners as the writer, Jack London, and the sea captain Paul Jones. (18) English at this level is not therefore used as a medium for spreading knowledge about contemporary English-speaking countries. It is, on the contrary, used to strengthen knowledge of the achievements of Soviet history and science. Where texts do concern life in an English-speaking country, they usually emphasise the obstacles which capitalist life has put in the way of great talent.

History. History is a subject which has a particularly important socialising role to play. As far as the formation of work attitudes is concerned, the importance of the history lesson is stated quite explicitly in the introduction to the history teacher's syllabus.

> As a result of studying historical material, very important aspects of pupils' world-view are formed:
> - they learn about the definitive role of the means of production in the life of society as the determining factor in the development of society
> - they learn about the laws of socio-economic change and the inevitability of the victory of Communism which will make the unlimited progressive development of society possible
> - they learn about the class struggle as the moving force in the development of any exploitative society
> - they learn about the role of the popular masses who are the real creators of history and about the significance of the individual in history.
> These ideas ... should turn into convictions which will define pupils' attitudes towards their own life in society and their own participation in the construction of Communism. (19)

other words, the history lesson is used primarily instruct pupils in the right philosophical titudes to work, legitimising Soviet society for em and providing them with a sense of history which nds importance and purpose to their own future as viet workers, however humble their jobs may be.

In practice the theoretical aims of the syllabus ich were quoted above are put into practice by aching history to children not as defined by the igns of particular monarchs but by dividing history to periods depending on the nature of the class lationships of the time. The significance of the le of the ordinary people is stressed as the major ctor in bringing about change throughout the story of the world. Pupils are taught about the story of many lands and the same Marxist historical ws are shown as applying whatever land or age is ing discussed.

cial Studies. The Social Studies course which is ken by senior schoolchildren backs up the lessons the history programme giving pupils their first rect instruction in Marxist philosophy. Pupils are ught in abstract terms about the theories which ey have seen illustrated in practice in the history ogramme. The final chapter of the Social Studies xtbook goes on to examine some concepts which are ld to be of key significance in Soviet society. bour is one of these - the others are peace, quality, freedom, brotherhood and happiness. In scussing labour, the textbook states:

> A person can work well, with enthusiasm, for a variety of reasons. Because he is counting on a rich reward for his labour. Because he is aware of his duty towards society. Because he is carried away by his work which allows him to discover his own creative potential. Finally, because work has become a habit for him, as natural and ordinary as the need to breathe or to have contact with other people. Bring all these reasons together and you have communist labour. (20)

he text adds that the reader of the text will robably be horrified at the idea of the communist eing motivated to work by the anticipation of aterial reward. It explains that the communist is ot, of course, concerned to earn as much as possible or himself, what he is interested in is the growth in the material wellbeing of the whole of society.

Lessons in psychology as well as in social studies have a part to play. A psychology textbook for pupils in senior grades addresses briefly the question of job choice and it gives the following advice:

> To find yourself and your correct place in life you must answer these main questions – what has my country today most need for, what does she expect from me, what am I capable of, in which sphere of activity shall I be able to discover myself most fully. These questions are inextricably linked; you will be of most use to your Motherland if you can unite your dreams, inclinations and abilities in the job to which you dedicate your life. (21)

This text clearly states the priority of a patriotic motive in job choice and the concept of work both as duty and as fulfilment.

Science Subjects. Science subjects are expected to do their bit for labour education by referring where possible to the links between what is being studied and the world of work; in other words the practical application of what is being studied is said to be of prime importance. To what extent does this really happen in the textbooks in practice?

If we look at the Nature Study coursebook for pupils in the second and third grades, we find that connection is openly made between nature study and work in a number of ways. The introduction to the coursebook sets out quite clearly the aim to make this link. Pupils are told:

> In the second class you will learn how nature changes with the seasons and how this affects people's work. You'll make observations and write them down in your 'Observation Diary' and on your calendar of nature and labour. (22)

In the above-mentioned diary and calendar pupils are asked to do various tasks throughout the course. For each season in turn these include things like 'Observe what jobs people do in autumn on the fields, in allotments, in gardens and in parks'. (23) Similarly for each season there is a text on the theme of people's work at that time of year and some questions to be discussed in class. The winter uestions are the following:

1. What do collective farmers do in winter on the fields? Why is manure put on the fields? Why is it very important to keep a snow cover on the fields?
2. What jobs are necessary in winter on the streets of a town? Why are the streets cleared of snow and sprinkled with sand?
3. What happens in vegetable stores in winter?
4. What happens in mechanical workshops in winter? Why are agricultural machines repaired in winter?
5. What winter work is particularly linked to the life of domestic animals?
6. Talk about your own observations on people's work in winter. (24)

he two-page text which follows these questions provides some of the answers and the teacher is expected to discuss the others with her pupils.

Zoology, like other science subjects, is given a certain work-oriented focus. The textbook for the 6th and 7th grades has a chapter dedicated to the Preservation of the Animal World'. This deals with man's influence on the natural world, pointing out how this has intensified in recent decades. It is added that not all that man has done is justified by necessity. Examples are drawn - from North America and Tasmania - to show how man has annihilated some very interesting species. The harm done by insecticides and industrial pollution is condemned. Regulations to reduce pollution introduced in the USSR are praised. An interesting paragraph says that 'The role of schoolchildren in the protection of the environment is great.' (25) Children are given basic countryside rules - they are told that it is not enough simply not to destroy birds' nests or anthills or to hurt useful insects. Neither is it sufficient just to make bird-tables in winter. Children must be very careful when lighting fires in the countryside; they should not sing or play musical instruments in the heart of the countryside - it could frighten animals and the children should themselves learn to listen to 'the natural music of the environment'. They also must never leave litter. Most of the zoology textbook is a standard account of the different species of the animal kingdom. The chapter described above, however, relates to the work theme in that it plays its part in trying to encourage

95

responsible attitudes to the world and an understanding of the interrelationships of man and the environment. Disciplined and thoughtful behaviour in the countryside will later lead, it is hoped, to disciplined and thoughtful behaviour at work - and in society at large, of course.

Other science subjects like physics and chemistry refer to Soviet achievements in these fields and teachers are constantly exhorted to emphasise the practical applications of the principles they are teaching. Formation of work attitudes in science lessons should not, however, be overemphasised; it does not seem to be the major preoccupation that it is, for example, in reading or history. Nor does it seem that in practice the practical applications of science subjects are emphasised quite as much as the pedagogues say they should be; learning the facts about the natural world is quite clearly the main objective of the science coursebooks analysed.

All other subjects in the curriculum are expected to contribute in some degree to the formation of the correct work attitudes. The new subject of computer studies is stated as being necessary because of the current campaign aiming at the intensification of the economy. The course in Soviet State and Law informs older pupils about, among other things, Soviet labour legislation. Geography is similarly given a Soviet flavour. This is done by giving a far greater importance to economic than physical geography - although the latter is certainly not ignored in the syllabus. The influence of different political systems on economic geography is also frequently discussed. In short, every single subject in the curriculum in Soviet schools serves in some way to put across the values which were identified in the first part of this chapter.

Method. Not only, however, does the content of the work correspond with these values, the methods used by the teachers work towards the same ends too. Thus classes are organised according to the principles of 'socialist competition' with groups such as classes, classroom rows or Octobrist 'links' (i.e. unit or team. Ed.) competing with each other; and rewards and punishments are awarded on a collective rather than an individual basis. The class collective plays a similar role to collectives later to be experienced in adult working life; the collective discusses the

96

performance of individuals in the group giving stern criticism or warm praise as it feels appropriate. The child thus experiences a microcosm of Soviet work organisation and learns habits which should stand him or her in good stead in the future.

Behaviour habits are moulded in other ways too by practice in the Soviet school. The School Rules, which are identical throughout the entire Soviet Union, do not simply deal with not running in corridors, they quite explicitly dedicate themselves to training attitudes to 'study and labour'. (26) Moreover, throughout the education process a child is given a mark for behaviour and an unsatisfactory mark here will hinder his progress through the school. The pupil's contribution to 'socially-useful labour' is one factor which will be taken into account when decisions are taken about the behaviour mark; in other words from the earliest age the child is expected to play a part in giving voluntary labour for the good of the community by, for example, tending the school garden or helping old people.

The above are just a few examples of how methods back up the content of the syllabus in attempts to form the correct work values. Given the thoroughness and the extent of the ways in which the Soviet authorities try to form the work values which they desire, it is necessary now to consider the degree to which their explicit socialisation in this area is successful.

How Successful is the Inculcation of Soviet Work Values?

It is very difficult to attempt to assess the effectiveness of any particular aspect of Soviet education. There are few large-scale pieces of sociological research into attitudes and behaviour. It is necessary to base general comments on small-scale surveys and on reports of an individual nature either from scholars in the field or from the press. There are, however, certain areas where it is clear that achievements do not match up to hopes. The work value isolated above which states that work must be disciplined and honest is the one where it is easiest to see a contrast between Soviet theory and practice. With the greater frankness of the press in the last two years, there have been numerous reports of dishonesty even at high levels. Articles in teaching journals clearly state that 'For schoolleavers discipline has not always become the norm, an internalised requirement for their own behaviour.'

97

(27)

Differential Job Status. The value that all jobs are equally deserving of respect is also one that has clearly not been fully assimilated even though the status of various types of work differs from their status in Britain and other Western countries. Of disturbingly low status as far as the Soviet economy is concerned are jobs in agriculture and in the service sphere. The low prestige of jobs in service industries is seen as being something that may cause particular problems in the future as the proportion of people employed in service rather than on production has been steadily growing; in 1940 88.2 per cent of all employed people worked in material production and 11.8 per cent in the non-production sphere - these figures changed to 77.1 per cent and 22.9 per cent in 1970 and 73.3 per cent and 26.7 per cent in 1984. (28) The current push towards the automation of industry is likely to speed up this trend. But, as economics professor, V. Kostakov, states 'It is no secret that the occupations associated with this sphere (service) are not considered prestigious, and that even the number of personnel working in it today is sometimes assembled with great difficulty.' (29)

The lack of success in attracting young people to stay in rural areas is similarly a cause of particular concern as there is an important need for dedicated and qualified workers to raise the level of Soviet agriculture. A number of surveys have been carried out in an attempt to discover how to improve the situation. One survey of young people found out that they were well aware of the advantages of rural life - 81 per cent of pupils and 54 per cent of workers aged between 17 and 25 valued highly such things as fresh air, the proximity to nature and a peaceful rhythm of life. However, only 12 per cent wanted to work in purely agricultural jobs. A number of factors are blamed for the situation. Firstly, there is inadequate knowledge in the schools about the variety of rural jobs needed; a study of schools in the Saratov oblast revealed, for example, that the directors of studies knew about the nature and conditions of only about one-quarter of the jobs which need doing in a modern agro-industrial complex. Secondly, there are not enough colleges training children in these jobs. This is particularly true for the rural specialisms which employ primarily girls. As a result, many young people, and especially girls,

98

cide to go into town for their post-school
aining. Once there, they rarely return to the
llages they came from. (30)

As with any system, it is difficult to draw a
onfident cause-and-effect relationship and state to
nat extent successes and failures in the formation
f work attitudes in the Soviet Union can be directly
tributed to the education process? There are, after
l, other influences on the formation of a citizen's
titudes towards his or her work. But if education
as gone wrong, where exactly is it to blame?
orbachev, as others before him, has criticised
oviet moral education for being at times too
ormalistic and tedious in its monotonous repetition
f what should be exciting ideas. (31)

eory v. Reality in School and the Work Place. One

arther reason why work values are not formed
atisfactorily is because there are numerous ways in
nich actual practice is at variance with the dreams
f pedagogues. An article in *Izvestiya* which looks at
ne progress of the 1984 School Reform notes with
oncern the difficulties being encountered by the
ourse in the fundamentals of computer studies which
s supposedly being prepared. It is also disturbed by
ne failure of industry to support the reform's
equirement that school students have experience of
ork in real working conditions. A shortage of
eachers is also a problem.

Similarly, some lack of success is due to the
act that the reality of life both in the Soviet
chool and, more especially, in the work place does
ot match the portrayal of life in the textbooks. In
chools there are reports of how corruption comes
to the classroom. Compositions can be bought from
ther pupils for five roubles, for example. (32) Even
eachers can show signs of corruption themselves. An
spection of one school in Turkmenistan, for
stance, showed that teachers' work in mathematics
d Russian language was at a very low level. In
enior grades studying Russian language, dictation
exts were chosen from the primary school syllabus,
ey were dictated word by word and even, on
casion, letter by letter. Despite this, in some
chools only 40 per cent of pupils wrote satisfactory
ctations. The reason for the low standards among
pils, it is claimed, is that teachers themselves
e semiliterate. (33) It is obvious that in labour
d other lessons things do not always happen as
noothly as they are presented in the textbooks and

99

the syllabus. The aims set by the Soviet educational
authorities are so high that their chances of
realisation are slight. Labour lessons, for example,
are typically criticised for being patchy and weak.
(34)

The very high expectation of the joys of work-
life which the Soviet schoolchild is given later
encourages disillusionment when reality does not
conform to the textbooks. The results of one
sociological survey show that an overwhelming
majority of people - 90 per cent of executives and 84
per cent of workers - felt that they could work
better under different economic conditions. The
conclusion of the surveyors was that 'When a person
receives the right to independence and initiative,
when his income is made directly dependent on the
quality of his labour, then not only productivity but
also responsibility will grow.' (35) In other words,
social conditions at work can alter any more positive
attitudes towards work that may have been created by
the socialisation process at school. The article
quoted above states in no uncertain terms that Soviet
practice does not correspond to the maxim of 'He who
gives more, gets more'; on the contrary, the writer
argues, the aim of many is now to give as little as
possible and to get as much as possible. More honest
young workers are disillusioned by seeing how, for
example, norms are deliberately lowered so that
workers can increase their wages by overfulfilling
the norms with the greatest of ease.

Similarly the ideal of working in a happy
collective for the good of the ultimate collective,
the Motherland, does not always work out in practice.
Sociologists have even seen fit to coin a new term,
'anticollective'. This refers to the feelings which a
team of workers develop for each other when the wages
of each of them depend on the overall performance of
the team - those who do not pull their weight are
resented, and the old and the young, who are less
able to work rapidly, suffer particularly. (36) This
anticollective attitude raises production but,
interestingly, it is nevertheless condemned by
Soviet sociologists as going counter to the spirit of
Soviet socialism. The press not infrequently
provides other illustrations of anticollective
behaviour. One boy was forced to leave his technical
school, for example, because of the repeated
beatings-up and robberies in his hostel. (37) Other
reports say the number of law violations among
teenagers is 'not decreasing'. (38) Schools are not
doing enough to combat alcohol and narcotics. (39)

100

Family Upbringing. The family is frequently blamed for the failure of the Soviet socialisation process to achieve all the aims it sets itself. Of all the agencies of socialisation the family is the most difficult to control and it is also, probably, the most effective. A report in <u>Pravda</u> examines work done in Latvia in response to legislation passed by the 27th Party Congress with the aim of 'strengthening the family and increasing its responsibility for children's upbringing'. The report criticises measures taken as being inadequate - young people are not satisfactorily morally prepared for becoming parents and organisations like clubs, work places and sports institutions are not doing what it is felt they should do to help improve the situation. (40) In drawing up further measures to try to eliminate problems the Latvian Supreme Soviet puts an emphasis on providing leisure and other facilities which will encourage families to spend their spare time together in ways approved by the state. It is hoped by this means to bring the family's upbringing activity more into line with that of the other state-controlled agencies of socialisation.

Some writers suggest that the reason for the unsatisfactory level of upbringing in the family may even be a result of the more successful socialisation of other values - like work values, for example - among young Soviet parents. These young people, it is stated, are 'vigorous, socially active young women and purposeful, energetic men. (They) steadily fulfil plans, the administration is pleased with them and they receive bonuses. Voters gladly elect them to Trade Union committees and Young Communist League bureaus.' As workers, in other words, they are model citizens. However, their devotion to their work makes them see their children as 'thorns in the flesh' getting in the way of their careers. As a result, children are ignored by parents and often left, when circumstances permit, to the grandmother to bring up. (41) Women receive particularly stern criticism for this behaviour.

'Visiting mothers' are now making their appearance alongside 'visiting fathers'. Young women who have yet truly to experience the joys of motherhood are buying their way free of their own children with expensive toys, pretty clothes, and ultimately, alimony paid to the grandmother. It's hard to understand who precisely they are at the age of 20 or 30. Daughters? Or mothers? Or just grown-up little girls, spoiled and pampered by life, who are 'playing dolls' in the age-old fashion? And they have no desire to grow up or to answer for their actions by recognising their duty to society - their duty as mothers. (42)

The need to educate women in particular to see their role as mothers as being at least as important as their role as workers is one that has been increasingly emphasised in recent years.

Bureaucratic and Organisational Failure. Planning weaknesses must also bear some of the blame for failures in the formation of the correct work attitudes. Firstly, it goes without saying that planners are fallible. In one area 67 teachers of English were assigned to Ashkhabad City Department of Education even though Ashkhabad had no need of them. Meanwhile 17 rural schools in a neighbouring district could not offer instruction in a foreign language because they had no teachers. (43) Even when the planners get everything right, it is not always so easy to make people fit into the plans. It is reported that in September 1985, 11 per cent of the graduates of teachers' colleges and 17 per cent of university graduates failed to turn up for their obligatory teaching posts. (44) Another report claims that in one area the children of 15 families living from 15 to 40 kilometres away from the nearest village did not know the way to school; no transport had been arranged for them to get to school and they had not even been enrolled in school. (45) Such examples are not untypical.

The extensive bureaucracy in the Soviet Union can have a stultifying effect on local initiative and action. A recent report on the progress of the 1984 Education Reform pointed to the fact that a mentality has formed in many schools whereby teachers and administrators wait for instructions from above but do not make any attempt to get on with implementing the spirit of the Reform off their own bat. People are too timid to make their own plans. (46) It is not difficult, of course, to understand why this timidity has arisen in the Soviet context - it is not unknown in the past for those who have used their own initiative to have suffered to some degree for it.

Work education is singled out for especial criticism. Links between school and work place are condemned in general terms as not yet being set up in a fully satisfactory way. Even the material basis for

abour education is not moving ahead in the planned
ay. In the last five-year plan the assignment for
he commissioning of vocational-technical schools
as fulfilled by only 71 per cent. (47) Figures show
hat in certain republics schools are much better-
quipped with metalwork and carpentry classrooms
han in other republics. In the USSR as a whole at
he beginning of the 1985/6 academic year 51.3 per
ent of schools had separate metalwork rooms and 55.8
er cent had woodwork rooms. Corresponding figures
or Latvia, the best-equipped republic in this
espect, were 78.3 per cent for both metalwork and
oodwork rooms. The figures for Georgia at the other
nd of the scale are 27.3 and 36.7 per cent,
espectively. Latvia is also well-provided with
laces for schoolchildren to do work at enterprises,
hereas Turkmenistan is relatively poorly supplied.
48)

he Black Economy. A final problem relates to the
ery nature of Soviet society. While there is a
hortage of consumer goods there is likely to be a
lack economy which will affect youngsters' work
ttitudes in a way different from that promoted by
he pedagogues. It would also seem that the
xaggerated bureaucracy of Soviet society encourages
hose with initiative to bend the rules and
iscourages many others from trying as hard in their
orking life as the authorities would like.
　　It is significant that there currently seem to
e moves not just to re-educate people but to change
ociety to fit the nature of the people in it. A
ecent *Izvestiya* article discusses the ways in which
arge numbers of people make extra income for
hemselves either by pilfering or, more honestly, by,
or example, cultivating a private plot. *Izvestiya*
eplores all dishonest means of adding to income but
tates that 'A law is being drafted on individual
abour activity. Its purpose is not to prohibit such
ctivity but, on the contrary, to develop it.' (49)
imilarly, moves are being proposed to increase the
roduction of such goods as spare parts, construction
aterials and consumer durables, which are in short
upply and which therefore tempt people to petty
heft and to black market activities. (50)
　　To modify the organisation of work life along
he lines mentioned above would seem to be the only
ay in which there could be hope of successfully
orming the attitudes outlined in the first part of
his chapter. Only by lessening the contrasts between

theory and practice, the discrepancies between 'real life' and the world of the textbooks, can there be hope of avoiding disillusionment and cynicism. Similarly, only by further improvement in the material conditions of Soviet life is there hope of removing the black economy so destructive to the sustaining of any positive work attitudes formed by the school.

Notes

1.   L.G. Grinberg et al., Osnovy kommunistech-eskoi morali (Moscow, 1980), pp. 91–110.

2.   Ibid., p.92.

3.   Ibid., p.94.

4.   Ibid., pp.97–8.

5.   I.M. Sokolova, 'Vospitanie soznatel'noi distsipliny', Vospitanie shkol'nikov, no. 5 (1985), p.25.

6.   Grinberg, Osnovy, pp.98–104.

7.   Ibid., pp.105–9.

8.   Ibid., p.110.

9.   L.Kh.Armaganyan, 'Glavnoe zveno trudovogo vospitaniya v shkole', Nachal'naya shkola, no. 5 (1986), pp.87–8.

10.   G.M. Starodubtseva 'Nravstvennoe vospitanie shkol'nikov', Nachal'naya shkola, no. 8 (1986), p.44.

11.   Many illustrations of these themes will be found in, for example, Kniga dlya chteniya 1 (Moscow, 1984).

12.   Kniga dlya chteniya 1 (Moscow, 1984), pp.151–2.

13.   Rodnaya literatura 4 (Moscow, 1981), pp.3–4.

14.   E.A. Men'shikova et al., Russkii yazyk dlya natsional'nykh shkol RSFSR 4 (Leningrad, 1984), pp.135–6.

15.   Ibid., p.197.

16.   Ibid., p.286.

17.   I.N. Vereshchagina and T.A. Pritykina, English III (Moscow, 1980).

18.   H. Weiser and A. Klimentenko, English (Moscow, 1976).

19.   Programmy vos'miletnei i srednei shkoly: istoriya (Moscow, 1980), p.4.

20.   Obshchestvovedenie (Moscow, 1980), p.311.

21.   Ya. L. Kolominskii, Chelovek - psikholo-giya (Moscow, 1980), p.198.

22.   Z.A. Klepinina and L.F. Melnakov, Prirodovedenie 2-3 (Moscow, 1981), p.5.

23. Ibid., p.9.
24. Ibid., p.65.
25. Zoologiya 6-7 (Moscow, 1981), p.217.
26. A. Kholodyuk 'Pravila dlya uchashchikh-sya', Vospitanie shkol'nikov, no. 4 (1986), p.20.
27. O.N. Maikina, 'Opyt vospitaniya distsip-linirovannosti u shkol'nikov', Sovetskaya pedagog-ika, no. 4 (1986), p.55.
28. 'One Person Must Work Like Seven', Sovetskaya kul'tura, 4 Jan. 1986, p.3, translated in Current Digest of the Soviet Press (CDSP), vol. 38, no. 3 (1986), p.1.
29. 'Man and Progress', Sovetskaya kul'tura, 1 Feb. 1986, p.3. translated in CDSP, vol. 38, no 3 (1986), p.23.
30. V.A. Zubkov and R.P. Kutenkov 'Profession-al'naya orientatsiya sel'skoi molodezhi', Sotsiolog-icheskie issledovaniya, no. 1 (1985), pp.103-6.
31. 'Uchit' po-novomu myslit' i deistvovat'', Izvestiya, 2 Oct. 1986, p.1.
32. 'The Supermen from the Bait', Izvestiya, 24 Feb. 1986, p.3., translated in CDSP, vol. 38, no. 11 (1986), pp.5-6.
33. 'Failing Grade for the Teacher', Pravda, 15 Apr. 1986, p.3, translated in CDSP, vol. 38, no. 15 (1986), p.23.
34. I.B. Pervin, 'Kollektivnyi trud shkol' nikov', Sovetskaya pedagogika, no. 2 (1986), p.24.
35. 'Work Brigades: A Good Idea Going Astray?' Sovetskaya Rossiya, 7 Jan. 1986, p.1, translated in CDSP, vol. 38, no. 2 (1986), pp.1-2.
36. 'Brigades at a Crossroads', Ekonomika i organizatsiya promyshlennogo proizvodstva, no. 8 (1985), pp. 151-91, translated in CDSP, vol. 38, no. 2 (1986), pp.3-8.
37. 'The Supermen from the Bait'.
38. 'Make the School Reform Thoroughgoing and Dynamic in its Effect', Uchitel'skaya gazeta, 3 July 1986, pp.1-2, translated in CDSP, vol. 38, no. 27 (1986), p.3.
39. Ibid.
40. 'In the Praesidium of the USSR Supreme Soviet', Pravda, 29 May 1986, p.2, translated in CDSP, vol. 38, no. 22 (1986), pp.4-5.
41. 'Playing Dolls', Sobesednik, no. 15 (1986), pp.12-13, translated in CDSP, vol. 38, no. 14 (1986), pp.29-30.
42. Ibid.
43. 'Failing Grade for the Teacher', Pravda, 15 Apr. 1986, p.3. translated in CDSP, vol. 38, no. 15 (1986), p.23.

44.   'Steps of the School Reform', <u>Izvestiya</u>, 7 May 1986, p.3, translated in <u>CDSP</u>, vol. 38, no. 18 (1986).
45.   'Failing Grade for the Teacher'.
46.   'Make the School Reform Thoroughgoing and Dynamic in its Effect'.
47.   Ibid.
48.   <u>Vestnik statistiki</u>, no. 5 (1986), pp.78-80.
49.   'About the Honest and Dishonest Rouble', <u>Izvestiya</u>, 2 June 1986, p.3, translated in <u>CDSP</u>, vol. 38, no. 21 (1986), p.3.
50.   'On Stepped-up Efforts to Combat Unearned Income', <u>Pravda</u> and <u>Izvestiya</u>, 28 May 1986, p.1, translated in <u>CDSP</u>, vol. 38, no. 21 (1986), p.5.

Chapter Five

GENDER AND SOVIET PEDAGOGY

Lynne Attwood

In the 1984/5 academic year, a course on 'sex-upbringing' entered the Soviet school curriculum. It constitutes the culmination of two decades of debate on whether a form of sex education was necessary or desirable in Soviet schools. It reflects growing concern over teenage pregnancies, venereal disease, the use of abortion as the main form of birth control, and the increase in divorce. However, the crucial factor in the subject's leap from journal to classroom is the so-called 'demographic crisis'. In the country as a whole there is a decrease in the birth rate, and this is particularly acute in the European republics, where the one-child family is now the norm.

The demographic crisis is seen as an unintended consequence of women's equality in the Soviet Union. In developing a work orientation, women have sacrificed their domestic and maternal orientation. This has resulted in a 'masculinisation' of the female personality. Traditional, nurturant female qualities are giving way to characteristics such as independence, rationality, and self-confidence, required by women in their professional lives.

This process has been accompanied by a parallel 'feminisation' of men. Men have lost their place in society. Women's mass entry into the work force means that men are no longer the sole breadwinners, and society itself has taken over most of their other traditional functions. They no longer have to mend the roof, chop firewood, or defend the honour of their womenfolk, for example. (1) The result is the loss of their sense of self-value, leading to apathy, indolence and alcoholism. This affects not only men's performance at work but also the birth rate; male alcoholism is a prime reason for divorce, and second

107

marriages, when these are attempted, are generally non-reproductive.

The school course, under the title 'The Ethics and Psychology of Family Life', tackles the demographic crisis simultaneously from two directions. On the one hand, it seeks to strengthen marriage and the family by changing young people's attitudes to it. This involves the inculcation of a stronger moral approach to sex, placing it firmly within the confines of marriage; a greater awareness of what conjugal life entails; and the understanding that marriage is not just a private matter but has great social significance.

The second approach is to re-socialise male and female personalities into traditional patterns of masculinity and femininity, which will fit better into family life. A feminine woman will subordinate her professional interests to those of the family and home. Her awareness of an innate need to nurture will encourage her desire for maternity and the establishment of a warm, cosy home. Her tenderness and emotional support will stimulate her partner's masculinity, and this, combined with the pleasant domestic atmosphere she creates, will make him more inclined to do things with and for his family. The result will be fewer divorces, more babies and a stable environment in which to rear them.

The attempt to resurrect polarised images of masculinity and femininity sits awkwardly alongside the Soviet Union's continued claim that women have complete equality with men. The definition of equality has, accordingly, been changed. Contrary to early Soviet thinking, the aspirations and abilities of men and women are now held up as innately different; the catch phrase is that 'being equal does not mean being identical, and everything that is traditional is not obsolete because it is traditional'. (2) Masculinity and femininity are presented not only as essential, but also as natural and inevitable.

In this chapter we will be tracing the development of Soviet thought on the subject of gender, concentrating mainly on the work of pedagogical writers. Since they often seek support from 'experts' in other disciplines, and the 'Family Life' course is generally portrayed as an interdisciplinary venture, we will also look briefly at the ideas on sex differences in personality to be found within psychology, sociology, and the medical profession. Finally, we shall see how these ideas are implemented in the course itself.

The Pedagogical Approach to Sex Differences in Personality

The early years of the Revolution were a period of innovation and experimentation in virtually all areas of life; relations between the sexes, both physical and psychological, were no exception. The Bolshevik woman turned her back on traditional femininity, adopting a military style of dress and a 'masculine' manner of behaviour, and her pleasure lay not in the fripperies of femininity but in the struggles of the Revolution. (3) This transformation was reflected in pedagogy, with girls and boys learning both manual and domestic skills in school. (4)

This modification of traditional gender stereotypes – or, at any rate, the 'masculinisation' of female personality – encountered a stumbling block when Stalin came to power. While Stalin recognised the essential role of women as workers in a rapidly industrialising country and made determined efforts to draw them into the labour force, he simultaneously sought to strengthen the family and institute a 'cult of motherhood'. The ravages of war, the drop in the birth rate brought about by the dislocation of the Revolution, and the growing awareness of a military threat from Germany, led to a pro-natalist policy which placed women firmly back in the home as well as in the work place. The fulfilment of their true natures apparently demanded a combination of multiple maternity and employment, unassisted – despite earlier promises – by state investment in social or domestic services. (5)

Theoretical Debate. The subject of psychological sex differences slipped from view for more than 30 years until the publication in 1964 of articles by the educationalists Kolbanovskii and Kostyashkin on sex education. (6) In the debate which they initiated, sex education – or 'sex upbringing' (polovoe vospitanie), as it was more commonly termed – struggled to find a definition. For some writers it meant (or included) something approaching sex education as understood in the West; others defined it as the process by which psychological sex, or gender, is formed in children.

Kolbanovskii's article concerns itself with both aspects. On the subject of sex, he laments the lack of information given to teenagers about sexual matters, and suggests a possible link between their ignorance and masturbation (which is still heavily frowned upon), sexual perversion (the content of which is not explained), and sexual crime. However, gender is apparently the root of the problem. If boys and girls develop appropriate male and female personalities, sex will take care of itself. 'There are certain norms of behaviour that are specific for boys and girls', he writes, 'which should regulate (their) mutual relations ... in the early age periods of their development. These moral standards and principles, along with hygienic recommendations, should constitute the specific character of sex upbringing.' (7) This has now become its standard definition. In the words of Khripkova, one of the more prolific of current writers on the subject, sex upbringing in the Soviet Union is not synonymous with the 'sex enlightenment' of the West, but is a programme of 'moral upbringing, ... with regard to one's membership of one or the other sex'. (8)

Khripkova is seemingly dismissive of early writings on sex upbringing. As late as 1981 she asserts, with her co-writer Kolesov, that 'in the available literature of the past 30 to 40 years we have not encountered any scientific work on this subject'. (9) However, although the more recent texts are usually couched in a more scientific language, the views expressed in them are little different from those put forward by Kolbanovskii and Kostyashkin. Sometimes we even read the same exhortations, word for word, in writings a decade apart. Hence it is possible to talk of a general pedagogical approach to sex differences in personality.

Biological inheritance stands in the centre. Some pedagogical writers acknowledge that this might seem unpalatable to those accustomed to an ideological framework which stresses the social construction of personality. However, in Kolbanovskii's words, 'if you drive nature out through the door, it will fly in through the window'. (10) Nature is primarily concerned with the different reproductive roles of men and women. These have a crucial effect on personality, engendering a range of psychological peculiarities relating to the woman's need to create a nest for her offspring, and the man's need to protect this nest. As Mikaberidze writes: 'In woman ... the qualities essential for creating and maintaining an atmosphere of family warmth, creating and preserving the happiness of loved ones, must be innate.' (11) Khripkova and Kolesov note that, 'girls are inclined towards caring activities - looking after people, nursing, showing concern, and so on ... This inclination may be seen as a manifestation appropriate to their age of the maternal instinct.' (12)

Many of the female personality traits have a less obvious link with reproduction, however. Girls are apparently more emotional, subjective, shy, modest and impulsive than boys. They are more sensitive, taking praise and censure more to heart. They are less brave, and less inclined towards investigative and inventive behaviour. They are more attracted to things concerned with the immediate environment - the home, and people known to them - while boys do better in unknown situations. When telling stories, they are more detailed than boys and inclined to digress. They are more concerned about their appearance, which can develop into a pathological conviction of physical inadequacy. They are neater, more accurate, conscientious, industrious and responsible. They are more likely than boys to seek help from figures of authority, and to adhere to accepted forms of behaviour. They are more passive than boys, which is reflected in choice of sport and reading matter. Girls prefer the gentler sports, those requiring 'flexibility and beauty of movement', while boys prefer the more active games of football, volleyball and ice hockey. Similarly, while 'boys seek action in books, girls are interested in the psychology of the heroes'. Favourite school subjects differ according to sex; girls prefer history and literature, while boys enjoy sport and practical activities. (13)

Most of these observations coincide with the popular myths about male and female personality in the West, which a study by the American psychologists Maccoby and Jacklin has convincingly refuted. (One interesting exception is the widespread assumption that men are naturally more aggressive than women. While Maccoby and Jacklin found some evidence to support this, in the Soviet pedagogical literature it has been argued that aggression is one male characteristic which does not have a biological basis, being instead a resilient legacy from the bourgeois ideology of the past!) (14)

Do Soviet writers deny that the social environment plays any role in the formation of these differences? Timoshchenko seems to grant it considerable prominence when she talks of the importance of role models in the development of appropriate personality traits. 'Consciously or unconsciously, boys and girls learn forms of behaviour which are considered typical for their sex. Boys, beginning from an early age, imitate primarily

111

men. Girls imitate their mothers, from whom they learn about female psychology, with the emotional-altruistic tint which is characteristic to them.' (15) Khripkova and Kolesov also acknowledge social influences when they suggest that boys are less capable than girls at performing domestic tasks partly because they have less practice. However, this is secondary; 'the chief thing ... is the fact that it is more difficult to train boys to do them than it is to train girls'. (16) Biology thus remains paramount. Upbringing can only 'promote ... that which the child already possessed from the moment of birth'. (17)

This leads pedagogical theory into a major confusion. While biology's role is vital, it is not deterministic. It leaves a sufficiently strong imprint on the personality to preclude the possibility of an absolute psychological identity of men and women, but it needs help if it is to successfully develop the tendencies contained in this imprint. Hence 'boys and girls need a differentiated upbringing. Pedagogy must not be sexless.' (18) While the autonomous influence of the environment on sex differences in personality seems pretty negligible, once it is harnessed to the purpose by parents and teachers it takes on a fundamental importance. Much of the recent pedagogical discussion is concerned with training and self-training of appropriate male and female characteristics, both in the school and the home. Teachers should understand the different personalities of boys and girls and how these are formed, to which end 'it is important to study the interaction of biological and social laws of development'. (19) In the West an understanding of the 'social laws' of gender development has been used by feminists to challenge the traditional roles of men and women; in the Soviet Union it has the opposite function of reinforcing them, since, once understood, social laws can be used to achieve a more successful inculcation of sex-typed characteristics. Assertions about the 'naturalness' of dichotomised personalities begin to seem like nothing more than a justification for sex-differentiated upbringing. The argument is that sex differences in personality are desirable because they are natural and, to some extent, inevitable; educationalists are not attempting to mould men and women to cultural stereotypes and perpetuate women's inequality, but are just helping nature to unfold her plans.

Failure to develop a sufficiently sex-typed

112

personality results in a number of negative consequences. Khripkova and Kolesov explain that

> the recognition of the character of one's own sexual group is the basis for the formation of the psychological structure, which defines the behaviour acceptable in a given society for members of the male or female sex. Therefore the formation of ideas about the necessary type of behaviour of a boy or a girl, a young man or woman, is an aim of upbringing. (20)

Failure to exhibit the appropriate characteristics apparently results in ostracism, even from the earliest age; kindergarten children have been seen to show hostility towards children of ambiguous sexual identity. (21) More importantly, an 'incorrect sexual orientation' results in the inability to perform one's essential roles in adulthood. According to Gudkovich and Kondratov,

> if the girl does not play with dolls, she frequently discovers, when she has become a mother, that her maternal feeling is weak; the child seems to her a burden and not a joy. In addition, she has few maternal habits. Boys, brought up by mollycoddling, become cowardly, delicate, weak and dependent. They want to play only with girls. And having grown up, they reap the sad fruits of such an upbringing, for the demands made on them are those made on men, and no-one will make allowances for "feminine upbringing". (22)

(The suggestion that fewer demands are made on women than on men in Soviet society is, to say the least, curious; a multitude of time-budget studies point to the opposite conclusion.)

Several of the supposed female characteristics seem decidedly unhealthy, however. Women's greater emotionality has been linked by pedagogical theorists with a tendency towards neurosis and to 'emotional scarring', and the peculiarly female interest in appearance with a pathological conviction of physical inadequacy. (23) While Soviet psychologists have talked of the possibility of eliminating negative personality traits in schoolchildren through training, (24) it is never suggested by pedagogical theorists that these negative female traits can be overcome. On the contrary, we find them urging parents and teachers to

113

assist nature in developing these very traits.

The main trait which should be instilled in boys is 'chivalry'. Kindergarten teachers should 'demand of boys that they defend girls, give up their places to them, let them go first, not allow them to do heavy physical work ...'. (25) This will apparently instill in boys 'a feeling of respect and regard for girls. Inasmuch as boys are physically stronger than girls, it is important to explain to them that man has been given his strength in order to protect the weak.' (26) Elsewhere we learn that nature has not actually given man strength, but merely the potentiality for it. This too needs to be 'developed from early childhood'. (27) Once nature has flown back in through the window, it is evidently likely to fly straight out again unless it is grabbed and held down by the combined forces of family and school.

Upbringing Practice. How should parents go about developing strength in their sons? The same instructions appear, word for word, in Kostyashkin's 1964 article and in another by V.A. Grigorova ten years later:

> The attitude towards the boys is stricter, demands on his physical strength and on a display of bravery are decisively higher, and defeats and failures are criticised more sharply. Even the food of the boy begins, from the age of fourteen or earlier, to be distinguished by fewer sweets and porridge, and a larger portion of meat. The boy's bed is harder, the mother's caresses are more restrained, the look of the father is more stern and punishment is stricter. And especially important is the continuous increase in the physical load, especially the workload. (28)

Kolbanovskii also recommends different levels of physical education for boys and girls: 'The norms for boys with respect to running, jumping, swimming, skating, skiing, and bicycling differ from those for girls. Some gymnastic exercises - weightlifting, pole-vaulting - and such types of sports as football, hockey, boxing and wrestling are contraindicated for girls, not only because of biological consider-ations, but also for aesthetic reasons'. (29) (Obviously it would not do to have girls looking strong.)

Teachers are urged to 'develop and affirm the

commanding masculine position' (30) by placing boys
in all the leading school and Komsomol posts, even
though girls - being more hard-working and diligent
at this age - seem on the surface more suitable.
Girls will not be upset at losing their prestigious
positions since they might 'like to command some
"assistants", but not a group or a detachment; and in
no event do they become accustomed to the role of
commander over boys ... Girls are fully satisfied
with a secondary role, and in fact quietly get on
with practically any job'. (31)

In girls, parents and teachers should
concentrate above all on inculcating traits
appropriate to motherhood. Here there are signs of a
change in perspective in the last 20 years.
Kolbanovskii thought it 'important that girls be
prepared for the experience of pure and honest love,
and for motherhood', but 'the main task' of teachers
was 'preparing girls for their future productive and
socially useful work'. (32) For current educational
theorists the emphasis has apparently shifted.
Timoshchenko places motherhood in the position of
primary importance; teachers should make girls aware
that 'the desire to prove oneself in adulthood, or be
the same as boys ("this is the age of equality!")
might end badly' (33). Schools in the past have
encouraged girls' professional aspirations to the
detriment of their maternal and domestic
orientation, she explains, so that now 'many girls in
the final year at school cannot imagine themselves in
the role of wife and mother. The majority of them
connect their future lives only with study and work'.
(34) Instead, the concentration should be on teaching
girls domestic skills - how 'to cook, sew, knit, and
fulfil other household duties quickly and with
forbearance; ... to look attractive; ... to radiate
warmth, light and kindness, and to support a buoyant
tone in the family'. (35) Belskaya writes in similar
terms that,

> our schools are to be praised for their
> successes in bringing up girls to be good
> workers and actively involved citizens, but it
> is time we paid more attention to making them
> more feminine and housewifely, more kindly,
> neat and gentle. They should be made more
> conscious of their supreme natural destiny as
> mothers, nurturers of children and keepers of
> the family. (36)

Support for a differentiated upbringing is

115

sought from within the pantheon of revolutionary
heroes. Makarenko, we learn, was supremely
chivalrous, always opening doors for his female
pupils; this gave boys a practical lesson in
masculine attentiveness, and raised in girls 'the
feeling of feminine dignity'. (37) The authority of
Marx is also invoked, to justify both the development
of strength in boys, and the stress on domestic
training for girls. Repeated references are made to
the answers he wrote (presumably in jest) on a
questionnaire asking for his favourite human
qualities; in men he claimed to value above all
strength, and in women weakness. (38) From
Timoshchenko we also learn that 'Marx and Jenny gave
much attention to the participation of their
daughters in housework. By the time she was a
teenager, Laura, who showed genuine talent in such
matters, was able to cook tasty pies and tarts, and
to prepare unusual sauces. The daughters sewed their
own sheets and dresses, embroidered and knitted'.
Marx did not confine his daughters' education to
domestic matters, of course. All three went to
business school, we learn, and became their father's
'secretaries'. (39)

It is girls' 'natural destiny' to be not only
mothers and domestic workers, but also the custodians
of morality. Kolbanovskii talks of 'maidenly honour'
as a vital female moral principle which teachers
should encourage and develop, counteracting the
'depraved view' of certain people that it is an
outdated prejudice. (40)

The advice Khripkova and Kolesov offer to
teenage girls about self-upbringing is one
indication that concern about the current fragility
of marriage and the family underlies the pedagogical
'theory' about sex differences in personality. They
are told that in order to succeed in marriage it is
necessary to exhibit appropriate feminine characteristics. Friendship is not the same as love, and the
qualities which allow women to develop a rapport with
men as friends are not those which will attract them
as husbands. The personality traits which men and
women apparently find attractive in each other
correspond with the 'natural differences'; men seek
in women modesty, shyness, emotionality and
sensitivity, for example, while women are impressed
above all by strength and logicality in a man. 'Of
course, femininity is a natural gift', they assure
readers; 'however, it is possible to develop or
suppress it in oneself'. (41)

Femininity not only attracts a man, but it also

116

rekindles his own flagging masculinity. 'On the one
hand, he becomes more masculine from the need to
protect and defend (the woman), and on the other
hand, sharp traits in his character soften; gradually
he becomes more tender and kind.' (42) This suggests
that women are being urged to act weak and helpless
in order to give men someone to protect. Any possible
reluctance to take on such a role is countered with
the assurance that 'there is great strength in
women's "weakness"'. (43)

Kolesov, for one, is aware that the views
expressed by current pedagogical writers contradict
those espoused in the early years of the Revolution.
It is the latter which are mistaken. They rested on a
disrespect for women, since men were always taken as
the standard of appropriate behaviour. Women were
expected to adopt men's clothes, hairstyles and
habits. In contrast, women of the present day are
equal not because they are identical to men, but
because they are members of a new and free society.
'If a woman is granted the "right" (which in fact
means she is forced) to do work which is unusual for
her, this is also inequality.' (44) This view is
echoed by a psychologist, Snegireva; she attacks
British feminists for placing what she sees as
impossible demands on schoolgirls by encouraging
them to aspire towards careers which are beyond their
natural capabilities. Women's professional achievements are quite sufficient as they stand, she argues
- providing a certain 'adjustment' is made for sex.
(45)

There is, it seems, a natural male or female
disposition for different types of work. In one of
the early pedagogical writings we find the assurance
that 'the girl prepares herself for a future work
activity just as the boy does; all paths of life are
open to her', but some are more open than others,
'especially those connected with women's nature -
treatment of the ill, the upbringing and teaching of
children'. (46) Since it is taken as unquestionable
fact that women have complete equality of opportunity
in the Soviet Union, any discrepancies in male and
female employment must be due to natural differences.
Kolesov can therefore offer as proof that men and
women are naturally inclined towards different kinds
of work the fact that many continue to be dominated
by one or the other sex. Citing the small numbers of
women electric drillers, timber workers, steel
foundry workers and blacksmiths, he exclaims, 'there
is special male work! The natural differences between
men and women do influence their division of labour!'

(47)

Opposing Views. Despite the apparent consensus of opinion which emerges from the above, there have been dissenting voices within pedagogy. An article published in the 1960s in the popular education journal <u>Sem'ya i shkola</u> provides a particularly clear example. (48) The article, by a teacher called Andreeva, would not look out of place in a Western feminist journal. It was not Western feminism which provided her theoretical framework, however, but the ideas propounded in the Soviet Union in the years immediately following the Revolution, when Andreeva was herself a schoolgirl. This shows the extent to which Soviet pedagogy has subsequently distanced itself from these ideas, despite the selective citing of early pedagogical works.

Andreeva rejects the call for a differentiated upbringing of boys and girls, claiming that this stems from a patriarchal ideology which sees women as weak creatures in need of chivalrous protection. This is both false and highly hypocritical, since the supposedly 'weaker sex' has a workload incomparably greater than that of the 'stronger sex'. 'At home, the gallant knights do nothing.'

Andreeva promotes an identical upbringing for boys and girls, which does not recognise separate spheres of male and female activity. Only then will adult men and women emerge who can relate to each other on the basis of mutual respect and comradeship. She finds support for her position in the work of the same early pedagogical theorists. Makarenko, for example, granted men an equal role in child-upbringing when he referred to it as the task of the entire family. Krupskaya thought it 'essential that both boys and girls are taught identically to do all necessary domestic work'. In the 1920s such ideas were put into practice; Andreeva describes her own childhood pleasure in learning manual skills at school, which she found 'incomparably more interesting than lessons on sewing and housekeeping'. However, they were defeated by the patriarchal notion of male superiority. 'In order to believe in his strength, the modern man requires weakness in his female partner, and in order to believe in his intelligence he needs her to be stupid. But this, in fact, is weakness - the need for self-affirmation through the abasement of another person'. Andreeva's words seem particularly pertinent 20 years later, with the 'feminisation' of men apparently at epidemic

118

levels and the proposed solution being the resurrection of feminine weakness and fragility.

It is also interesting to note that <u>Sem'ya i shkola</u> published Andreeva's article alongside that of a pedagogue called Ryabinin, whose views tally with those we have been discussing above. They were presented as two possible interpretations of the woman question, and readers were invited to judge for themselves which was right. In contrast, opposing voices to the main approach are now few and mild, and are not to be found in the pedagogical press but in journals like <u>Literaturnaya gazeta</u>, known for their comparative liberalism.

Other Academic Disciplines on Sex Differences in Personality

The discussion on sex differences in personality is not confined to pedagogy. Contributions have also been offered by psychologists, sociologists and the medical profession. As will be quickly apparent, these differ little from the views put forward in pedagogical texts.

Psychology. Psychology's interest in the subject has generally been slight. It has produced a few rather physiological studies, such as those by Anan'ev on the role of sex differences in ontogenesis. (49) But little attempt has been made to establish a comprehensive theory of gender development.

I.S. Kon is one exception. Described in different texts as a social psychologist, sociologist, ethnographer and even 'sexologist', he has become an acknowledged expert on the subject of sex differences in personality. At first glance, his ideas look similar to those of Western exponents of socialisation or social learning theory, with which he is evidently familiar. He talks, for example, of sex-role stereotypes, and draws a distinction between a person's biological sex and his or her gender. However, Kon is forced into even greater theoretical confusion than his pedagogical colleagues through an attempt to combine Western theories with the Soviet ideas we looked at above. On the one hand, he appears fairly liberal. He talks with disapproval of the hierarchical structure of traditional sex roles, and welcomes their erosion; he would like to see a more diverse combination of masculine and feminine traits within an individual, and in particular the possibility of men coming to

119

value the 'softer' qualities in themselves – tolerance, emotional responsiveness, and the ability to understand the feelings of another person.

However, this should not go too far. He rejects the 'androgeny' sought by Western feminists, which runs counter to both nature and Marxism. 'Marx himself, naming the most valuable qualities of man and woman, gave in the first case "strength", and in the second "weakness"'. (50) The usual banners are raised; 'quality does not mean identity', and 'not everything which is traditional is wrong'. (51) Biology, again, is granted the crucial role in the development of gender.

Kon's theory is that natural differences between the sexes caused the initial division of labour between men and women, and that this then engendered a further series of psychological differences. These, in turn, produced corresponding stereotypes in people's minds, which influence the self-image and behaviour of each generation. Although such stereotypes are exaggerations and not themselves direct descriptions of reality, they are rooted in natural differences. They can be modified with changes in the sexual division of labour, but they will not disappear. (52)

All the same, teachers and parents are exhorted to 'train, and train again, girls to be girls and boys to be boys, so that we will then see in them the women and men we want to see'. (53) The women and men we want to see are presumably those of the traditional stereotypes, but with some modifications, so that professionally competent women and emotionally responsive men can exist.

Kon is careful to stress that a child's individuality should not be stifled by a teacher's overzealous adherence to the norms of masculinity and femininity, and that personality should be developed on two fronts – 'the front of general development (including the professional aspect) of the personality, and the front of the particularly "female" (or "male")'. (54) Unfortunately he gives no further explanation of what the front of 'general development' should include. It seems, in fact, to include very little. In the case of girls, it should evidently not be permitted to encroach on male psychological territory. Kon talks with concern of the '"feminisation" of the male character, the undermining of the foundation of "masculinity" in the family and in society', and cautions that 'women ... are not always taught about the great sensitivity of men towards everything which is connected with their

ideas about masculinity; a too energetic and
assertive woman (especially in love) is involuntar-
ily perceived as a transgressor of male
"sovereignty"'. (55)

It could be that Kon is forced to walk a narrow
tightrope between what he wishes to say and what he
has to say to accord with the current line on sex
differences in personality. This would explain why
his more traditional statements fit so uncomfortably
with those inspired by Western theories. The
possibility is supported by the otherwise
inexplicable fact that at a time of evident interest
in sex differences in personality, Kon's own weighty
tome on the subject has not been accepted for
publication in Russia (though it has circulated round
the psychology community in Moscow in manuscript
form). It has, on the other hand, appeared in both
Hungarian and Estonian, the languages of two of the
more liberal enclaves within the Eastern bloc.

Sociology. Sociologists are virtually alone amongst
social scientists in the Soviet Union in voicing a
cautious acknowledgement that women have yet to
achieve equality with men, regardless of how one
defines it. However, they have devoted little
attention to the development of gender, looking more
at the difference in male and female roles in the
family and work place.

Zoya Yankova has made some reference to the
development of female personality. Her main point is
that in order to develop all-round, harmonious
personalities - which is the professed aim for all
Soviet citizens - women need to be involved in both
the professional and familial worlds. Work outside
the home has developed in the female personality some
qualities formerly associated with men (independence, initiative, and self-confidence, for example),
but their different reproductive roles ensure that
men and women will never be psychologically
identical. 'The function of motherhood has formed and
will continue to form in women such character traits
as tenderness, attentiveness, concern, softness,
emotionality.' (56) These qualities, essential for
family happiness, also benefit the woman's work
environment, since she is able to understand the
moods of her colleagues and offer them emotional
support. Women's equality in the Soviet Union enables
them to nurture a work collective as well as a
family.

Later, however, we read that women are in danger

of losing their feminine qualities if a psychological balance is not maintained between their old and new qualities. The problem develops when

> equality is understood as identity - women begin to perform work which is difficult and dangerous to their organism, to become coarse, and to take on masculine patterns of behaviour, patterns which lead to family conflicts. They lose their taste for domestic behaviour and the interpersonal intimacy verified by the centuries. The weakening of femininity inevitably has an adverse effect on the psychological climate of the family, and often leads to complex collisions and frustrations in the work collective. Femininity is therefore an important mechanism for stabilising and strengthening the family, protecting and deepening in it a pleasant emotional and spiritual atmosphere, and is an important characteristic of a socialist female personality. (57)

Medicine. The medical profession has become pedagogy's staunchest ally in the struggle to preserve, or resurrect, traditional masculinity and femininity. The health journal <u>Zdorov'e</u> frequently carries articles on the subject, many of which are indistinguishable from those appearing in pedagogical journals and whose link with health issues is far from obvious. These often refer to the 'scientific work' of certain pedagogical writers, who in turn cite the writings of medical 'specialists' to support their views. <u>Zdorov'e</u> is the most widely read of Soviet journals, with a distribution of over sixteen million. Could its interest in sex-upbringing reflect a Party concern to reach a larger audience than pedagogical texts could themselves achieve?

Some articles do manage a connection between gender and health. We read, for example, that an increasing number of men are choosing not to marry because women are not sufficiently feminine, and single men are more often ill and have a higher death rate than their married counterparts. (58) Marriage is no guarantee of health and happiness, however, again because of women's lack of femininity. A strong, practical and independent woman challenges and erodes a man's masculinity, and according to Sysenko (whose work is among the recommended texts for the 'Family Life' course), many men turn to alcohol if they are deprived of their rightful role as head of the family. (59) Women will also be unhappy in the absence of traditional roles, since they need to feel themselves under the protection of their husbands. The solution is in their own hands; t is their 'business ... to support man's masculinity'. (60) Evidently if femininity is reinstated, masculinity will automatically follow.

A particularly interesting discussion of sex differences is to be found in the work of A.I. Belkin, head of Moscow's Institute of Psychiatry. Primarily an endocrinologist, Belkin is also the Soviet specialist in the treatment of 'hermaphrodites'. Most of Belkin's patients have a gender identity which does not correspond to their biological sex; because of a congenital physical abnormality they were assigned the wrong sex at birth, and brought up accordingly. The mistake generally comes to light at puberty, with the appearance of the wrong secondary sex characteristics. Belkin claims to successfully reconstruct the gender identities even of his adult patients (contrary to Western wisdom, which holds that gender is irrevocably fixed by the age of four). He does this according to a rigid model of sex-role stereotypes, arguing that a person's psychological wellbeing rests on the strength of his or her gender identity. (61) A person who is not sufficiently masculine or feminine will experience a sense of depersonalisation', a lack of belonging; and 'this intolerable feeling of "sexlessness" expresses itself in anti-social behaviour such as alcoholism, drug-taking and homosexuality'. (62)

The labelling of homosexuality as an antisocial activity, and its placement on a par with alcoholism and drug-taking, can also be linked to the demographic crisis. Homosexuality is seen as antisocial partly because it is non-reproductive; homosexuals are not performing their demographic duty.

Ethics and Psychology of Family Life' Course

The introduction of the course on 'the Ethics and Psychology of Family Life' was no spontaneous move. Years before its inception its aims and outline were under discussion in education journals and articles in the popular press. Preparatory studies were conducted on, for example, children's perceptions of masculinity and femininity and their level of family orientation prior to the course. (63) In 1982 a

123

recommended course outline, designed by members o
the Academy of Pedagogical Sciences and approved b'
the Ministry of Education, appeared in the educatio
journal <u>Vospitanie shkol'nikov</u>. A year later this wa
followed by a detailed, lesson-by-lesson programm
for teachers of the course, with advice about how t
handle individual topics, how to involve pupils i
discussions, and what homework to set. Before it
adoption in schools throughout the country it wa
tested in certain schools in Moscow and the Balti
republics.

Articles about the course usually begin with th
declaration that the family is the most importan
cell of socialist society. (64) Its functions have
been listed (not always in this order) as th
regulation of reproduction, the satisfaction o
people's domestic and daily-life needs, th
organisation of their leisure activities, and th
upbringing of the next generation. (65) In the 197'
Constitution it was 'taken under the protection o
the state'; the 'Family Life' course is evidentl
part of this protection. (66)

The increase in divorce has been blame
primarily on poor preparation for family life; o
'the inability of the partners to develop thei
relationship, and false ideas on the part of youn
people about the role of men and women in th
family'. (67) The course therefore includes muc
discussion of 'the nature of the relationship betwee
partners, masculinity and femininity, and mora
attitudes within the family', in order to bette
prepare young people for marriage and develop in the
'the ability to create the correct family relations'
(68)

It is seen as a distinct departure from th
normal school curriculum. It is concerned not wit
education but with upbringing; not with th
communication of knowledge, but with the formation o
moral qualities appropriate to future marriag
partners. (69) It is, in fact, primarily a programm
of sex-role socialisation. As Yufereva explains, 'u
to now, school-children's ideas about th
psychological differences of men and women have bee
formed by chance. With the introduction of the ne
school subject, teachers will be directed towards th
upbringing of children according to the laws o
personality development connected with their sex.'
(70) Psychologist Tat'yana Snegireva similarl
asserts that the course will help children 'becom
aware of themselves and their special male and femal
roles'. (71)

These roles are different but complementary, based on the balance of male and female personalities. In a handbook for course teachers, Krasovskii explains that 'women are more emotional, that feelings are more clearly expressed by them; men, on the other hand, are more rational and, as a rule, the intellect rules over feelings in them. Logical thought in men is generally counterpoised by intuition in women.' (72) Similarly, the 'strength' of man is balanced by the 'weakness' of woman. Like Khripkova and Kolesov, Krasovskii sees great strength in woman's 'weakness', if it is correctly handled:

> The strength of woman lies not in her ability to curb her husband and direct him like a marionette, but in her "weakness" - in femininity, in softness, sympathy and kindness. A woman must above all respect in herself these qualities, and manifest them ever more in family life. The husband, in turn, must try to be strong, masculine, active, decisive, and energetic. The formation of such relations between husband and wife is one of the most important paths of achievement of harmony in family life and family happiness. (73)

The course is also concerned with inculcating a socialist sexual morality. This disdains bourgeois notions of 'free love', 'short-term marriage' and 'changes of partner', and recognises that marriage and sexual relations are not a purely personal matter but have great social significance. Failure to acknowledge this 'is particularly to blame for the sharp current demographic problem'. (74)

Course Outline for Teachers. The course takes place in the ninth and tenth grades (15-17-year-olds), for two hours per week. Teachers begin by establishing its aims, the importance of the family, and the state's concern for it. One of the pupils is called on to explain what the state's protection of the family actually means. This involves writing on the blackboard the laws and benefits regarding the family, such as the period of paid maternity leave, moves to establish a shorter working day for mothers with small children, recent improvements in preschool institutions and extended-day school facilities, domestic services, and the privileges and allowances granted to large families. (75)

Next comes a series of lessons on 'the Personality, Society and the Family'. This is divided into three sub-sections: 'the personality and self-upbringing', 'the personality, work collective and society' and 'the personality and the family'. This section is introduced with the statement that one of the basic aims of socialist society is the all-sided and harmonious development of the personality of each person. Students are told that Marxism sees personality as a social phenomenon, formed and transformed through interaction with society. Next they learn that there are certain innate features in a male or female personality regarding cognitive tendencies, interests, and emotional responses.

Although sex-role socialisation appears throughout the course, it is at its most overt under the heading 'the moral basis of the mutual relations between boys and girls'. This subject only forms a two-hour component on the course, but is afforded by far the most detailed analysis in <u>Vospitanie shkol'nikov</u>'s guide for teachers. It begins with an enumeration of the benefits achieved by women in the Soviet Union, and a discussion of their equality in work and study. A week before the class, students are set the task of writing about their understanding of masculinity and femininity, the qualities they most value in men and women, and which they would most like their future spouse to possess. The children's essays provide a starting point for a lesson on the desired content of masculinity and femininity.

Pupils learn that 'the modern boy' has 'an understanding of masculinity, and of the duty to protect and preserve the virtue and honour of the girl'. (76) He should be honest, responsible, intelligent, brave, decisive, noble; he should possess self-control, a love of work, a readiness to defend the weak and take on himself the most difficult and demanding jobs. This is true in the domestic as well as the work situation. Hence 'helping' his wife with the housework - at least, certain types of housework - is presented as not incompatible with the man's masculine pride. It is suggested that teachers read aloud in class some of the letters which appear in the popular press on women's perceptions of masculinity, such as: 'An intelligent man might not be a knight, but he understands that he must offer his seat to a woman. He might not be able to prepare a tasty meal, but he understands that he must help with the housework'. Children must also learn to recognise 'incorrect notions of masculinity', those which link it with a indless pursuit of fashion, rudeness, use of lcohol, and speech littered with swearwords and lang. (77)

A discussion on the 'modern girl' should be receded with an outline of the role of women in the amily and society, and about the qualities which omen should possess in order to manage this ifficult combination. (No such mention is made of a ombination of male roles, even if they are expected o help more now with the housework.) The works of ducational writers such as Timoshchenko (who, as we ave seen, stresses the domestic and maternal roles f women above their professional activities) are ecommended for use as course textbooks. The changing tatus of women throughout history is analysed; the arly matriarchal cultures, the male acquisition of ower, the contradictions of the Renaissance period when men idolised women and fought duels for them ut treated them as slaves and playthings), apitalism with its double oppression by husbands and mployers, and finally the achievement of equality nder socialism. This is contrasted with women's ontinuing oppression in the capitalist countries.

Teachers then explain that equality has brought n its wake a problem. 'The new male and female roles n the family and society have entered into ontradiction with traditional ideas about the kind f qualities men and women should possess'. (78) In hedding their dependence and subordination, women ave sometimes also shed their femininity - their indness, concern for others, softness, tenderness, houghtfulness, and their ability to concede to thers. Men, on the other hand, have lost their ormer role of breadwinner, and sometimes with it heir masculinity, becoming indecisive and weak of haracter. This is disastrous for society. uriously, teachers are expected not to explain here bout the demographic crisis, but that 'femininity nd high morality are indivisibly-united concepts', nd that if women are no longer 'the custodians of ocial morality', (79) society will collapse into oral turpitude. Fortunately, the problem can be olved without sacrificing women's equality because t is now known that 'equality does not mean dentity'.

Again, teachers are told to draw on letters in he popular press to illustrate the qualities ssential in women. A debate in <u>Komsomol'skaya ravda</u>, for example, established that 'the modern oman' should be kind, affable, able to understand ther people, tender, sincere, natural, trusting,

127

modest, sensitive, loyal, intelligent; she should possess a high level of morality, the ability to love, and the ability to be a housekeeper. These traits are all essential, but different ones may be prioritised by different people; hence while some people put intelligence in first place, others see more importance in the ability to do housework. (80) (The authors mention this with no trace of criticism or irony; it is apparently not a bizarre notion that in a society which has achieved equality for women some people still see the ability to do housework a women's greatest quality.) Teachers should also discuss with pupils the meaning of 'maidenly honour' and 'female virtue'. (81)

The final section in the first year of the course is 'Marriage and the Family'. This covers 'what being prepared for marriage means', 'the Soviet family and its functions', and 'special features o the young family'. In these lessons, children are guided step by step through courtship and marriage and are presented with a single model of conjugal bliss. Evidently the course designers have taken to heart the opening line of <u>Anna Karenina</u>: 'All happy families resemble one another ...'. There is considerable discussion in this section of the outline for teachers about the demographic crisis but it is not clear if this should be relayed to pupils or is offered as background information for the teachers themselves. What is evident is that an appeal to reproduce solely on these grounds is not seen as sufficient. Teachers are told to make children aware that a one-child family is not a real collective, and is doomed to breed excessive anxiety in the parents and egoism in the child. (82)

In the first class of the tenth grade the focus of the course shifts to the family's relationship with the external world. It begins with 'the Basic Values of the Family'. This looks at its ideological values, moral foundations, its role as a collective the work atmosphere within it, its budget and economy, its domestic organisation, and the social consequences of a breach in family relations. Children should be taught that not only their future happiness, but also their physical health rests on their successful creation of a family; as articles in <u>Zdorov'e</u> have claimed, married people live longer and are less often ill. (83)

The final section deals with children. Subjects to be discussed are society's concern for children, the family's role in their upbringing, the different roles of mothers and fathers, and the family's relationship to other upbringing institutions. Again, the benefits mothers and children have achieved under socialism are enumerated, and the new measures which have been introduced to help women combine their two roles (in other words, to have more children). Motherhood is eulogised; it is the highest social value, women's great mission. (84)

Conclusion

We have noted that there is a virtual consensus about sex differences in personality across interested disciplines in the Soviet Union, and that this is reflected in the school course on the Ethics and Psychology of Family Life. It is reasonable to assume that this is not mere coincidence. In the 1960s there is some evidence of a debate around the subject; now, although there are differences of opinion, they fit within a single framework.

There is some disharmony within the framework itself, however. This is particularly clear in the conflict between the insistence on the one hand that sex differences in personality are natural and will never disappear, and on the other that they will fail to appear without determined training on the part of parents and teachers. The reality is that the transformation of society has brought about changes in personality, particularly in female personality, and this is a source of concern because the collapse in clearly defined sex-roles – men as providers, women as homemakers – is blamed for the fragility of marriage and the drop in the birth rate. The perceived solution is to reverse this trend and, perhaps in anticipation of accusations that this is contrary to the notion of equality between the sexes, it is supported by an insistence that sex differences in personality are natural and inevitable.

Evidently the pedagogical approach to sex differences is informed by social and demographic concerns and not by Marxism (despite references to Marx's predilection for strong men and weak women, and his encouragement of pie-making abilities in his daughters). The Marxist stress on the social construction of personality is certainly at odds with the insistence that sex differences in personality are fixed by nature.

The socialist aim of developing all-round, harmonious personalities also stands in conflict with pedagogy's attempt to develop primarily those aspects of personality considered appropriate to a person's sex. Some sociologists have tried to deal with this contradiction by suggesting that the feminine side of women's personalities is in danger of becoming under-developed. They explain that 'the character and structure of a woman's personality will be incomplete if she abstracts herself from her family functions, and especially from the function of maternity, and that 'the process of the harmonious development of a woman's personality presupposes not only her participation in creative labour, but also the cultivating of typically female traits of character such as pride, virtue, maternal care for near and dear ones, gentleness, etc.' (85) However, there is little suggestion (apart from Kon's somewhat timid venture) that men's personalities could similarly benefit from the development of a nurturant aspect. Also, as we have seen, writers are agreed that the development of those qualities in women's personalities connected with their professional work should not be allowed to intrude too far into male psychological territory and thus erode his masculine dignity. Masculinity and femininity are paramount; and one-sided as these are, the development of all-round personality has to fit itself around them.

According to Andreeva, the reversal of early socialist aims regarding male and female education and personality development began in the Stalin era, notably with the return to single-sex education from 1943 to 1954. However, the programme of rapid industrialisation, and the deficit of workers during the war years, ensured a continued need for women's participation in the work force. Now, women's work outside the home has been placed in a secondary position. It is charged with having removed her, both physically and psychologically, from her function of motherhood.

The instability of marriage and the decrease in the birth rate can obviously be linked to other factors in Soviet society besides the demise of masculinity and femininity. Numerous sociological studies have shown that a sharp imbalance exists in the amount of time spent by working women and men on housework, and the pressure on accommodation in large cities in the European republics means that couples wanting to have more than one child will often have insufficient living space to do so. Although high by Western standards, the provision of preschool institutions is still not sufficient, and their reputation for poor quality care deters many women from using them.

The government is aware and concerned about these problems. Its response has been to appoint a woman, Alexandra Biryukova, to the Party secretariat - the first woman to hold a senior party post for 25 years - to deal primarily with family issues, and to introduce a number of resolutions in the 27th Party Congress concerning the improvement of the material, domestic and living conditions of families. Despite a declared commitment to the combination of motherhood and the active participation of women in work and social activities', the new measures, with the exception of the provision of more kindergarten places, reinforce the pedagogical attempt to develop women's domestic orientation at the expense of the professional. They include the increase of part-paid maternity leave to 18 months, the establishment of more part-time jobs, and the possibility of working from home. While the school course aims to develop in girls the necessary qualities to create a cosy home, these measures will install her in it.

It remains to be seen whether the moves to resurrect traditional masculine and feminine characteristics will succeed. So far the course has had a mixed reception. Psychologists in Moscow have complained that materials are grossly inadequate and teachers hopelessly unprepared (though this will no doubt change when the planned course on the subject is introduced in teacher-training colleges). In contrast, the headmistress of a school I visited in Moscow in December spoke with enthusiasm about the high level of student motivation and participation in the course, and an already noticeable improvement in family awareness.

Notes

1. T. Afanas'eva, 'Muzhchina doma', <u>Nedelya</u>, no. 22 (1977), p.6.

2. T. Snegireva, 'Ne predopredelenie, a vybor', <u>Literaturnaya gazeta</u>, 23 May 1984, p.12.

3. See R. Stites, <u>The Women's Liberation Movement in Russia</u> (Princeton University Press, Princeton N.J., 1978), pp.321-2.

4. E. Andreeva, 'Protiv patriarkhal'nykh nravov', <u>Sem'ya i shkola</u>, no. 1 (1977), pp.6-9.

5. For fuller discussion, see L. Attwood and M. McAndrew, 'Women at Work in the USSR' in M.J. Davidson and C.L. Cooper (eds), <u>Working Women</u> (John Wiley, Chichester, 1984), pp.269-302.

6. I.V. Pershaeva, 'Podgotovka devochek-starsheklassnitz k lichnoi zhizni v sisteme raboty klassnogo rukovoditelya', <u>O ratsionalizatsii uchebno-vospitatel'noi raboty v shkole</u> (Sverdlovsk,

1977), p.143.

7.   V.N. Kolbanovskii, 'The Sex-upbringing of the Rising Generation', Soviet Education, vol. 1 (1964), p.4.

8.   A.G. Khripkova, 'Neobkhodima mudrost' (polovoe vospitanie - grani problemy)', Sovetskaya Rossiya, 16 December 1979, p.3.

9.   A.G. Khripkova and D.V. Kolesov, Devochka - podrostok - devushka (Moscow, 1981), p.72. (This book is also partly serialised in the journal Sem'ya i shkola, Aug-Dec 1979.)

10.   Kolbanovskii, 'Sex upbringing', p.9.

11.   A. Mikaberidze, 'Osobennosti vospitaniya devochek', Kalendar' dlya roditelei 1980 (Moscow, 1979), p.97.

12.   Khripkova and Kolesov, Devochka - podrostok - devushka, p.76.

13.   Ibid., pp.73-80, and L. Timoshchenko, 'O vospitanii devochki', Vospitanie shkol'nikov, no. 6 (1980), p.37.

14.   Kolbanovskii, 'Sex upbringing', p.7.

15.   Timoshchenko, 'O vospitanii devochki', p.38.

16.   Khripkova and Kolesov, Devochka - podrostok - devushka, p.79.

17.   Ibid., p.76.

18.   A.G. Khripkova, 'A kakov vklad pedagog-iki', rabotnitsa, No. 19 (1979), p.14.

19.   Ibid.

20.   Khripkova and Kolesov, Devochka - podrostok - devushka, p.84.

21.   Ibid., p.83.

22.   L.N. Gudkovich and A.M. Kondratov, O tebe i obo mne (Stavropol, 1977), p.18.

23.   See I.S. Kon, 'Muzhestvennye zhenshchiny? Zhenstvennye muzhchiny?', Literaturnaya gazeta, 1 Jan. 1970, p.12; Timoshchenko, 'O vospitanii devochki', p.38; and Khripkova and Kolesov, Devochka - podrostok - devushka, p.80.

24.   See L. Attwood, 'The New Soviet Man and Woman - Soviet Views on Psychological Sex Differences' in Barbara Holland (ed.), Soviet Sisterhood (Junction, London, 1985), p.59.

25.   The same advice, word for word, appears in V. Aleshina, 'Chtoby vyros nastoyashchii muzhchina', Sem'ya i shkola, no.4 (1964), pp.4-5, and A.G. Khripkova, Voprosy polovogo vospitaniya (Rostov on Don, 1969), p.53.

26.   Kolbanovskii, 'Sex upbringing', p.4.

27.   E.K. Kostyashkin, 'Pedagogicheskie aspekty polovogo vospitaniya', Sovetskaya pedagogika, no. 7

(1964), p.48.

28. Ibid., p.47, and V.A. Grigorova, quoted in J. Peers, 'Workers by Hand and Womb' in Holland, Soviet Sisterhood, p.37.

29. Kolbanovskii, 'Sex upbringing', p.4.

30. Kostyashkin, 'Pedagogicheskie aspekty', p.51.

31. Ibid., p.51.

32. Kolbanovskii, 'Sex upbringing', p.7.

33. L. Timoshchenko, V sem'e rastet doch' (Moscow 1978), pp.58-9.

34. Timoshchenko, 'O vospitanii devochki', p.38.

35. Ibid., p.40.

36. G. Belskaya, 'Where Bad Wives Come From', translated from Literaturnaya gazeta in Current Digest of the Soviet Press, vol. 29, no. 37 (1977), p.13.

37. Aleshina, 'Chtoby vyros nastoyashchii muzhchina', p.5.

38. For fuller discussion of this, see L. Attwood, 'The New Soviet Man and Woman', pp.65-6.

39. Timoshchenko, V sem'e rastet doch', p.89.

40. Kolbanovskii, 'Sex upbringing', p.7.

41. Khripkova and Kolesov, Devochka - podrostok - devushka, p.121.

42. A. Baskina, quoted in Khripkova and Kolesov, ibid., p.120.

43. Ibid., p.120.

44. D.V. Kolesov, Besedy o polovom vospitanii (Moscow, 1980), p.178.

45. Snegireva, 'Ne predopredelenie', p.12.

46. I. Gyne, 'Zhenstvennost' in P. Peter, V. Shebek and I. Gyne, Devushka prevrashchaetsya v zhenshchinu (Moscow, 1960), p.12.

47. Kolesov, Besedy, p.221.

48. Andreeva, 'Protiv patriarkhal'nykh nravov', pp.6-9.

49. B.G. Anan'ev, Chelovek kak predmet soznaniya (Leningrad, 1968), pp.168-175.

50. I.S. Kon, 'Polovye razlichiya i differentsiatsiya sotsial'nykh rolei' in Sootnoshenie biologicheskogo i sotsial'nogo v cheloveke (Moscow, 1975), p.773.

51. Ibid., p.773.

52. Derived from the above work (see note 50), plus: I.S. Kon, Lichnost' kak sub'ekt obshchestvennykh otnoshenii (Moscow, 1966); I.S. Kon, 'Psikhologiya polovykh razlichii', Voprosy psikhologii, no. 2 (1981), pp. 45-57. I.S. Kon, 'Adam, Eva i vek-iskusitel', Literaturnaya gazeta, 1 Jan. 1979,

p.11; I.S. Kon, <u>Psikhologiya starsheklassnika</u> (Moscow, 1980); Interview with Kon in L. Kuznetsova, <u>Zhenshchina na rabote i doma</u> (Moscow, 1980), pp.177-91.

53. Kuznetsova, <u>Zhenshchina na rabote</u>, p.191.
54. Ibid., p.191.
55. Ibid., p.189.
56. Z.A. Yankova, <u>Sovetskaya zhenshchina</u> (Moscow, 1978), p.123.
57. Ibid., p.128.
58. I.V. Dorno, 'Muzhchina za 30', <u>Zdorov'e</u>, no. 11 (1985), p.22-3.
59. V.A. Sysenko, 'Zhenshchina i muzhchina', <u>Zdorov'e</u>, no. 1 (1980), pp.14-15.
60. Ibid.
61. A.I. Belkin, 'Biologicheskie i sotsial'nye faktory, formiruyushchie polovuyu identifikatsiyu' in <u>Sootnoshenie biologicheskogo i sotsial'nogo v cheloveke</u>, pp.777-90; and A.I. Belkin and V.N. Lakusta, <u>Biologicheskaya terapiya psikhicheskikh zabolevanii</u> (Kishinev, 1983).
62. A.I. Belkin, 'Muzhchina i zhenshchina; stiranie psikhologicheskikh granei?', <u>Literaturnaya gazeta</u>, 1 Aug. 1973, p.13. The same article appears under the name 'Masculine, feminine or neutral?' in The Unesco Courier, August-September 1975, pp.58-61.
63. T.I. Yufereva, 'Obrazy muzhchin i zhenshchin v soznanii podrostkov', <u>Voprosy psikhologii</u>, no. 3 (1985), pp.84-90; and M.S. Matskovskii, 'Podgotovka podrostkov i molodezhi k budushchei zhizni' in <u>Sem'ya v sisteme nravstvennogo vospitaniya: Aktual'nye problemy vospitaniya podrostkov</u> (Moscow, 1979), pp.204-13.
64. For example, 'Etika i psikhologiya semeinoi zhizni - tipovaya programma kursa dlya uchashchikhsya IX - X klassov (eksperimental'nyi variant), <u>Vospitanie shkol'nikov</u>, no. 1 (1982), p.28; and 'Etika i psikhologiya semeinoi zhizni', <u>Vospitanie shkol'nikov</u>, no. 1 (1983), p.32.
65. A.S. Krasovskii, <u>Eticheskie besedy so starsheklassnikami o brake i sem'e</u> (Minsk, 1983), pp.3, 24.
66. A frequent reference to Article 53 of the 1977 Constitution - 'The family enjoys the protection of the State.'
67. Yufereva, 'Obrazy muzhchin i zhenshchin', p.84.
68. Ibid.
69. Krasovskii, <u>Eticheskie besedy</u>, p.6.
70. Yufereva, 'Obrazy muzhchin i zhenshchin', p.90.

71. Snegireva, 'Ne predopredelenie', p.12.
72. Krasovskii, <u>Eticheskie besedy</u>, p.21.
73. Ibid., p.58.
74. Ibid., p.25.
75. The following is taken from the series on 'Etika i psikhologiya semeinoi zhiz'ni' in <u>Vospitanie shkol'nikov</u> nos. 1 and 2 (1982) ('experimental version') and nos. 1-6 (1983) (course outline for teachers).
76. <u>Vospitanie shkol'nikov</u>, no. 1 (1982), p.29.
77. Ibid., No. 1 (1983), p.36.
78. Ibid., p.37.
79. Ibid., p.37.
80. Ibid., p.37.
81. Ibid., p.38.
82. Ibid., No. 3 (1983), pp.28-9.
83. Ibid., No. 4 (1983), p.36.
84. Ibid., No. 1 (1982), p.32.
85. Quoted by J. Peers, 'Workers by Hand and Womb', p.138.

Chapter Six

THE ROLE OF YOUTH ORGANISATIONS IN COMMUNIST UPBRINGING IN THE SOVIET SCHOOL

Jim Riordan

Introduction

Ask any Soviet or even former Soviet person if they remember the day they joined the children's movement and likely as not they will say it was the happiest moment of their lives. It was and is a most moving and memorable occasion even for those remote from politics - rather like confirmation for Christians. And early years spent in the Octobrists and Pioneers are generally happy and absorbing, providing both an outlet for the exuberance of childhood and something solemn and responsible, a link with the wider society.

The Soviet children's movement is one of the links in the chain of socialising agencies that shape the values and behaviour of young people: 'the entire country teaches children, brings them up, tempers and cares for them, and enriches them culturally. Each link in mature socialist society, however, be it family or school, cultural or health institution, social organisation or mass media, has its own specific part to play, its place and designation in regard to children.' (1)

Unlike children's organisations in the West, the Soviet children's movement embraces virtually <u>all</u> schoolchildren, it is based on the school, it has no rivals and the values it seeks to instil fully coincide with those of other official agencies. What is more, its goals are explicitly political. As Lenin put it in his policy-forming address to the Young Communist League (<u>Komsomol</u>) in 1920, 'It is the job of the Youth League ... to educate communists. The whole purpose of training, educating and teaching young people today is to imbue them with communist ethics.' (2) Not religious ethics, not faith in other-worldly matters. Not a Protestant ethic of thrift, modesty and hard work. Elements, certainly, of both. From religion a faith in the Party and the future, in the writings of Marx and Lenin often learned as a catechism and used as a sacred blessing, in Lenin as a model for personal conduct and a personification of abstract values. From a work ethic the sort of earthy values one would expect in a society in turbulent transition from farming to industrialising, from village to city. But with further ingredients from Russian and other ethnic traditions, the consensus needs of a developing society and the inspiring vision and communist principles of Marx and Lenin (not to say Stalin!).

While schooling is basically, though not exclusively, concerned with academic learning (obuchenie), the children's organisations are largely concerned with character training (vospitanie). As the early Soviet educationalist Nadezhda Krupskaya once put it, 'while schools focus attention on study, the Pioneer movement focuses on vospitanie. The two are closely connected, they complement one another, they intertwine, yet none the less constitute two separate entities.' (3) In fact, the relationship between school and the children's movement, between obuchenie and vospitanie has shifted over the years and even today is not always clearly differentiated.

In the early Soviet years, some eager young communists had put forward the slogan of 'Down with school!', campaigning for the transfer of education to the children's movement. Krupskaya rebuked them, pointing out that there had to be a close alliance between school and the children's movement which 'provides school with new child material. The Pioneer movement immeasurably enhances in children an awareness of their human worth and their desire for and interest in knowledge, developing a serious attitude to study and disciplining them. The teacher finds it much easier to work with such children.' (4)

All the same, up to the 1930s, the Pioneers had a residential and occupational base, possessing only 'outposts' (forposty) in school. But from the educational reform of 1931, the Pioneer base moved to schools: the first seven grades were assigned to the Pioneers, grades eight-ten to the Komsomol. Both were expected to encourage study and good conduct. (5)

What is the Children's Movement?
While the children's movement is a vital link in the chain of socialisation, it also forms a three-link chain in its own right, encompassing young people

from the age of seven to 28, as follows:

1. The Octobrists (<u>Oktyabryata</u>): 6-9 (grades 1-3)
2. The Pioneers (<u>Pionery</u>): 10-15 (grades 4-8)
3. The Komsomol: 16-28 (grades 9-11).

Virtually all children in the relevant age groups are members of the Octobrists and Pioneers. In 1984 the Pioneers had a membership of 19,506,000 (6); but Komsomol membership in 1983 was 41,802,565 or roughly 60 per cent of the 16-28-year-olds. (7) Membership diminishes with age and Soviet sources are vague over the exact membership figures; one source gives 90 per cent of schoolleavers as members (8), another cites 80 per cent of 16-17-year-olds (9), another over 75 per cent of Komsomol-age schoolchildren (10), while another gives 'more than 50 per cent'. (11) Apparently, a significant and growing number of young people see their <u>rites de passage</u> not extending beyond the Pioneers to the Komsomol.

The Pioneers lead the Octobrists, the Komsomol leads the Pioneers, and the Communist Party leads the Komsomol. And children move naturally from one young people's organisation to the next as they grow up. The youth programme, tailored to the needs and desires of specific age groups, is said to be based on the psychological characteristics of each age group, as determined by educational psychologists. This <u>Orientir</u> (Orientation) Programme divides young people into five age groups: 6-9, 10-11, 12-13, 14-15, and 15 plus, with recommendations for youth training via the appropriate youth organisation for each group.

The Octobrists. Soon after commencing school, the child automatically becomes an Octobrist. The name was given to the first seven-year-old members who joined in 1924, seven years after the October Revolution, two years after the formation of the Pioneers and six years after the Komsomol. Today, the initiation ceremony, known as the 'Little Red Star Ceremony', traditionally takes place on 7 November, the anniversary of the Revolution. It is a festive occasion to which adult guests of honour are invited and for which Pioneers put on a concert, perhaps inviting the novitiates 'to tea and cakes prepared by the girl Pioneer leaders', as a <u>Pioneer Handbook</u> puts it. (12)

During September and October prior to the
ceremony children are prepared for entry, the aim
being to make membership a special occasion and an
honour to be earned. In that two-month period they
learn about the Revolution, their country's
revolutionary history, Lenin, and living in the
collective. (13) The accent in this early period of
character training is on group play and games. As
Krupskaya wrote, 'In group games children learn how
to organise, to lead, to be able persistently to
strive for a goal and attract others after them.'
(14) The group games are not dissimilar from those
played by the Brownies and the Cubs; indeed, some are
based on the games of the old Russian Scout movement.

Krupskaya it was in the early 1920s who took the
Komsomol to task for their unqualified condemnation
of everything connected with the Boy Scouts (at the
Komsomol 2nd and 3rd Congresses in 1919 and 1920).
She advised the Komsomol to learn from the Scouts,
setting out many of the Scout games worthy of
emulation: 'Scouting has something that irresistibly
attracts young people, gives them satisfaction,
binds them to the organisation.' She listed its
attributes as a careful study of young people's
psychology, interests and needs, the attraction of
ceremony and ritual, the clever use of children's
group feelings, and the employment of lively forms of
activity, especially games.

> The Komsomol, if it seriously intends to educate
> the younger generation and is to have even the
> slightest understanding of the colossal tasks
> which confront this generation, and if it is not
> to confine itself to childish aping of grown
> ups, must as soon as possible incorporate these
> methods into its own practice. (15)

Although the Russian Scout movement was to be
banned, the Komsomol did heed Krupskaya's advice and,
when forming the first Pioneer and Octobrist
detachments, engaged former scoutmasters 'who
accepted the principles of work of the Pioneer
organisations'. (16) The Pioneers, initially called
'Red Scouts' or Young Communists-Scouts also took
over from the Scouts their salute and motto 'Be
Prepared' (though Krupskaya later claimed it was
invented by Lenin (17)), the fleur-de-lys emblem
which evolved into three flames, the organisational
structure of <u>otryad</u> (troop), <u>druzhina</u> (council) and
<u>vozhaty</u> (leader) and various rituals. As Krupskaya
said, 'symbolism and ritual are what emotionally

attract young people: parades, red neckerchiefs,
song and drumbeating.' (18) Of the three Scout
principles of militarism, patriotism and religion,
therefore, only the third was discarded and replaced
by 'communism'.

As a symbol of membership at the initiation
ceremony, the new Octobrist receives a little red
enamel five-pointed star badge with a picture of the
three-year-old Lenin inside the star. A Pioneer pins
the badge to her/his left lapel in ceremonial
fashion. From now on until they join the Pioneers at
ten, the children will be under the supervision of
Pioneers whose job it is 'to help the Octobrists with
their lessons, to perform their first assignments, to
teach their young comrades to be friendly and to do
group social work, to abide by the Octobrist Rules
and to prepare them for joining the Pioneers' (19)
(see Appendix 6.1 for the Octobrist Rules).

After reciting the rules, the next task is to
divide the class of 30-35 children into small groups
of <u>zvezdochki</u> (little stars) made up of five to six
children, one of whom will be put in charge as
<u>komandir</u>. Ideally, all the 'little stars' will take
turns as commander during the school year. And a
Pioneer will take charge of each 'little star' and
present it with its red standard (<u>flazhok</u>).

The overall objective of the Octobrists is said
to be to get each member 'to learn to behave in a
lively and independent way within the group, to be
responsible for the common cause, fairly to assess
their own behaviour and that of classmates, and to
learn to be a reliable helper to Komsomol and Party
members'. (20) After the 'Little Red Star' ceremony,
the Pioneer leader gives each member of the Octobrist
group an assignment, such as 'flower tender',
'cleanliness monitor', 'library monitor' and
'teacher's chief assistant.' As an example, the
'cleanliness monitor' is required 'to see that all
the Octobrists in the group are neat and tidy,
properly washed, do their keep-fit exercises and keep
tidy satchels.' (21) The 'teacher's chief assistant'
helps classmates prepare their lessons, hands out and
collects exercise books, and so on.

Such role-playing is said to be highly salient
in that 'it is invariably social, the child taking on
the role of the adult and reproducing the adult's
life'. (22) This is a point made about the children's
movement by Ronald Hill, 'the authorities attempt to
inculcate the value of collectivity rather than
personal development. They simultaneously prepare
future citizens for involvement in the adult

political world.' (23)

Once or twice a month all the Octobrist zvezdochki have an hour-long assembly (sbor) or parade led by their Pioneer leaders in full dress uniform (khaki uniform with forage cap and leather shoulder strap and belt; 'all are keen to wear the cap and belt as soon as possible' (24)). Normally, the senior Pioneer leader (vozhatyi) calls the roll, leads off an Octobrist song, then gives a seven-to eight-minute talk on a particular theme, say, the work of miners, fishermen, pilots, builders, postal workers, the militia, fire brigade. If convenient a guest is invited along to talk about his or her job. The example given in the Pioneer Leader's Handbook (Kniga vozhatogo) is on border guards:

> A week before the assembly coloured posters appear in the Octobrist Corner, with such questions as "Do you know the secret of soundless walking? Can you see in the dark? Would you like to meet a real border guard? Would you like to know how border guards outwitted a saboteur?" Under the questions is the legend: so many days remain until the parade. (25)

Children may be reminded that 'dozens of border violators were apprehended on signals from Pioneers', and that they can earn themselves a Border Guard's Young Friend badge for vigilance. (26) It is worthy of note here that a recurring theme of socialisation in loyalty and patriotism is the accent on imperialist attempts to subvert Soviet young people and to 'drive a wedge between the generations, between them and their Party'. (27)

As with Cub and Brownie meetings, there are plenty of 'stories, songs, role-playing and games, some common work and group discussion'. (28) If possible, the meetings should take place out-of-doors: 'Let the Octobrists see for themselves at work places how knowledge and skill are needed in every job and endeavour.' (29) The aim here is for children to understand how the work of manual and mental workers fits the needs of the community, to appreciate that physical work is as vital and respected as any other.

The first two years of school teach the child to live in a collective and to study hard, all the while observing Octobrist rules. The third year of school is intended to prepare them for the Pioneers. By now they know they have to work hard, be honest and help

141

the aged and the very young; but their broader civic
and political knowledge would be relatively weak. Now
they begin to learn the rudiments of politics,
starting with the state emblem (a red star above the
hammer and sickle against the background of a globe
and over a rising sun, all clasped within two
wheatsheaves containing the inscription 'Workers of
the World Unite' in the 15 Republican languages).
They are told:

> The five-pointed red star is the symbol of unity
> of the working people of the five continents.
> The hammer and sickle symbolise the
> unbreakable alliance of worker and peasant.
> The rising sun represents the radiant
> future of humanity under Communism.
> The wheatsheaves are the country's wealth
> and prosperity.
> The slogan 'Workers of the World Unite'
> demonstrates the international solidarity of
> Soviet peoples with the workers of the world.
> Altogether, the state emblem symbolises
> the voluntary union of equal Union Republics in
> a single state and the equality of socialist
> nations.

Further, they learn about the Communist Party,
with examples that show the Party as hero, good
friend, pioneer, part of Lenin's family. Finally,
they learn about Communism as 'lofty moral relations
between people, requiring everyone to be honest,
hard-working, respectful of their elders and
solicitous to the young, with fraternal feelings for
the working people of other nations'. (30)

The Pioneers. Towards the end of the third year at
school the Octobrist should be ready to step up to
the next rung of the ladder and become a Pioneer. By
now the child is ten (or, exceptionally, nine) and
eager to become a Pioneer. Although all Octobrists
become Pioneers, emphasis is laid on first having to
merit the honour by being a model pupil, disciplined
and conscientious in completing all assignments. A
pride is taken in being the first 'little stars' in
the class to be deemed worthy of becoming Pioneers.
This is decided at a meeting of the school Pioneer
council (druzhina); those chosen are invited to
attend a Pioneer troop (otryad) meeting at which the
Pioneer leader of the appropriate 'little star'
introduces each of the pupils to the troop,

142

explaining the record of each. Then the council votes
on whether to admit them. No more than ten Octobrists
at a time can be taken. Those successful are
congratulated and invited to attend the ceremonial
handing over of the Pioneer neckerchief.

It is this ceremony that is probably the most
memorable occasion in a child's life. It normally
takes place in the school museum or local Pioneer
Palace in the presence of parents, teachers, Komsomol
friends, pensioners and ex-servicemen. The parade
opens with a bugle fanfare and drum roll as the
children march in, the Pioneer leaders bearing red
standards. When all the children have lined up, each
Pioneer leader reads out the decisions: 'The Chkalov
Detachment (each detachment has its own name after a
particular hero) of Grade Six has unanimously elected
Tanya Orlova to the Pioneers. She has taken a
prominent part in the life of the little star,
carried out her assignments well, is a good pupil and
well respected by her classmates.' Another Pioneer
leader then announces, 'The Yurii Gagarin Detachment
of Grade Five admits Vova Balashov and Rashida
Davletshina into the Pioneers.' And so on.

After that, the big moment has come for the red
neckerchief to be presented and for each new member
to recite the text of the Solemn Promise (see
Appendix 6.2 for the Promise and Pioneer Laws).
Following the Promise, the Pioneer leader orders
'Present neckerchiefs!', the various Pioneer leaders
of the detachment step forward and, to bugle and drum
accompaniment, tie the red neckerchiefs about the
necks of the new Pioneers, declaring, 'Pioneer, Be
Prepared to Fight for the Cause of the Communist
Party!' (31)

'Always Prepared!', comes back the answer as
the new Pioneer gives the salute, right hand raised
slightly above the head, fingers together,
symbolising 'the unity of interests of the homeland,
the Party and working people's children of all five
continents.' (32)

The new recruit also receives on the left lapel
the Pioneer badge: a five-pointed star containing the
picture of Lenin above the words 'Be Prepared' and
below three flames, symbolising the 'unbreakable
alliance of the three generations: the Pioneers, the
Komsomol and the Communists, true to Lenin's teaching
and ready to fight for the Party cause'. (33)

From now on the Pioneer has the right to wear
the Pioneer dress uniform at parades: white shirt for
younger Pioneers, light blue for older Pioneers,
bearing the red star and three-flames badge on the

143

sleeve, blue-grey skirt or trousers, light blue forage cap, white socks (girls), yellow belt with metal buckle. Pioneer leaders have a little star or stars on their sleeve above the Pioneer badge, denoting their rank. On non-dress occasions, the Pioneers wear their Pioneer badge and red neckerchief.

Since 1972 the Red Neckerchief ceremony has taken place at the start of a nationwide Octobrist Week, beginning on Lenin's birthday on 22 April and finishing on 28 April. Each day features a new theme: a school exhibition of Octobrist work, school-made craft and toy display, book exhibition and quiz, sports day (including the <u>zarnitsa</u> - 'summer lightning' - paramilitary game), friendship and peace day, manual work day and, finally, a day of concerts that brings the week to a festive close.

As youth leaders the world over would appreciate, the rituals and symbols are intended to provide an emotional colouring to serious moral and political messages. The rituals of parades and marches accompanied by bugles and drums, as well as the various symbols of badges, motto, the Promise and Laws, red flags and neckerchiefs, salute and heroes all

> lend a revolutionary-romantic atmosphere to Pioneer life and work; they help to strengthen the group organisationally and ideologically, to invest Pioneer work with an emotional élan ... They express in a form accessible to children political ideas and the spirit of struggle for socialism and Communism. (34)

Pioneer Aims and Structure. According to its rulebook,

> the Pioneer organisation together with school, family and community trains Pioneers and schoolchildren to be dedicated fighters for the cause of the Party, it develops in them a love for work and learning, the initial habits of communal living, it helps shape the younger generation in the spirit of communist awareness and morality, collectivism and comradeship, patriotism, friendship among peoples of the USSR and proletarian internationalism. (35)

It is beyond the scope of this chapter to make any profound comparative analysis of the goals of

144

citizen training. Suffice it to make two points.
First, reference to 'Communism' and the 'cause of the
Party' can be variously interpreted as shorthand
terms for honest living and other rules for life as
inscribed, for example, in the Ten Commandments or
the Koran, and also in terms of 'the building of
Communism' - the transformation of the social,
economic and political fabric and character of Soviet
society. Second, while the scope and goals of citizen
training in Soviet and Western schools are similar in
many respects - the objective being to instil in
young people approved ways of thinking and acting
politically, they are broader and more comprehensive
in the USSR. In a comparison of such goals in
American and Soviet schools, Charles Cary made the
interesting distinction that

> American educators view citizenship primarily
> in terms of <u>state</u> citizenship - the membership
> of an individual in an organised political
> community. This concept of citizenship refers
> only to an individual's relationship to the
> political system. Soviet educators conceive of
> citizenship in terms of <u>societal</u> citizenship -
> membership of an individual in a society, which
> in the Soviet case is <u>coterminous with the</u>
> <u>organised political community</u>. This concept of
> citizenship encompasses <u>all</u> aspects of an
> individual's relationship to the social system
> (my italics - JR). (36)

The latter is likely to be the case with all
modernising societies.

Once a child joins the Pioneers, it becomes part
of a link (<u>zveno</u>) of between five and eight friends
and classmates (in the ten-13 age group) or seven to
12 classmates (in the 14-15 group). Each link (see
Figure 6.1) has a Pioneer meeting each week, with a
leader elected by the link members to coordinate
meetings (the class teacher supervises the link as
part of his or her work). Each link combines with two
to three other links in the class to form a troop
(<u>otryad</u>), making up at least 20 children, which meets
two or three times a month. All the troops in a
school form the council (<u>druzhina</u>) which has an
elected board (<u>sovet</u>) of at least three older
Pioneers; in turn the board elects a chairperson. The
board's work is under the direction of the senior
Pioneer leader (<u>starshii vozhatyi</u>), teachers and the
school head teacher.

The senior Pioneer leader, sometimes known as

Figure 6.1: Pioneer Organisational Structure

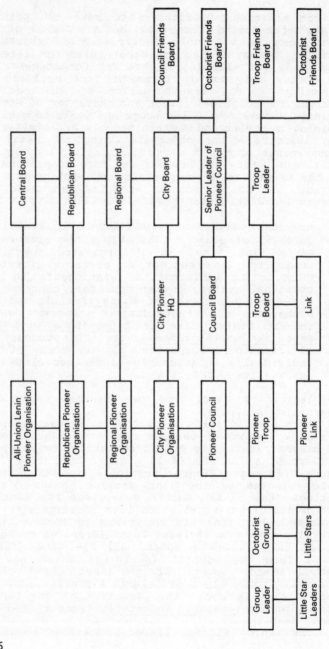

Source: Kniga vozhatogo (Moscow, 1985), p. 649.

146

he 'Pioneer commissar', is vital here in that she or
e is a full-time, usually paid, trained youth
orker, at least 18 years old, who has received
raining at one of the 25 institutes of education
pedinstituty) that offer special five-year courses,
r one of the 160 colleges of education
peduchilishcha) training such senior Pioneer
eaders. (37) In 1981 they trained over 120,000
ioneer leaders. (38) The Pioneer leader would
ormally be a Komsomol official, thereby ensuring a
irm link between the Komsomol and the school Pioneer
rganisation:

> The Pioner vozhatyi is a political leader and
> experienced older friend, a campaigner
> (agitator) and youth specialist (metodist), an
> organiser and direct participant in Pioneer
> affairs, a member and leader of the children's
> group. The leader is a link between the Pioneers
> and teachers, between the school and district
> Komsomol. (39)

t is the senior Pioneer leader who, along with the
chool head, coordinates all Pioneer activities in
chool and sees that the youth programme is carried
ut. The leader is a member of the school educational
oard and, for the sake of continuity, is supposed to
tay at the school for a minimum of two or three
ears. As badge of office, male leaders wear a khaki
rmy-type uniform, while women wear a brown check
ress and olive blouse.

ioneer School Activities. While the new Pioneer
embers are being gradually introduced to Pioneer
ctivities, play and responsibilities during the
arly weeks of membership, older Pioneers on the
chool board are planning activities for each school
erm under the guidance of adults who have already
ecided on the annual plan at a series of meetings
nvolving teachers, the school head teacher, senior
ioneer leaders and representatives of the local
omsomol committee. After deciding on the general
bjectives of the year's work, the adults call the
ouncil members together and inform them of the
hemes and broad activities of the coming period.
hen, together, the adults and Pioneers draw up
etailed plans for projects, dividing responsibility
for their fulfilment among the links and troops. The
inks, finally, hand out assignments to individual
ioneers and even provide a plan of recommended daily

activity (see Appendix 6.3).

Once again, detailed work with children i
tailored to age ability and inclination. Thi
'scaling the heights' youth programme sets target
for each 'height': 10-11, 12-13 and 14-15, with eac
'height' leading up to the next. The overall Pionee
programme now introduces practical projects an
proficiency tests in personal improvement an
community work. For example, Pioneers collect scra
metal and waste paper for various nationwid
campaigns. Thus, they are told that Pioneer
collected scrap metal for building 100,000 'Pioneer
tractors in the 1960s, and for rails, trains an
bridges for the Baikal-Amur Railway project in th
1970s. (40) In this way, they are making a direct an
tangible contribution to the nation's wellbeing an
work effort.

Similarly, individual betterment and civic
mindedness are combined in a nationwide physica
fitness programme known significantly as 'Ready fo
Labour and Defence', introduced in 1931. The Pionee
is expected to take achievement tests in physica
skills such as running, jumping, skiing, swimming
gymnastics and camping through the appropriate fou
age levels: 6-9, 10-11, 12-13 and 14-15. For thos
over 14 the programme includes defence skills such a
shooting, wearing a gas mask for 30 minutes, civi
defence training and first aid. Further, grou
singing, dancing, games, excursions and natur
rambles are all intended to foster togetherness
resourcefulness, courage, *joie de vivre*, and to ac
as an outlet for youthful energies. Many of the game
activities differ little from those engaged in by th
Cubs/Scouts or Brownies/Guides - though without th
obvious sex division and stereotyping of the latter

Good school work receives praise on the Pionee
wall newspaper or in front of the troop; on the othe
hand, poor work, slackness or disobedience ar
publicly criticised, with group pressure put o
culprits to pull up their socks. An exemplary Pionee
is often assigned to a 'slacker' to help improv
performance. This mutual aid is also intended t
develop in all pupils a sense of persona
responsibility for all others in the Pioneer group
Later the same quality is encouraged at the workplac
where leading workers are expected to help thos
lagging behind.

Out-of-school Pioneer Activities. Although based o
school, the Pioneers have a wide range of out-of

school activities, especially in the Pioneer houses
and palaces which offer a broad spectrum of
educational and recreational opportunities to
supplement the school programme. It is well to
remember that Soviet schools mostly finish each day
by 2.00 p.m., leaving the afternoons and early
evenings free for more or less freely-chosen
activities and hobbies at the local Pioneer club. In
1984, over 5000 such Pioneer houses and palaces
served some four million Pioneers and Octobrists.
(41)

In addition, summer Pioneer camps are available
under Pioneer and Komsomol supervision for 7-15-
year-olds. In 1983, there were 68,863 camps for
13,368,000 children - roughly one in three of the
Pioneer age group. (42) For an example of activities
in the summer Pioneer camps, see Appendix 6.4.

At the age of 15 or 16, after eight years of
taking part in the Octobrist and Pioneer
organisations, children leave the Pioneers and the
basic part of their schooling; the great bulk of them
join the Komsomol.

The Komsomol. While the Octobrists and Pioneers are
not directly under Communist Party tutelage, no bones
are made about Party control of the Komsomol and
explicit political socialisation of the 15 plus age
group. The Komsomol is 'the active assistant and the
reserve of the CPSU, the active conductor of Party
directives. Its strength lies in Party leadership, in
ideological conviction and dedication to the Party
cause.' (43) The top Komsomol body, its Central
Committee, is directly subordinate to the Party
Central Committee, and the local Komsomol is under
local Party supervision. The highest office in the
Komsomol, the first secretary of the Central
Committee, is traditionally held by a member of the
Party Central Committee and is a Party assignment.
Furthermore, besides carrying out for the younger
generation the work of political education that the
Party engages in for the adult population, the
Komsomol has the specific role of Party recruitment
and serves as a valuable training ground for Party
members and future Party leaders (including
Gorbachev).

In terms of membership, the Komsomol is formally
rather more selective than the Pioneers in that it
accepts only 'advanced young people between the ages
of 15 and 28 dedicated to the Soviet homeland.' (44)
Somewhat contradictorily, however, it also aims 'to

149

encompass and organise the entire younger generation'. (45) Even so, it does impose an initiation rigmarole in which applicants have to fill in a questionnaire about themselves and be proposed by at least two Komsomol members with year-long membership or by a Party member. True to the old Bolshevik tradition in the wrangle with Mensheviks over membership, the Komsomol is open to 'anyone who accepts Komsomol rules, actively takes part in building Communism, works in a Komsomol organisation, carries out Komsomol decisions and pays dues'. (46)

At school, if a class has more than ten members in the Komsomol it elects its own three-to-five-member bureau which, in turn, elects the school Komsomol committee for a period of a year; the committee, consisting of between three and 11 members, is supposed to meet no less than once a month.

The stated Komsomol aims in regard to school children are principally as follows:

1. to encourage study and see to it that all young people complete full secondary education;
2. to encourage a diligent attitude to all forms of work, including physical work, to give young people vocational guidance, and to ensure sufficient schoolleavers fill state-needed jobs;
3. to harness the energies and loyalties of young people to communist ideology and to steel them against bourgeois ideas and morality;
4. to socialise young people into vigilance against hostile outside forces, and into the need for military training;
5. to improve the moral guidance of the Pioneers, teaching them to be upright citizens, and avoiding and eradicating anti-social behaviour. (47)

To deal with each of these, the school Komsomol would normally elect individuals to take charge of each sector of work and issue assignments to all of its members. Each schoolleaver's character reference from the Komsomol usually contains a record of fulfilment of such assignments and responsible posts held.

The most difficult and controversial aspect of Komsomol work is that of political education. This is carried out by means of lectures, study groups, school exhibitions and wall newspapers, political information and literature. In regard to literature, it is apposite to mention here, by way of comparison, that while virtually all children's and teenage periodicals in the West are commercially - rather than educationally - oriented, often purveying values at odds with those of school, the Komsomol controls all Soviet children's and young people's periodicals. It owns three publishing houses, with an annual output of 50 million copies of books and brochures, and over 230 newspapers and magazines for children and young adults, with a total print run of over 75 million copies. They include the prestigious daily newspaper Komsomol'skaya pravda with a daily circulation of ten million. (48)

The major form of political education in school today is the All-Union Leninist Test - a combination of knowledge about Lenin, Party and Komsomol history, youth work with the Pioneers, performance of voluntary work and social assignments, and participation in 'agitation brigades' (peripatetic political campaigns). An abundance of evidence (see below) shows, however, that many young people are turned off politics, partly by Marxist-Leninist 'bible-punching' young communists, partly by Komsomol 'radishes' (red on the outside only), partly by general apathy. So urgent is the problem that the 27th Party Congress called for a 'review of political study' in schools. (49) All the same, to get on, especially to gain admission to college and university, all schoolleavers need a reference from the Komsomol and 'it is in the tenth grade within the framework of the socio-political certificate (attestatsiya) of the All-Union Leninist Test that work on compiling a reference for each schoolleaver begins and ends'. (50) So at least lip-service has to be paid to political ideology and passive attendance has to be made at a minimum number of political lectures, and Komsomol meetings.

How Effective are the Youth Organisations? Soviet youth organisations have historically played their part on behalf of the adult leadership in the political control of young people, in developing the values and skills appropriate to a modernising economy, in acting as a new socialising agency in a period when rapid social transformation was eroding the traditional foundation of socialisation - through the family, kinship groups, local community

151

and religious organisations - and in creating the cultured, honest personality who aspires to live up to the ideals of the new socialist person. Any assessment of the effectiveness of youth organisations, therefore, has to be measured at least in part against these guiding criteria.

The first conclusion to draw is that the youth movement does seem to have helped young people cope with many of the stresses and strains engendered by the transition from rural <u>Gemeinschaft</u> to urban <u>Gesellschaft</u> relationships; the level of juvenile delinquency, drug-taking (excluding alcohol and tobacco), suicide, violence and alienation appears to be significantly lower in the USSR than in other nations that have undergone or are undergoing modernisation. For example, the bullying and suicide of schoolchildren reported in Japan has no parallel in Soviet schools. (51)

Second, by not offering (or permitting) many competing values, organisations and cultural styles, the Soviet leadership's centres and sources of authority have not been seriously challenged by youth; as a result, Soviet society appears to be more stable than any in the West. This may well be because, besides discouraging non-conformist behaviour in or out of school, it actually incorporates young people <u>through their own organisations</u> into the larger political undertaking of building a new society. And that can be a satisfying experience engendering a strong sense of belonging. Some Western scholars have remarked on this integrational function. Thus, David Lane writes that 'the process of inclusion helps to create feelings of social and political solidarity'. (52) Allen Kassof has said of the youth programme that 'it gives official recognition to young people as a partner in the larger societal undertaking and thereby provides a sense of identification and purpose that so often is lacking among young people in modern societies'. (53) Nevertheless, it is a view that does not go unchallenged in the West. Unger talks of the 'ritualistic character of participatory activities' (54) in the Komsomol, while Cary maintains that 'although the youth organisations initially represent institutionalised peer groups that are coopted for political education, they become a setting for a "teen culture" that is not so purposefully directed'. (55) Without further evidence it is difficult accurately to gauge the influence of peer groups on the political socialisation of young people or the nature of their participation in the wider society.

Third, the youth organisations would seem to be powerful backup forces to teachers in encouraging diligence, hard work, discipline and enthusiasm, which are probably all the more effective coming from the peer group itself rather than being imposed by adults (though it is, of course, adults that ultimately set the standards). In Western society, the overtly adult-imposed values and sanctions, allied to the pluralistic divisions within the community, often produce a 'them versus us' relationship between teachers and taught, resulting in the villain as hero and the swot as 'creep' within the peer group. Urie Bronfenbrenner has written that not only are 'Soviet children much less willing to engage in anti-social behaviour than their age-mates in three Western countries (the USA, Britain and West Germany), but that among Soviet schoolchildren 'their classmates were about as effective as parents and teachers in decreasing misbehaviour'. (56) It should be noted that Bronfenbrenner collected his comparative data from 12-year-olds. The Soviet educational psychologist A.I. Lavrinenko has collected data on 16-year-olds which show that once Soviet children move from the Pioneers to the Komsomol they develop a set of values partially independent of adult values and more representative of a youth culture autonomous of, and sometimes at odds with, that conveyed by the Komsomol. (57)

Fourth, and following on from the above, available evidence demonstrates a clear distinction between the effectiveness of the Octobrists and Pioneers, on the one hand, and that of the Komsomol, on the other, between the voluntary nature of Pioneer activities and the 'ritual participation' or what Unger has called the 'voluntary compulsion' of Komsomol involvement. (58) There seems to be a cut-off point about the age of 14 or 15 at which the youth movement's influence diminishes sharply. Not only is this reflected in declining membership, in critical resolutions on the Komsomol at successive Komsomol and Party Congresses and in recent sociological studies, but the more open criticism starting in the mid-1980s has opened up a veritable Pandora's box of youthful ills and complaints, from apathy and cynicism to infatuation with Western culture and 'consumerism' (commodity fetishism), from ideological deviance right across the political spectrum, even to flirtation with anarchism and fascism (59), to an abiding curiosity from a small section of young people about religion. What the evidence reveals is that while the youth movement has integrated many young people into socialist construction, it has estranged a section of youth through excessive bureaucracy, discipline, routine and invasions of personal life styles. Times and needs are changing, while youth organisations are slow to adapt. The Revolution was 70 years ago and it is hard to maintain revolutionary enthusiasm among girls and boys born in the 1970s. Nor is it easy to bring up young people in what they perceive as old-fashioned, parochial values at a time when modernisation, and increasing exposure to Western youth culture and the growing restlessness of urban teenagers are leading to a polarisation of values between the younger and older generations. Religion and the established youth organisations are encountering similar problems in the West. A disaffected youngster, Andrei S., articulates the Soviet situation well in a recent letter to <u>Molodoi</u> <u>kommunist</u>:

> The Komsomol is increasingly losing its influence over young people ... The younger generation today has no faith in the ideological-theoretical foundation on which the Komsomol bases its entire work, which is now out of step with reality and the demands of the time ... As a result, youth is starting to chase after material goods or engage in interminable wrangles about life and even in God-seeking. (60)

The increasing signs of youthful rebelliousness and discontent with the Komsomol have evoked varying responses from the authorities: from greater efforts to expose and deter 'bourgeois ideology' and to instil a firmer faith in communist ideology, Lenin, the Party and homeland, on the one hand, to attempts to provide less didactic and supervised facilities through clubs, discos, rock concerts and more entertaining mass media (like the popular weekly youth magazine <u>Sobesednik</u> founded in 1984) - 'we must replace insipid, frontal didactics and tutelage by more subtle forms of influencing group behaviour.' (61) There are signs, too, of consideration of a shift of the youth-organisation base from school into the residential locality.

Even in a society with such a unifying set of values and a political monopolisation of children's organisations as the USSR, it is evidently not easy to raise the younger generation according to a prescribed pattern, to induce and sustain a dedication to officially-set ideals, and to revolutionise the minds of the young. Life is more complex than dogma, to paraphrase Lenin.

Appendix 6.1: Octobrist Rules

Octobrists are future Pioneers
Octobrists are hard workers, love school and respect their elders
Only those who love work are Octobrists
Octobrists are honest and bold, clever and skilful
Octobrists are friendly children, read and draw, play and sing, and enjoy life.

Source: <u>Kniga vozhatogo</u> (Molodaya gvardiya, Moscow, 1985), p.12.

Appendix 6.2: Pioneer Promise and Laws

I (Orlova, Tatyana), enrolling in the ranks of the All-Union Pioneer Organisation named after Vladimir Ilich Lenin, in the presence of my comrades do solemnly promise fervently to love my country, to live, study and strive as the great Lenin willed and the Communist Party teaches us, always to carry out the Laws of the Pioneers of the Soviet Union.

A Pioneer is devoted to the country, the Party and Communism
A Pioneer prepares to become a Komsomol member
A Pioneer emulates heroes of struggle and labour
A Pioneer reveres the memory of fallen fighters and prepares to defend the country
A Pioneer is persistent in study, work and sport
A Pioneer is an honest and loyal comrade, always steadfastly standing up for the truth
A Pioneer is a comrade and leader for the Octobrists
A Pioneer is a friend to Pioneers and working people's children of all lands

Source: <u>Kniga vozhatogo</u>, pp. 64a and 64d.

Appendix 6.3: Recommended Daily Plan for Pioneers

Get up, do exercises, wash and make the bed	7.00 a.m.
Have breakfast	7.30
Walk to school	7.50
Do lessons, Pioneer and social work	8.20

Walk home	2.00 p.m.
Go for a walk and play in fresh air, Pioneer activities in club, domestic chores and free time	3.00
Do homework with 5-10 min. break every 45 mins	5.00
Supper, domestic chores, free time	7.40
Prepare for bed	9.30
Bed	10.00

Source: <u>Tovarishch. Sputnik pionera</u> (Moloday gvardiya, Moscow, 1984), p.224.

Appendix 6.4: Seven-day Schedule for 11-12-year-old at the Mayak Pioneer Camp in 1982

Day 1 1. Walk in woods - search for 'Flower Rainbow glade
        2. Sports hour
        3. Arranging campfire site
        4. Evening round campfire: 'Legends of ou camp'

Day 2 1. Meeting the sunrise. Fishing
        2. Drawing competition: 'Hello Sunshine'
        3. Soccer and volleyball matches <u>v</u>. Voskho Troop
        4. Work in clubs
        5. Operation 'Fairy Tale for Kids'

Day 3 1. Pathfinder game (to help Octobrists)
        2. Compiling troop songbook
        3. Talk around campfire: 'Lads and lasses'
        4. Talk: 'Summer day feeds the year'

Day 4 1. Preparing concert for farmworkers
        2. Concert in the harvest field
        3. 'Learn to dance' evening

Day 5 1. Work in farm orchard. Operation frui salad
        2. Work in clubs
        3. Defence of fantasy projects: 'Our troop o Planet Vega'
        4. 'Little flame' on day's work. Film

Day 6 1. Prepare for hike-relay
        2. Talk on 'Warpaths of commissars'
        3. Nature and fantasy competition
        4. Campfire evening: 'Favourite books'

Day 7 1. Prepare for hike. Rehearsal of Agitbrigade
          concert
       2. Talk on 'Pages from <u>Pioner pravda</u>'
       3. Soccer and volleyball games

Note: A comment is made on this programme that it
includes activities that children like best:
campfire, fishing, nature rambles, dancing, games,
independent activity. 'But independence, creativity,
work and games are not just for oneself; they are for
all children, the entire camp, for the farmworkers.'

Source: <u>Kniga vozhatogo</u>, p.262.

Notes

1. <u>Kniga vozhatogo</u> (Molodaya gvardiya,
Moscow, 1985), p.4.
2. V.I. Lenin, <u>Zadachi Soyuzov molodezhi.</u>
<u>Rech'ina III Vserossiiskom s'ezde Rossiskogo</u>
<u>Kommunisticheskogo Soyuza Molodezhi 2 oktyabrya 1920</u>
<u>g</u> (Molodaya gvardiya, Moscow, 1980), p.7.
3. N.K. Krupskaya, 'Pionerdvizhenie kak
pedagogicheskaya problema' (1927) in N.K. Krupskaya,
<u>O vozhatom i ego rabote s pionerami</u> (Molodaya
gvardiya, Moscow, 1981), pp.31-2.
4. N.K. Krupskaya, 'Shkola i pionerdvizhenie'
(1924), ibid., p.115.
5. See <u>Desyatyi s'ezd Vsesoyuznogo Leninskogo</u>
<u>Kommunisticheskogo Soyuza Molodezhi, 11-21 aprelya</u>
<u>1933 goda. Stenograficheskii otchet</u> (Partizdat TsK
RKP (b), Moscow, 1936), vol. 2, p.195.
6. <u>Zhenshchiny i deti v SSSR</u> (Finansy i
statistika, Moscow, 1985), p.116.
7. <u>Vsesoyuznyi Leninskii Kommunisticheskii</u>
<u>Soyuz Molodezhi. Naglyadnoe posobie</u> (Molodaya
gvardiya, Moscow, 1985), p.39.
8. Ibid., p.5.
9. B.M. Bagandov, <u>Obshchestvenno-politiches-</u>
<u>koe vospitanie starsheklassnikov</u> (Pedagogika,
Moscow, 1982), p.83.
10. V.A. Sulemov (ed.), <u>Istoriya VLKSM i</u>
<u>Vsesoyuznoi pionerskoi organizatsii imeni V.I.</u>
<u>Lenina</u> (Prosveshchenie, Moscow, 1983), p.5.
11. B.N. Pastukhov, 'XVIII s'ezd VLKSM',
<u>Pravda</u>, 26 April 1978, p.3.
12. <u>Kniga vozhatogo</u>, p.246.
13. See <u>Rodnaya rech'</u> (Pedagogika, Moscow,
1974), p.33.
14. N.K. Krupskaya, 'Yunye pionery i igra'
(1923) in Krupskaya, <u>O vozhatom i ego rabote s</u>

pionerami, p.111.

15. N.K. Krupskaya, 'RKSM i boiskautizm' (1923) in N.K. Krupskaya, Pedagogicheskie sochineniya (Pedagogika, Moscow, 1959), vol. 5, p.26.

16. Ibid., p.42.

17. N.K. Krupskaya, 'Bud' gotov!' (1924), in N.K. Krupskaya, O vozhatom i ego rabote s pionerami, pp.145-6. She writes that Lenin coined the phrase in his What is to be done? written in 1902. Could Baden-Powell have borrowed the motto from Lenin?!

18. Quoted in V.V. Lebedinskii and T.N. Malkovskaya (eds), Metodika vospitatel'noi raboty s pionerami i oktyabryatami (Prosveshchenie, Moscow, 1984), p.10.

19. Kniga vozhatogo, p.12.

20. Ibid.

21. Ibid., p.247.

22. Ibid.

23. Ronald J. Hill, The Soviet Union (Frances Pinter, London, 1985), pp.127-8.

24. Kniga vozhatogo, p.248.

25. Ibid.

26. Vsesoyuznaya pionerskaya organizatsiya imeni V.I. Lenina. Dokumenty i materialy (Molodaya gvardiya, Moscow, 1974), p.120.

27. V.M. Chebrikov, 'Bditel'nost' - ispytannoe oruzhie', Molodoi kommunist, no. 4 (1981), p.29.

28. Kniga vozhatogo, p.248.

29. Ibid., p.249.

30. See Tovarishch. Sputnik pionera (Molodaya gvardiya, Moscow, 1974), p.31. See also Kitty Weaver, Russia's Future. The Communist Education of Soviet Youth (Praeger, New York, 1981), pp.9-10.

31. The 1923 motto adopted by the then 'Spartacist Young Pioneers' was 'Be Prepared to Fight for the Workers' Cause'; this lasted until the present motto was adopted in 1967 (see Vsesoyuznaya pionerskaya organizatsiya imeni V.I. Lenina, p.22).

32. Kniga vozhatogo, p.16. The initial salute was identical to that of the Scouts.

33. Ibid.

34. Lebedinskii and Malkovskaya, Metodika vospitatel'noi raboty, p.7.

35. Cited from Ustav VLKSM, articles 52 and 53, in Vsesoyuznyi Leninskii Kommunisticheskii Soyuz Molodezhi, p.164.

36. Charles D. Cary, 'The Goals of Citizenship Training in American and Soviet Schools', Studies in Comparative Communism, vol. 10, no. 3 (Autumn 1977), p.290.

37. G.M. Ivashchenko, Ideino-politicheskoe

ospitanie yunykh lenintsev (Prosveshchenie, Moscow, 985), p.100.

38. L.P. Ivanova, Pionerskii vozhatyi v hkole. V pomoshch' uchitelyu (Prosveshchenie, loscow, 1981), p.3.

39. Ibid., p.109. The book also provides examples of a model day's work plan for the senior ioneer leader.

40. Ibid., p.37.

41. Zhenshchiny i deti, pp.118-19.

42. Deti v SSSR. Statisticheskii sbornik (Statistika, Moscow, 1984), p.51.

43. Vstupayushchemu v Komsomol (Molodaya vardiya, Moscow, 1976), p.35.

44. Organizatsionno-ustavnye voprosy komsomol-skoi raboty (Molodaya gvardiya, Moscow, 1975), .58.

45. Ibid., p.59.

46. Ibid., p.58.

47. See Bagandov, Obshchestvenno-politicheskoe ospitanie starsheklassnikov, pp.78-9, and S.V. Jarmodekhin, Komsomol'skaya rabota v shkole, (Prosveshchenie, Moscow, 1980), pp.24-5.

48. N.A. Petrovichev et al., Vazhnyi faktor vozrastaniya rukovodyaschei roli KPSS (Politizdat, Moscow, 1979), p.147.

49. See 'Politucheba: uroki, mysli i Jeistviya', Molodoi kommunist, no. 6 (1986), p.43.

50. Bagandov, Obshchestvenno-politicheskoe vospitanie starsheklassnikov, p.85.

51. The Guardian, 1 March 1986, reported that in 1984 as many as '572 juveniles under 19 committed suicide in Japan, 220 of them over "school matters"'. Further, 'in the first half of the 1985 school year, 68 per cent of the country's junior schools reported serious bullying cases, resulting in physical and psychological damage to the weakest children in the class'.

52. David Lane, The Socialist Industrial State (Allen & Unwin, London, 1979), p.80.

53. Allen Kassof, The Soviet Youth Program. Regimentation and Rebellion (Harvard University Press, Cambridge, 1965), p.174.

54. Aryeh L. Unger, 'Political participation in the USSR: YCL and CPSU', Soviet Studies, vol. 33, no. 1 (January 1981), p.121.

55. Charles D. Cary, 'Peer groups in the political socialization of Soviet schoolchildren', Social Science Quarterly, vol. 55, no. 2 (1974), p.461.

56. Urie Bronfenbrenner, Two Worlds of

Childhood: U.S. and U.S.S.R. (Allen & Unwin, London, 1971), p.78.

57. A.I. Lavrinenko, 'Izuchenie ustoichivosti moral'nykh suzhdenii u shkol'nikov', Voprosy psikhologii, no. 16 (1970), pp.143-150. Quoted in Cary, 'Peer groups', p.459.

58. Unger, 'Political participation in the USSR', p.111.

59. For young people with overt sympathy with fascism see 'Shalunishki i predatel'stvo', Sobesednik, no. 21 (1986), p.6. For 'anarchists', see Chebrikov, 'Bditel'nost'', p.29.

60. Yurii Kovalev, 'Znayu, pis'mo moe vy ne opublikuete', Molodoi kommunist, no. 6 (1986), pp.49-50.

61. A.G. Kharchev and V.G. Alekseeva, Obraz zhizni. Moral'. Vospitanie (Politizdat, Moscow, 1977), p.75.

Chapter Seven

PEACE EDUCATION IN THE SOVIET UNION

Wendy Rosslyn

Peace education is still a new field in the Soviet Union, just as in the West, and Soviet policy for it dates only from the early 1970s. (1) It is also an area of great topical importance, and one where new developments continue to take place.

One such development is the peace lesson (<u>Urok mira</u>) which, since 1983, has been the first lesson of the school year for all classes; this is in recognition of the fact that 1 September, the traditional starting date, is also World Peace Day. Since peace lessons are a new phenomenon, it may be of interest to give an account of two of them in some detail. (2)

The lessons described took place in a Moscow school specialising in the teaching of English. The beginning of the school year was marked by an assembly of all the children in the playground in front of the school steps. The grades (years) lined up in order, from those starting school for the first time to those shortly to graduate, with the classes in each grade together. There was then a short ceremony, in which the Pioneer and Komsomol banners were paraded, and the whole school was addressed first by the headteacher, and then by a representative of the local soviet, a representative of the <u>shefy</u> (the factory or other institution which has 'adopted' a given school), and by our delegation of British Quakers. The uniformed children, laden with flowers to give to their teachers and the visitors, then dispersed to their classrooms for the peace lessons.

The lesson for the tenth grade was, quite appropriately, arranged around the British delegation and consisted of two short talks on peace, the dangers of the arms race, the peace initiatives taken by the Soviet Union, and on Soviet contacts

161

with Quakers, which are of long standing and are felt by the Soviet Peace Committee to be a valuable contribution to peacemaking between East and West. As is often the case on such ceremonial occasions, the pupils were polite but bored, but became animated in the following question-and-answer session. Their own contributions seemed spontaneous and also displayed an impressive grasp of the facts of the topic.

The lesson for the ninth grade was more ordinary and not planned in expectation of the presence of a foreign visitor. The lesson consisted of a series of short talks given by the pupils themselves on subjects including Lenin's views on peace, just and unjust wars, the military-industrial complex, the peace movement in the West, and the class's own work for peace. The teacher concluded by speaking about the sacrifice of Soviet lives in the Second World War and, by asking how many of the class had lost relatives in the war (the majority), reminded the pupils of their own connection with it. The lesson finished with some stirring music from the record-player. Posters put up for the occasion in the classroom carried such slogans as 'The union of the working classes of various countries in the final analysis must make war between peoples impossible' (Marx) and 'Remember! Every day of peace has been paid for by twenty million lives of Soviet people.' The lesson was also attended by the representative from the <u>shefy</u> who had earlier addressed the assembled school. Here again, the pupils were very well informed, which was the more remarkable since they had apparently not been prepared by the teacher. It was therefore a pity that they presented their material in a rather mechanical and unattractive way, that there was no discussion, and that the class was restless and not attentive. Perhaps the unexpected foreign guest was a disruptive factor; nor of course is it an easy matter to speak spontaneously on such complex political topics. Moreover, the politicians on whom the pupils may have modelled their presentation are often not noted for the liveliness of their speeches.

There have to date been only three annual peace lessons, and teachers are helped to prepare for them by local peace committees (<u>komitety zashchity mira</u>). There are 120 of these, headed by the All-Union Soviet Peace Committee, and though their activities are naturally in harmony with party and government policy, they are funded by the Peace Fund and are not official organisations. The Soviet Peace Committee noted with satisfaction in 1984 that it was currently

he only Soviet public organisation to belong to the
pecial Committee of Non-Governmental Organisations
n Disarmament at the UN. (3)

It was possible to obtain the briefing issued to
eachers for this purpose by the Leningrad Regional
eace Committee, (4) a booklet of eleven pages in
hotocopied typescript. This begins with the
elebration of the 40th anniversary of 'the victory
f the Soviet people in the Great Fatherland War' and
he defence of peace as one of the lessons taught by
he war. (5) It then goes on to speak of the peace
essons themselves:

> They aid the communist education of the
> generation growing up, and the further drawing
> of youth into the ranks of the active fighters
> for peace throughout the world.
>   Peace lessons are intended to help pupils
> realise the character and scale of the military
> threat, and their sources, and to understand the
> consistent and persistent struggle of the
> Communist Party and the Soviet government for
> the maintenance and strengthening of peace and
> against the threat of nuclear war. In the course
> of peace lessons it is essential to give pupils
> general information about the peace movement at
> the present stage, to tell them about mass
> antiwar actions and the activities of the
> Leningrad Regional Peace Committee, and to pay
> particular attention to the forms of
> participation of Leningrad youth in the
> struggle for peace.
>   As practice shows, places for conducting
> the lessons may be classrooms, museums, Pioneer
> rooms, memorial locations, etc. It is good to
> decorate the places for conducting the lessons
> with posters and drawings done by the pupils. It
> is possible to use printed posters, film
> materials, and slides, and to show documents and
> materials from museums and the exhibition halls
> of schools and vocational-technical colleges
> (PTU). It is appropriate to invite the
> participation in peace lessons of party,
> soviet, trades union and Komsomol workers,
> representatives of social organisations,
> adoptive enterprises and military units,
> workers, war and labour veterans, and exponents
> of the arts and literature.

The document then goes on to a detailed exposition of
the material which it has recommended for teaching in

the lessons. The ninth-grade peace lesson conformed closely to the pattern set down here.

It is rather ironic that this peace lesson, special on account of its association with the beginning of the year and with World Peace Day, is probably less effective as teaching than a lesson given on an ordinary day; and this is the more ironic since this is the only peace lesson as such in the school year.

The Russian for 'peace education', 'education in the spirit of peace' (<u>vospitanie v dukhe mira</u>) (6) is a pointer to the fact that peace education is not a separate subject in Soviet schools; it is an element of various other timetabled subjects, and is mostly taught in history lessons, but also in biology (in the form of ecology and conservation), physics (atomic power, for example), chemistry and literature. It is also part of the child's moral education, that is training the child to feel part of the community and to be socially active.

The teaching of peace education is determined, of course, by the Soviet understanding of peace. In the Soviet view the causes of war are not such factors as the pursuit of <u>lebensraum</u>, innate human aggressiveness, religious discord, or ethical failings, but socio-political and economic factors, amongst them the 'artificial kindling of international and religious discord and policies of colonialism, racism and apartheid'. (7) Lenin's policy condemning wars of aggression has been upheld; thus national liberation movements are not felt to be sources of war. Because wars are caused by socio-political and economic factors, socio-political means of averting them can be found. War is not therefore inevitable.

Some states have social systems which lead to political and economic equality for people, to friendship among nations, and to the removal of national, religious and other conflicts. (8) Others are imperialist and a threat to peace. Given that the world is divided between different social systems, peace is preserved by such factors as the UN, the peace movements of all countries, and the parity of the Warsaw Pact and NATO. (9) The requirements assumed for peace are:

> consideration of peaceful coexistence as the renunciation of war as a means of settling disputes between states; the need to settle such disputes through negotiations on the basis of equal rights, mutual understanding and trust

among states, taking into account the interest of all the parties concerned; noninterference in the domestic affairs of others; recognition of the right of each nation to self-determination; strict respect for the sovereignty and national integrity of all countries; the development of economic and cultural co-operation on the basis of complete equality of rights and mutual benefit. (10)

It must be borne in mind that 'social processes, particularly such processes as the elimination of colonialism, the struggle against neocolonialism and the struggle of peoples to establish progressive democratic regimes in place of racist regimes and foreign occupation, are objective in character and cannot be interpreted as the exporting of revolution or interfering in domestic affairs.' (11) No economic reason is found to exist which would make war between socialist and capitalist states inevitable, but peace is threatened by the arms race, the existence of the military-industrial complex, and the doctrine of limited nuclear war. (12) In a divided world, peaceful coexistence is the aim.

Peace education in the Soviet Union therefore includes study of the socio-political and economic factors involved in war and peace, consideration of socialism and Communism as forces for peace, study of the UN and peace movements, and participation in the effort to avert war. It also believes that peace is to be achieved by 'maintaining the present parity of strategic forces, while simultaneously adopting measures to limit and reduce them' and by negotiating reduction of conventional weapons. (13) Pacifism and nonviolence have no place here.

Professor Yu.K. Babansky, Vice-President of the Academy of Pedagogical Sciences, outlines broad and narrow definitions of peace. The broad definition involves (in addition to politics and economics as such) questions of the environment, personal relations, North and South, women and men, the generation gap, man and technology. The narrow definition is that peace is life in the absence of war, and active mutually beneficial co-operation between countries. Peace education in the Soviet Union concentrates on the narrow definition. The education system does, however, pay some attention to the broader one, even if not under the heading of peace education. For example a new course 'The Ethics and Psychology of Family Life' (*Etika i psikhologiya semeinoi zhizni*) was introduced in 1984, and ecology was introduced into the biology syllabus in 1983.

A tentative syllabus for peace education proposed by the Soviet Union at UNESCO includes the following topics: peace as a human right; outlines of international law; the causes and consequences of war; why war can be prevented; problems of doing so; the work of the UN, UNESCO, and the peace movement; specific examples of how wars have been prevented; documents of the Helsinki Conference and 'other forums of peace-loving forces'; the arms race, the arms industry, limited nuclear war; ways of achieving general disarmament; confidence-building measures; current peace talks; the link between the peace movement and social progress and the struggle of peoples for their rights; methods of peace work. (14)

As in the West, it is felt that the teaching methods used for peace education must be consistent with the overall aim, and that attitudes must be instilled as well as information conveyed. In the Soviet Union role-play and co-operative games (to take two examples) appear to be little known and more formal teaching methods seem to be the norm. It is clearly more difficult to adopt new methods especially suited to peace education when peace is taught as and when it arises, in the course of teaching other subjects; a compensating advantage of Soviet teachers over their Western counterparts is, however, the reinforcement outside school of what is taught inside it, and this is very much the case with peace education. Research on the diversification of teaching methods is in hand, and a recent article on pair work in schools finds that the latter is more efficient than individual learning, and that it leads to a high level of co-operation. (15) However, the undesirability of competitiveness is less strongly felt in the Soviet educational system than by Western teachers of peace education.

Soviet teachers are aware that there is a danger of frightening children with discussion of war, and to judge from anecdotal evidence, children do often become upset. It is felt that the danger of arousing anxiety is most acute in the youngest age group, before the child is able to understand the causes of war and to be socially active in trying to prevent it. Another danger is of giving the impression that the problem of war, because it is soluble, is easily dealt with. The aim is to give the child optimism, the feeling that with much work the problem can be overcome, and confidence that the Soviet government will avert war. The children are also told about the efforts of peace movements in the Soviet Union and other countries.

Peace education for the youngest age-group in school begins with immediately relevant and practical things, such as encouraging good relations between the children, and care for animals. The discussions prescribed for the first grade include: 'What you can do for peace', 'How your parents fight for peace', and 'Friendship with the peoples of other countries'. After this come: 'The unity and friendship of working people the world over', and 'The struggle of our people for peace'. (16)

Pupils of secondary-school age then take a more analytical approach, and from the fourth grade onwards peace education is concentrated in history and social science courses. The fourth-grade course 'Introduction to the History of the USSR' covers (amongst other things) the Decree on Peace of October 1917; Lenin's foreign policy; Russia's withdrawal from the First World War; the struggle against Fascism; efforts for arms reduction; the peaceful coexistence of nations. The course on postwar history covers the worldwide peace movement, the aims of the UN and UNESCO, and 'the struggle of the peoples of the whole world for peace and security'. 'Fundamentals of the Soviet State and Law' describes the foreign policy of the Soviet Union in relation to peace, and the legal basis for resolving issues of war and peace. It also discusses peace in relation to the Soviet constitution. Courses on modern history deal with human rights, and study Rousseau, Voltaire, the American Declaration of Independence, the 1789 Declaration of the Rights of Man and the Citizen, and the abolition of slavery in the USA. The course on history of the Soviet Union deals with human rights in pre-revolutionary Russia.

In social studies (obshchestvovedenie) the tenth grade works on the foreign policy of the Soviet Union and topics such as peaceful coexistence, detente, arms limitation proposals, condemnation of racism, elimination of the theatres of war created by imperialism, and international co-operation on the environment, communications, the prevention of diseases, and the exploration of space and the oceans. One chapter in the textbook is devoted to peace questions.

The literature course for grades eight to ten has the topic 'Soviet literature in the struggle against the threat of war, for peace and friendship amongst nations', and the works studied here include B. Vasil'ev's The Dawns Are Quiet Here, V. Subotin's How Wars End, and V. Bykov's An Alpine Ballad. Prior to the formulation of policy on peace education in the early 1970s, the literature course for the tenth grade in 1969/70 included a survey, allotted four hours of class time, of the literature of the period of the Great Fatherland War. (17) Secondary school examinations in Russian literature for the 1967/8 school year included, out of 50 questions, four on topics of peace and war:

> The love of freedom and patriotism in the creative work of M.Yu. Lermontov.
> The heroism and patriotism of the Russian people in the novel <u>War and Peace</u> by L.N. Tolstoy.
> The Soviet Union on guard of peace.
> The poem <u>Vasilii Terkin</u> by A.T. Tvardovsky - a truthful depiction of the severe war-life conditions of Soviet soldiers.

Examination papers in Russian literature for the tenth grade for the 1968/9 school year included, out of 66 questions, five on these topics, to be answered orally, as usual:

> The problem of true and false patriotism in the novel <u>War and Peace</u> by L.N. Tolstoy.
> The theme of Soviet patriotism in the poetry of V.V. Mayakovsky. Recite from memory one of the poet's poems.
> <u>War and Peace</u> by L.N. Tolstoy as a heroic epic.
> The depiction of the beauty of the soul and the character strength of the Soviet man, fighter and toiler, in the story 'The Fate of a Man' by M.A. Sholokhov.
> The theme of the Great Fatherland War in Soviet poetry. Recite from memory one poem on this topic. (18)

No Soviet textbook on peace education yet exists, but the Soviet Union proposes to use the UNESCO manual on peace education, due to be published shortly; this is a collective work to which various countries, including the Soviet Union, have contributed. In discussions at the Academy of Pedagogical Sciences, the Soviet side floated the idea of intervisitation by British and Soviet specialists on peace education and the study of each other's textbooks, as is already done for history and geography by a Soviet-American commission.

Closely connected with peace education is

international education, which in the Soviet Union is taught in the same way - not in its own right, but as part of other subjects, in this case history, geography, literature, Russian, foreign languages, and social studies. In the Soviet view, international education is not the description of all features of a given national culture (inside or outside the USSR), but is about the 'democratic and socialist elements' of other cultures. It involves developing not only respect for other peoples, but specifically a sense of responsibility for the fate of socialism all over the world, and understanding of the obligation of Soviet citizens to support national liberation and anti-imperialist movements. The task of the teacher is to harmonise national and international education, and to develop pride in the multinational Soviet Union.

In higher education disarmament is again part of the compulsory social science syllabus. According to the Soviet response to a UNESCO survey, disarmament topics enter into obligatory courses on international relations, international law, contemporary history, historical materialism, scientific communism, political economy, the economics of foreign countries, and the history of the Communist Party of the Soviet Union. These occupy somewhat over 190 hours during the first four years of the university curriculum. The main topics are disarmament and detente, peaceful coexistence and co-operation between states, nuclear disarmament; new types and new systems of weapons of mass destruction and the problem of banning them; disarmament and social progress; disarmament and employment; international military detente; disarmament control; non-proliferation of nuclear weapons; nuclear-free zones; the theory and practice of other states in the field of disarmament; disarmament and international law; European law; the causes of the arms race. (19) Just as with peace education in the schools, disarmament enters into courses in physics, chemistry and biology, history, geography, international law and journalism. (20)

Research is carried out by various public bodies into questions such as peaceful coexistence, detente, disarmament, general and regional security, ways of settling international conflicts, the effect of science and technology on peace, development and peace, economics and peace, peace movements, and peace education. The centres involved are research institutes of the Academy of Sciences, the Academy of Social Sciences and the Academy of Pedagogical

Sciences, universities, government institutions, and organisations such as the Soviet Pugwash Committee and the Soviet Peace Committee. The coordinating body is the Scientific Research Council on Peace and Disarmament. (21)

As can be appreciated from this survey of syllabuses, the factual material taught to Soviet schoolchildren and students is wide in scope and complicated in detail. To judge from the performances of the pupils in the peace lessons, it is, even so, effectively taught.

Personal relations is an area which does not come into peace education in the narrower of the Soviet definitions, but which is part of the broader definition, and of Western conceptions of peace education, and therefore deserves some attention. This field, new to Soviet schools, comes in the course called 'The Ethics and Psychology of Family Life' which takes up 17 hours in each of the ninth and tenth classes, following a (new) 17-hour course in the eighth grade on hygiene and sex education. (22)

The teacher's manual states that the basic aim of the course

> is the formation in young men and women of the need to create a family, of readiness to enter into marriage, of the ability to build relationships within the family correctly and to bring up future children; the education of an implacable attitude to bourgeois conceptions of the family. (23)

Preparation for family life is considered both as contributing to the formation of a well-developed personality and as the acquisition of the knowledge and skills required for a happy married and family life. It is also a response to the currently perceived need for better preparation for parenthood and for new views about the relations between men and women and about family life. The need to lower the rate of divorce and raise the birth rate is also to the point.

Of particular interest in the context of peace education is the question of conflict. The possibility of conflict in marriage and family life is, of course, acknowledged, and the approach is to set before the pupils models of behaviour which will avoid it. For example, feelings of hurt, it is stated, can be avoided if criticism of a person is offered in a comradely manner, with concern, respect,

and a desire to help. (24) Prevention of conflict is
also a technique to be applied in the classroom:

> In cases when (class) self-government is not
> developed, when only part of the class is
> active, often the same pupils, and the others
> find themselves in the position of passive
> observers or critics, often the former and the
> latter experience feelings of dissatisfaction,
> resentment, sometimes indignation and envy.
> These negative feelings, gradually accumulat-
> ing, lead to the creation of an unpleasant
> psychological climate, which is characterised
> by an aggressive attitude to one another, or, on
> the contrary, to a subdued mood in the members
> of the collective. It is therefore absolutely
> essential that all in the class should be
> active, and that the activeness should have an
> emotionally positive colouring, then the
> psychological climate will be characterised by
> involvement, enthusiasm, happiness and a
> buoyant mood. (25)

The manual also issues practical advice on
dealing with conflicts which have arisen in spite of
the preventive measures, for example to ensure
harmony in marriage. It states that 'the internal
strength of the family depends to a great extent on
both partners seeking mutual understanding' (26) and
quotes nine 'commandments' which help to preserve
peace in the home. These are axioms such as 'Do not
hurry to say a bad word, but be quick to repeat good
words' and 'Every step to meet (each other) equals
many days of happiness'. Advice on resolving marital
conflict includes being tolerant, patient, willing
to give way, and self-control. Techniques used by
happy couples to resolve conflicts are noted and
include:

1. Restricting the area of conflict to a
   minimum, i.e. not recalling past
   incidents.
2. Speaking about each other's faults gently
   and with good will.
3. The ability and will to understand the
   other person in the argument 'from the
   inside' as it were to put oneself in his
   place. (27)

There is here, as with other aspects of Soviet peace
education, an emphasis on rote-learning of

171

principles and facts, which is perhaps not the most effective method of teaching skills of conflict resolution. (28)

Avoidance of conflict may fail, and advice be forgotten or go unheeded, and the course, to judge, at least, by the manual, rather rarely encourages the teacher to involve the class in experiential learning. The class can be invited to look at a given conflict from the point of view of each of the participants, (29) but it is to do so in written form. The teacher is, certainly, invited to explain the concept of the psychological climate of a group by taking the class as an example, and it is proposed that the class be set the task of analysing some concrete class activity from the point of view of the mood in which it was carried out. (30) But in general such suggestions are not numerous. It must be said, however, that the manual advises teachers to avoid the exhortatory approach, and aim for a frank exchange of views, a collective search for the truth, analysis of real facts and events, and in recognition of the nature of the course marks are not to be given. (31)

The book for pupils which accompanies the course (32) contains relatively little on conflict within the family. Much of what there is consists of sociological observations and there is hardly any practical advice on dealing with conflict. Recommendations again take the 'prophylactic' approach, and include not raising the voice during the discussion of controversial questions, treating the weaknesses and faults of one's partner as a parent treats the incapability and immaturity of the child, and taking into account the fact that women are psychologically and emotionally older than men of the same age. (33)

The course does not discuss conflict in relationships in terms of the psychological make-up and history of the individuals concerned. By the same token great emphasis is put upon the place of the individual, couple, and family in society. Changes in behaviour are expected to come about by individuals emulating the ideal set before them, helped by the collective, and not by experiential learning or psychological means.

The teacher's manual for the course is aware that parents work with the teacher in preparing children for family life and are often in need of help in the task, and special classes for parents are advised. (34) As part of the School Reform, schools are setting up courses for parents with the aim of guiding them and improving their pedagogical correctness and effectiveness. Classes meet nine times every year that the child is in school. Family conflict is on the syllabus, but peace education as such does not figure. (35)

The approach of the 'Ethics and Psychology of Family Life' course is to describe circumstances in which conflict can be forestalled, often those where the individuals have shared goals. Collectivism does not entirely rule out conflict, but it is felt that the conflicts which do arise should be resolved to the advantage of the group, not to the advantage of a single person.

Soviet schools, like schools everywhere, have difficult pupils, their troublesome behaviour caused perhaps, it is felt, by their home background or peer group. Here too the approach is to deal with this behaviour by prophylactic means and by improving the child's relationship with adults. One procedure with disruptive pupils is to elucidate the causes of their behaviour, to make recommendations for removing these (including changing adults' relationships with the child), to get agreement to the recommendations, teach all concerned to carry them out and to monitor the process; the child, family, and school are all involved, so as to change the environment in which the child lives. These functions will be performed by the educational psychology service (psikhologo-pedagogicheskaya sluzhba) now being set up. (36)

A different approach to therapy for family conflict, owing not a little to Carl Rogers, is outlined by V.A. Smekhov, who concentrates on the client's subjective perceptions of the situation and aims to analyse and correct the factors within the personality which determine the interactions in the family. The psychologist's diagnosis is presented to the client 'not in traditional monologue', but in the form of a dialogue, with the client actively participating in the process. Conclusions arrived at co-operatively are found to be more effective in correcting the problem. Psychologist and client work on real-life conflicts, and not on artificial problems set up for the purpose of diagnosis. The client is helped to reflect upon what he and his opponent said, did, thought, felt, and tried to do, and what they would have preferred to do and felt they should have done. The aim is to construct a picture of the conflict consisting of the client's understanding of the objective circumstances determining the conflict, his conception of himself and others, and his conception of the causes of the

173

conflict. This then helps the client to change his
response to conflict. (37) Such an approach does
indeed impart skills for the resolution of conflict,
and, moreover, is careful to use terms and language
accessible to the client; it would seem able to offer
an important and effective technique for pupils of
the 'Ethics and Psychology of Family Life' course.

The educational psychology service, hitherto
experimental, is being set up in schools as a
practical response to need, and its aims are still
being defined, but they are, at least in part, to
provide an ongoing psychological diagnosis of the
pupils, to assess the psychological climate of the
classroom and to advise teachers on difficult
problems in the class. Some schools have a
professional psychologist on the staff; in others the
work is done by an experienced teacher, ideally the
headteacher. (38) A pilot scheme is also offering a
service to families to strengthen relationships,
correct parental errors in bringing up the children,
and remove the causes of family conflict, most of
which turn out to be connected with the
unpreparedness of young people for marriage, family
life and bringing up children. The representatives of
this pilot scheme in schools are the teachers of the
'Ethics and Psychology of Family Life' course. The
possibility is foreseen that senior pupils taking
this course may be formed into groups to work with
difficult pupils lower down the school. (39)

The participation of pupils in pastoral
activities is a long-established custom. From grade
four onwards, when the primary system of a single
teacher for all subjects is replaced by a system of
specialist subject teachers, each class is allotted a
member of staff (klassnyi rukovoditel'), who is
responsible for such matters as the coordination of
the work of individual subject teachers, contacts
with parents, and counselling. But the class also
elects a self-governing 'class administration'
(klassnoe upravlenie), whose responsibility is to
deal with issues of concern to the class as a whole,
including the academic progress of all the pupils,
their social activism, and the relationships within
the class and the class's relationships with other
groups. The 'elder' (starosta) of this body is the
contact between the class and the supervising
teacher, and also liaises with the Komsomol or
Pioneer organisations, which have units in all
classes. Anecdotal evidence suggests that membership
of this committee can be a great test of sensitivity,
integrity, and psychological insight, the more so

since the 'elder' may be caught between pressures from the supervisor and pressures from the class, and since a given group may remain together in the same class from starting school at six to leaving eleven years later.

Peace education, whether broadly or narrowly defined, is not felt in the Soviet Union to be incompatible with military training, for the reason that the pursuit of detente and disarmament goes hand in hand with the policy of maintaining parity with NATO forces:

> The education of Soviet youth in a spirit of patriotism rules out the inculcation of militarism, chauvinism, the desire for territorial aggrandizement or for enslaving or destroying other peoples. But, at the same time, educating our young people in a spirit of peace and friendship and in support of disarmament does not preclude the inculcation of a readiness on the part of the younger generation to defend their homeland and fight for its security. So long as the forces of reaction and imperialism are at work fomenting wars of aggression and territorial aggrandizement, the people are compelled to defend their freedom and national independence. (40)

In the Soviet view the USA seeks military superiority over the Soviet Union, and has from the outset been responsible for initiating each new phase of the arms race; Soviet peace proposals have for the most part not evoked a co-operative response, and so, in spite of Soviet citizens' horror of war and desire for peace, the Soviet Union cannot risk unilateral disarmament.

Basic military training (140 hours in all) is therefore given to all young men between the ages of 14 and 17, as preparation for conscription, normally two years' service at the age of 18. Much of this training is given in school, and under the new curriculum it is allotted two hours per week in the final two years. The training includes party policy on national defence, military law, tactical and weapons training, drill, map-reading, and civil defence. (41) The textbook shows that pupils are themselves involved in civil defence. Civil defence units operate in all 'units of the national economy', industrial enterprises, farms, and schools too. Depending on their size and type, and on the available equipment, secondary schools can set up

175

rescue groups, chemical and radiation monitoring posts, preservation of public order groups, and civil defence units for refuges and shelters. These sections consist of pupils, as well as teachers and ancillary staff. (42)

In accordance with Soviet political thinking, at the same time as senior pupils, male at least, are engaged in military training, they are also taught how they can contribute to the prevention of war, and are encouraged to take an active part in so doing, both in and out of school. Teaching about peace matters in school is reinforced outside by the youth organisations, peace committees, the media and so on.

Examples of activities taking place in school are those enumerated by the ninth grade in their peace lesson: making peace posters, participating as helpers in the XII International Festival of Youth and Students (held in Moscow in the summer of 1985), giving weekly briefings to the class on the current political situation in the world, and contributing to the Soviet Peace Fund some of its earnings from summer work on a farm. The Peace Fund is the result of huge numbers of contributions from individuals and collectives and it is run by about five million volunteers. It is common, for example, for shifts of workers, industrial or agricultural, to work a 'peace day' and donate their wages for it to the Fund. The money raised is used to finance the peace committees, to sponsor research and the Scientific Research Council on Peace and Disarmament, for disaster relief abroad, and to help 'the victims of imperialist aggression'. (43)

For the most part, however, the activities in which children participate are broadly similar, whether initiated by the school or by other bodies. Children join with their parents in events organised by the Peace Committees (90 million people took part in demonstrations during Disarmament Week in October 1984.) They make posters and banners, and raise money for the Peace Fund by collecting medicinal herbs, waste paper and scrap metal, by making things to sell and putting on concerts, as well as by working in agriculture. Children also take part in events associated with special days in the Soviet calendar, such as Day of the Young Anti-Fascist Hero, United Nations Day (24 October) and Human Rights Day, along with Disarmament Week (observed since 1978). Similar days are International Youth Solidarity Day (24 April), International Day of Co-operation (5 July), World Youth Day (10 November), and International Students' Day (17 November). During Young Anti-

Fascists' Week in February schools hold meetings to protest against nuclear war and the arms race, competitions are held for the best poster, drawing and composition on peace themes, and exhibitions and concerts of political songs are held. In 1984 an essay competition on the topic 'I vote for peace' was organised by the Komsomol, the Ministry and the Soviet Peace Committee, and certificates and diplomas were awarded to the winners. Also in 1984 Leningrad schoolchildren collected more than half a million signatures on protests addressed to the heads of Western governments.

International education in school is complemented by International Friendship Clubs (<u>kluby internatsional'noi druzhby</u>) in schools and Pioneer Palaces. There are some 700 of these in Moscow alone. The clubs provide opportunities to find out about foreign countries, organise correspondence with groups of children abroad, hold political briefings and demonstrations, and raise funds for aid to foreign children, in the same ways as for the Peace Fund.

Propaganda and agitation extends to children no less than to adults, via schools, youth organisations, and the media. There are, for example, 157 children's newspapers in the Soviet Union, <u>Komsomol'skaya pravda</u> printing ten million copies, and <u>Pionerskaya pravda</u> thirteen million. Thanks to these joint efforts, children are well aware of the Soviet position on issues of peace and disarmament, and join in peace activities, both to a greater degree than in the West. What cannot, of course, be gauged is the extent to which these facts are the result of responding to official propaganda, of the pressure for social conformity, and/or of considered acts of personal will.

Since in the Soviet system peace education extends beyond the classroom and into the outside world, it is also necessary to consider its psychological and social context.

A number of general points can be made about the extent to which Soviet society is militarised and the military and civilian spheres integrated. Defence, which consumes a large proportion of public expenditure, is accorded a higher priority than consumer needs. The whole population, including children, is (at least in theory) trained in civil defence, the Civil Defence organisation being part of the armed forces. The revolutionary festivals of 7 November and 1 May are marked with military parades. The military is accorded much recognition in the

Soviet calendar, which marks 23 February as the Day of the Soviet Army and Navy, 13 April as the Day of Soviet Anti-Aircraft Defence Forces, 9 May as the Day of Victory of the Soviet People in the Great Fatherland War, 27 July as Navy Day, 17 August as Soviet Air Force Day, 14 September as Tank Forces Day and 19 November as Rocket Forces and Artillery Day. Days connected with peace and co-operation are given rather less prominence.

Propaganda constantly reminds the public of the horrors of the Second World War. Children, who are too young to remember it, have, as one teacher said, memories created for them. Schools have museums with exhibits commemorating pupils who died or distinguished themselves in the war. Similarly, Pioneer Palaces have museums commemorating their members. Children are taken to visit war memorials, visits to which have also become a conventional part of Soviet weddings, when the bride lays her flowers on the Tomb of the Unknown Soldier. Children are encouraged to remember and honour members of their family who fought or died in the war, and to feel their debt to the nation's sacrifice.

It is indicative that the chapter on family traditions in the teacher's manual for the 'Ethics and Psychology of Family Life' course mentions labour, socio-political, family, and cultural traditions, but devotes most attention to patriotic ones. The 'revolutionary festivals' include not only the anniversary of the Revolution and 1 May, but also the Day of the Soviet Army and Navy, and Victory Day. These are felt to occupy an important place in the family's spiritual life, along with the family relics - that is to say, documents, photographs, letters and medals relating to the war and the five-year plans. But the mention of the five-year plans is perfunctory and the emphasis of this passage is otherwise entirely on the significance of the war as an example and inspiration to the younger generation in its definition of its values. Peace activities are not mentioned. (44)

The effect of propaganda, blunted, of course, by frequent repetition, is twofold: to keep alive the horror of war inspired by experience, and, by so doing, to stimulate mental preparedness to fight, should an enemy start a war - which would be far more horrendous than that already known. Propaganda also spreads respect for and gratitude to the armed forces.

Soviet sport also has a distinct military bias, with which children come into contact. DOSAAF (The

Voluntary Society for Aid to the Army, Air Force and Navy) offers young people facilities for training in any sport which might have a military application, and claims a membership of 80 million. The GTO national fitness programme includes civil-defence and gas-mask training, and serves, amongst other things, as pre-conscription fitness training. In its civilian aspect the GTO is a set of minimum standards in running, jumping, throwing, shooting, skiing and gymnastics, conducted through schools and sports clubs. Each year it awards badges for reaching its standards of performance to some 18 million citizens, mainly the young.

Peace education exists, therefore, in a context where military and civilian are often closely connected. To the Quaker pacifist this might seem a situation fraught with paradox. But pacifism and nonviolence are not principles of Soviet peace education. The assumption of government policy, and thus of propaganda, peace education, and social organisation alike, is that peace coexistence must be pursued whilst maintaining strong defences. There is thus no contradiction in giving military training at the same time as peace education.

Indeed, the language of peace propaganda itself contains military metaphors. The Soviet Peace Committee is in Russian the 'Soviet Committee for the Defence of Peace', and General Secretary Gorbachev has remarked, to take just one example, that understanding where aggression can lead 'raises more and more detachments of progressive democrats for the struggle against the threat of war'.

Peace education in the Soviet Union is in many ways unlike its Western equivalents. It does not seek to impart practical skills of conflict resolution, or to make peaceful and unpeaceful relationships the subject of experiential learning: little attention is paid to personal conflicts and to conflict within the self because peace is conceived in social and political terms. Children are well informed about the facts of disarmament and peace policy and take part in large numbers in the peace movement. And peace education, far from attracting opposition from anxious parents and local councillors fearful of political indoctrination, is a quite unexceptionable activity. In the Soviet Union peace is a universal preoccupation which attracts the support of state and individuals alike; by the same token peace education forms part of a coherent and cohesive policy designed, among other things, to support Soviet foreign policy.

179

Notes

1. A survey of the Soviet peace education programme, together with a critique of peace education in the West can be found in I.V. Ivanyan, 'Education and Disarmament', in V.S. Shaposhnikov (ed.), <u>Problems of Common Security</u> (Progress, Moscow, 1984), pp.333-48.

2. Much of the material for this article was gathered during a visit to the Soviet Union by a delegation of the Religious Society of Friends (Quakers) at the invitation of the Soviet Peace Committee. The visit, which took place in September 1985, was for the specific purpose of studying peace education in the Soviet Union. The views expressed here are those of the author and not those of Quaker Peace and Service.

3. P.N. Fedoseyev (ed.), <u>Peace and Disarmament. Academic Studies 1984</u>, (Progress, Moscow, 1985), p.280; the activities of the Soviet Peace Committee are described on pp. 275-81.

4. <u>Leningradskii oblastnoi komitet zashchity mira. Metodicheskie rekomendatsii v pomoshch' uchitelyu po provedeniyu v shkolakh i proftekhuchil- ishchakh "Urokov mira" (sentyabr' 1985 goda)</u>.

5. It is interesting that the reference to the Great Fatherland War is followed by the statement that 'on 1 September 1939 with the perfidious attack of fascist Germany on Poland there began the most bloody war in human history, lasting more than 5 years'. The Great Fatherland War is traditionally dated 1941-45.

6. The term for peace studies, as distinct from peace education, is <u>obuchenie miru</u> or <u>izuchenie problem mira</u>.

7. Yuri K. Babansky, 'Methodological Approaches to Peace and Disarmament Education in the USSR', in <u>UNESCO Yearbook on Peace and Conflict Studies 1982</u> (UNESCO, Paris, 1983), pp.15-16.

8. Ibid., p.17.

9. Ibid., pp.17-19.

10. G.I. Morozov and I.P. Blishchenko, 'The Methodology of Peace Research in the USSR' in <u>UNESCO Yearbook of Peace and Conflict Studies 1981</u> (UNESCO, Paris, 1982), p.18.

11. Ibid.

12. Babansky, 'Methodological Approaches', pp.17-19.

13. Ibid., p.19.

14. Ibid., pp.20-1.

15. V.V. Andrievskaya, G.A. Ball, Z.G. Kisarchuk and S.A. Musatov, 'Psikhologicheskie

predposylki effektivnosti sovmestnoi uchebnoi raboty mladshikh shkol'nikov', Voprosy psikhologii, No. 4 (1985), pp.38-45. The article includes references to other work on co-operative learning.

16. Most of the information on the syllabus is taken from Babansky, 'Methodological Approaches', pp.21-3.

17. N.N. Schneidman, Literature and Ideology in Soviet Education (Lexington Books, Lexington, Mass., Toronto and London, 1973), pp.91-2.

18. Ibid., pp.101-10.

19. 'Disarmament Education in the USSR (University Level)' in UNESCO Yearbook on Peace and Conflict Studies 1981, pp.235-8.

20. For further details, see I.P. Blishchenko and I.V. Ivanian, 'New Approaches in the Teaching and the Scientific Study of Problems Related to Detente and Peaceful Coexistence since the Adoption of the Final Act of the Conference on Security and Co-operation in Europe' in UNESCO Yearbook on Peace and Conflict Studies 1980 (UNESCO, Paris, 1981), pp.100-14.

21. For details, see G.I. Morozov and A. Kalyadin, 'Soviet Organizations Dealing With the Problems of Peace' in UNESCO Yearbook on Peace and Conflict Studies 1980. pp.278-81 and G.I. Morozov and I.P. Blishchenko, 'The Methodology of Peace Research', pp.15-23. Much information on the work of the research institutes of the Academy of Sciences is to be found in V.L. Shvepov, 'USSR: Peace and Disarmament Research Centres in the Soviet Union' in UNESCO Yearbook on Peace and Conflict Studies 1981, pp.376-88.

22. Details of the course are taken from I.V. Grebennikov (ed.), Etika i psikhologiya semeinoi zhizni. Probnoe posobie dlya uchitelya (Prosveshch-enie, Moscow, 1984).

23. Ibid., p.7.

24. Ibid., pp.63-4.

25. Ibid., p.167.

26. Ibid., p.103.

27. Ibid., p.125-6.

28. Ibid., p.56.

29. Ibid., p.48.

30. Ibid., pp.166-7.

31. Ibid., p.8.

32. T.M. Afanas'eva, Sem'ya. Kniga dlya uchashchikhsya starshikh klassov (Prosveshchenie, Moscow, 1985).

33. Ibid., p.109.

34. Ibid., p.7.

35. The content and methods of these ten one-year courses are described in I.V. Grebennikov, Shkola i sem'ya. Posobie dlya uchitelya (Prosveshchenie, Moscow, 1985).
36. S.G. Shuman and V.P. Shuman, 'Psikhologo-pedagogicheskaya sluzhba pri gorodskom Sovete narodnykh deputatov', Voprosy psikhologii, No. 4 (1985), pp.76-7.
37. V.A. Smekhov, 'Opyt psikhologicheskoi diagnostiki i korrektsii konfliktnogo obshcheniya v sem'e', Voprosy psikhologii, No. 4 (1985), pp.83-92.
38. A.D. Alferov and E.A. Lugovoi, 'Uchitel' v sisteme psikhologicheskoi sluzhby v shkole', Voprosy psikhologii, No. 4 (1985), pp.74-5.
39. This pilot scheme is described in Shuman and Shuman, 'Psikhologo-pedagogicheskaya sluzhba', pp.77-8.
40. Blishchenko and Ivanian, 'New Approaches', p.106.
41. For deatils, see the textbook: A.I. Averin, I.F. Vydrin, N.K. Endovitskii and others, Nachal'naya voennaya podgotovka, 6th edn (DOSAAF, Moscow, 1983).
42. Ibid., p.182.
43. For further details, see Anatoly Karpov, 'Soviet Peace Fund' in Peace and Disarmament. Academic Studies 1984, pp.288-291.
44. Grebennikov, Etika i psikhologiya semeinoi zhizni, pp.140-3.

Bibliography

Afanas'eva, T.M. Sem'ya. Kniga dlya uchashchikhsya starshikh klassov (Prosveshchenie, Moscow, 1985)
Alferov, A.D. and Lugovi, E.A. 'Uchitel' v sisteme psikhologicheskoi sluzhby v skhole', Voprosy psikhologii, No. 4 (1985), pp.74-5
Andrievskaya, V.V., Ball, G.A., Kisarchuk, Z.G. and Musatov, S.A. 'Psikhologicheskie predposylki effektivnosti sovmestnoi uchebnoi raboty mladshikh shkol'nikov', Voprosy psikhologii, No. 4 (1985), pp.38-45
Averin, A.I., Vydrin, I.F., Endovitskii, N.K. and others Nachal'naya voennaya podgotovka, 6th edn (DOSAAF, Moscow, 1983)
Babansky, Yu.K. 'Methodological Approaches to Peace and Disarmament Education in the USSR' in UNESCO Yearbook on Peace and Conflict Studies 1982 (UNESCO, Paris, 1983), pp.13-24
Blishchenko, I.P. and Ivanian, I.V., 'New Approaches in the Teaching and the Scientific Study of Problems

Related to Detente and Peaceful Coexistence since the Adoption of the Final Act of the Conference on Security and Co-operation in Europe' in UNESCO Yearbook on Peace and Conflict Studies 1980 (UNESCO, Paris, 1981), pp.100-14

'Disarmament Education in the USSR (University Level)', in UNESCO Yearbook on Peace and Conflict Studies 1981, pp.235-8

Fedoseyev, P.N. (ed.), Peace and Disarmament. Academic Studies 1984 (Progress, Moscow, 1985)

Grebennikov, I.V. (ed.) Etika i psikhologiya semeinoi zhizni. Probnoe posobie dlya uchitelya (Prosveshchenie, Moscow, 1984)

Grebennikov, I.V. (ed.) Shkola i sem'ya. Posobie dlya uchitelya (Prosveshchenie, Moscow, 1985)

Ivanyan, I.V. 'Education and Disarmanent', in V.S. Shaposhnikov (ed.), Problems of Common Security (Progress, Moscow, 1984), pp.333-48

Karpov, A. 'Soviet Peace Fund' in Peace and Disarmament. Academic Studies 1984 (Progress, Moscow, 1985), pp.228-291

Leningradskii oblastnoi komitet zashchity mira. Metodicheskie rekomendatsii v pomoshch' uchitelyu po provedeniyu v shkolakh i proftekhuchilishchakh "Urokov mira" (sentyabr' 1985 goda)

Morozov, G.I. and Blishchenko, I.P. 'The Methodology of Peace Research in the USSR' in UNESCO Yearbook of Peace and Conflict Studies 1981 (UNESCO, Paris 1982), pp.15-23

Morozov, G.I. and Kalyadin, A. 'Soviet Organizations Dealing With the Problems of Peace' in UNESCO Yearbook on Peace and Conflict Studies 1980, pp. 278-81

Schneidman, N.N. Literature and Ideology in Soviet Education (Lexington Books, Lexington, Mass., Toronto and London, 1973)

Shuman, S.G. and Shuman, V.P. 'Psikhologo-pedagogicheskaya sluzhba pri gorodskom Sovete narodnykh deputatov', Voprosy psikhologii, No. 4 (1985), pp.76-8

Shvepov, V.L. 'USSR: Peace and Disarmament Research Centres in the Soviet Union' in UNESCO Yearbook on Peace and Conflict Studies 1981, pp. 376-88

Smekhov, V.A. 'Opyt psikhologicheskoi diagnostiki i korrektsii konfliktnogo obshcheniya v sem'e', Voprosy psikhologii No 4 (1985), pp.83-92

Chapter Eight

MULTICULTURAL EDUCATION IN THE USSR

Nigel Grant

Cultural Identity: Some General Considerations

Identity is a notoriously complex concept, even though its manifestations may on occasion seem starkly simple. A group may be identified, or identify itself, by reference to citizenship, nationality, language, religion, or some other prominent characteristic chosen from a whole cluster of them for particular emphasis. But this is a 'marker', not a total description; behind that badge or label may be a host of values, attitudes and customs that make up the identity of that group. Before going on to examine the issues in the USSR, it may be useful to consider a few examples nearer home.

In Belgium, the principal marker is language, to the extent that it may override citizenship; a great many feel themselves to be Flemings or Walloons before they are Belgians, becoming Belgians mainly when they feel the need to distinguish themselves from the Dutch and French respectively. But language is not the whole story, for social class, political affiliation and historical traditions may be involved as well; speaking Dutch or French may be a conspicuous label and an emotional commitment, a convenient shorthand way of labelling identities too complex for ready analysis. In Northern Ireland, tragically, there is a division, often violent, between two groups usually described as Protestant and Catholic. But their disputes have little to do with theology - no one seems to be trying to <u>convert</u> anyone. They may also identify themselves as Unionist or Nationalist, declaring loyalty to the British Crown or to Ireland; but again this is incomplete, since neither group (or at least the more vocal leaders) feel in the least bound by the politics or attitudes of the United Kingdom or the Irish Republic if these prove to be inconvenient. What we are

witnessing is a conflict between two historical
communities, with ancient grudges and complex
allegiances; the religious affiliations do not, in
themselves, <u>explain</u> their behaviour - after all,
Protestants and Catholics manage to live together
elsewhere without wanting to kill each other or even
quarrel; but they do <u>summarise</u> the identity of these
two groups in this specific situation.

It may prove advisable to identify groups in
order to attend to their interests and avoid
conflict. Yugoslavia's prewar attempt to run a multinational state like a homogeneous one proved to be a
disaster; during the war, the internecine feuding was
even bloodier than that between the partisans and the
Germans. The postwar federal structure, with
extensive decentralisation, was in part an attempt to
reduce these tensions, or at least to prevent them
from getting out of hand again. Yugoslav policy
distinguishes between the 'peoples of Yugoslavia'
and the 'nationalities'. The nationalities are the
non-Slav ethnic minorities, normally definable by
linguistic criteria, such as the Albanians, Turks,
Hungarians, Romanians, Italians and others. The
'peoples' are the various South Slav groups after
whom the country is named, each with its own republic
in the federation. Of these the Slovenes in the north
and the Macedonians in the south can be distinguished
by language readily enough, but the others present
something of a problem, since they all speak a
language which can reasonably be described as Serbo-
Croat in spite of its varieties. (1) The Croats,
perhaps, can be most easily distinguished from the
others; there are some consistent linguistic
differences, they use the Latin rather than the
Cyrillic alphabet, and there are cultural
differences which include the Catholic Church and a
history of Habsburg rather than Ottoman rule. The
Bosnians distinguish themselves from the Serbs by
describing themselves as Muslims in the census
returns. Other Muslims, such as Albanians and Turks,
do not do this, using the nationality label instead.
Once again, in the Bosnians we have an example of a
group using religion as a summary of a more complex
identity. For the Montenegrins, the smallest of the
'peoples', neither language nor religion can be used
in this way, as they are the same in these respects
as the Serbs. Nevertheless, it is unwise to call a
Montenegrin a Serb; he is different because his
history, traditions and way of doing things tell him
so, and because he says so.

Actually, this situation is quite common. All

the countries of Latin America, apart from Brazil, are Spanish-speaking and Catholic, but that has never prevented a sense of distinctiveness, and often open hostility, between one country and another. In their case, citizenship serves as the most obvious marker. Similarly, English-speaking Canadians do not like to be called Americans, nor Austrians Germans, nor New Zealanders Australians. The terms 'Britain' and 'England' are often used interchangeably, but never in Wales or Scotland, where this causes great offence. The identity of the Welsh and Scots does not rest on citizenship, language or religion. Whether they like it or not, they all share United Kingdom citizenship with their English neighbours. There are some religious differences, but not enough to make this a distinguishing feature, since in all of the countries concerned religious practice is diverse and followed by a minority anyway. Wales does have an indigenous language, but only a minority speak it. Scotland has two, but even smaller minorities speak them. In both cases the majority speak only English; certainly, they tend to speak it differently from the English, but such differences can be found within England as well. Yet the Welsh and the Scots are emphatically not English; their history, their social mores (and, in Scotland, their institutions) tell them so. (2)

In many countries in the industrialised world the question of identity has not figured prominently until recently, in education or anything else. Most Western European countries have had cultural minorities within their borders since they first took shape. (3) There are Bretons, Occitans and Corsicans in France, Andalusians and Galicians in Spain, and Catalans and Basques in both; there are Gaels in Ireland and Scotland, Lapps or Saame in Norway, Sweden and Finland, Frisians in the Netherlands, Germany and Denmark. The very drawing of borders had left Dutch and German speakers in France, German-speaking Belgians and Danes, Danish-speaking Germans, Finnish-speaking Swedes and Swedish-speaking Finns, German speakers in Italy and Slovene speakers in Austria. Switzerland, Belgium and Luxembourg, by their very nature as multilingual countries, have always had to accept pluralism, and respond accordingly in public policy and education. Elsewhere, the general response to minority cultures has been either neglect or, more commonly, suppression. Policies have ranged from exclusion to attempted assimilation, but have rarely accepted minority cultures as having any value or viability of

heir own. In virtually every European country, the
authorities and the majority populations have worked
on the assumption that only their cultures, norms and
languages were valid. (4)

During the last couple of decades or so, there
have been a number of developments challenging these
perceptions - and, sometimes, making some impact on
policies as well. One has been the growing
disinclination of minorities to relinquish their own
identities as the price of participation in the
larger polity. The end of the colonial empires since
the Second World War has undermined belief in the
superiority of the metropolitan cultures, and the
increasing internationalisation of institutions -
whether through such organisations as the EEC or more
informal connections - has demonstrated the
viability of pluralism, at any rate at the
supranational level. It is perhaps no accident that
the reassertion of autonomy by the Catalans, Basques
and Galicians in Spain has coincided with the
development of supranational organisations. Also,
modern linguistic research, which has effectively
demolished the notion of the 'bilingual deficit', has
established functional bilingualism as a reasonable
objective without damage to general educational
attainment. (5)

Furthermore, many European countries have now
become multicultural in a more conspicuous sense.
Since the war, Britain has received settlers from
parts of the former colonial empire, as has France,
and these groups have now established firmly-based
communities, a large and growing proportion of which
are locally born and bred. Elsewhere, notably in
Germany, foreign workers originally brought in to
take jobs that locals were unwilling to do, have put
down roots and produced communities of German-born
Turks and Greeks, Dutch-born Moluccans, and so forth.
Easy assumptions that these groups would simply
assimilate into the local majority population have
not worked out. For one thing, they have rarely been
allowed to; many individuals who have attempted this
still meet discrimination on the basis of the one
thing they cannot change, namely their physical
appearance. Many, therefore, return to a cultural
environment where they can be accepted. Further, many
see little reason to abandon their religions,
languages and customs just to acquire the skills for
survival in the host community; increasingly, they
feel that they can do that <u>and</u> retain their own
identities. Some majority communities see this as a
'problem', others see possibilities in developing

187

multicultural education as a general preparation fo
living in an inevitably pluralist world. Either way
the fact of cultural pluralism is there, and (th
efforts of racist and extreme right-win
organisations notwithstanding) will not go away
Thus, more and more countries are having to come t
terms with the existence of various groups, whethe
indigenous or immigrant-descended, and are beginnin
to suspect that the traditional unitary an
integrationist assumptions no longer hold good.

It has already been observed that languag
serves as a major marker of identity, which is hardl
surprising, given the depth of emotional attachmen
and the intimate relationship between language an
thought. It has also been noted that earlier notion
that knowledge of one language necessarily impair
the learning of another – the basis of many policie
of suppressing minority languages to make room fo
the majority one – have been discredited. I
principle, bilingualism is perfectly feasible as a
educational objective, and it is to be expected tha
recognition and use of their own languages should b
a prominent aspiration of cultural minorities. Ther
remains the question of the suitability of som
languages for use in an industrialised society
including educational use. (6)

It is sometimes argued – usually by speakers o
majority languages, though members of minoritie
have often acquiesced in this – that some language
are intrinsically incapable of handling the concept
of a modern society. The authorities in the days o
the British Raj took this view of Indian vernaculars
and used this argument to construct an English-mediu
educational system. The same logic was used elsewher
in the British Empire, in the French Empire, an
indeed in Britain and France themselves to devalu
their own minority languages. Much was made of th
heavy borrowing from English into Welsh or Gaelic, o
from French into Breton.

A closer look casts doubt on the logic of thi
assumption. Of course minority languages borrow fro
others; and so, in their day, did the others. An
language, at any given point of time, is likely t
develop the vocabulary necessary for the lives of th
people who speak it. The vocabulary of Innui
(Eskimo) is rich in words for snow in variou
conditions, Arabic makes fine distinctions i
different words for camel which most other language
find unnecessary, medieval French had a bewilderin
range of words for different kinds of battlements an
pieces of armour, and so forth. When new needs arise

here are two ways of meeting them. There is _alquing_, making up new words from native material, the method favoured by Chinese, Arabic and German; and there is the borrowing of new roots and words, adapting them phonetically, and incorporating them into the native vocabulary - the method favoured by Persian, Romanian, Swahili and a host of others, notably English. Borrowings are normally taken, naturally enough, from the nearest available culturally or technologically dominant language. Gaelic, Welsh and Hindi borrow from English, as English did in its turn, heavily, from French and Latin, Latin in its turn from Greek. In the Soviet Union, less 'advanced' languages obviously borrow from Russian, as _some_ of them did in the past from Arabic and Persian.

It is, then, misleading to argue that any language is _intrinsically_ unsuitable for any needs. If a written form is lacking, this can be devised, as has been done for hundreds of languages in modern times. Vocabulary-building, however, can take time, and if it happens on a massive scale there can always be the danger of swamping the language with alien material, failing to adapt it to the phonetic and morphological structure of the minority language and thus weakening its capacity to develop in its own way. There has been some of this with the minority languages in the British Isles, and also with some Indian languages such as Hindi, where masses of unassimilated language material remain incomprehensible to less 'educated' speakers. In such circumstances, even native speakers of the language may switch completely to the dominant tongue when discussing matters related to the metropolitan culture, even amongst themselves. French is widely used in this way in Africa, as is English there as well as in the British Isles; Russian, likewise, is similarly used among many of the smaller and more scattered language communities in the USSR.

The Linguistic and Ethnic Composition of the USSR

The population of the USSR is such that it has never been possible to ignore cultural diversity. In the West, the terms 'Russian' and 'Soviet' are still widely used interchangeably, even by bodies that should know better, like the BBC. The common usage, however, is wildly inaccurate, since the Soviet Union is a multilinguistic and multinational state by definition as well as in fact. The Russians, to be sure, are by far the biggest single group, but they

Table 8.1: Nationalities over 1 million: Number (000s) 1979, Percentage Increase or Decrease since Previous Census, Language Family and Script

Nationality	Nos. (000s) 1979	% +/-	Family	Script
Russians	137,397	8.5	Slavonic (IE) (a)	Cyrillic
Ukrainians	42,347	3.9	Slavonic (IE)	Cyrillic
Uzbeks	12,456	35.5	Turkic	Cyrillic
Byelorussians	9,463	4.5	Slavonic (IE)	Cyrillic
Kazakhs	6,556	23.7	Turkic	Cyrillic
Tatars	6,317	6.5	Turkic	Cyrillic
Azerbaidzhanis	5,477	25.0	Turkic	Cyrillic
Armenians	4,151	16.6	Armenian (IE)	Armenian
Georgians	3,571	10.0	Caucasian	Georgian
Moldavians	2,968	10.0	Romance (IE)	Cyrillic
Tadzhiks	2,898	35.7	Iranian (IE)	Cyrillic
Lithuanians	2,851	7.0	Baltic (IE)	Latin
Turkmens	2,028	33.0	Turkic	Cyrillic
Germans	1,936	4.9	Teutonic	Latin
Kirgiz	1,906	31.3	Turkic	Cyrillic

Table 8.1: continued

Nationality	Nos. (000s) 1979	% +/-	Family	Script
Jews	1,811	-15.8	Teutonic (IE)	Hebrew (b)
Chuvash	1,751	3.4	Turkic	Cyrillic
Peoples of Dagestan	1,657	21.4	various	Cyrillic
Latvians	1,439	0.6	Baltic (IE)	Latin
Bashkir	1,371	10.6	Turkic	Cyrillic
Mordvin	1,192	-5.6	Uralic	Cyrillic
Poles	1,151	-1.4	Slavonic (IE)	Latin
Estonians	1,020	1.3	Uralic	Latin
Total USSR	262,085	8.5		

Note: (a) IE = Indo-European Family. (b) Yiddish, spoken by a minority of Soviet Jews; most are Russian-speaking.

Source: 1979 Census (see Note 7 below).

form a bare majority (52 per cent according to th
1979 census.) (7) There are 103 separat
nationalities listed, ranging in size from th
Russians (137 million) to the Yukagir and Aleut, wh
number only a few hundred. Many of these peoples ar
tiny, and are found mainly in the Far North, the Fa
East, the Pamirs and the Caucasus, but many ar
substantial. There are over 42 million Ukrainians
over 12 million Uzbeks and over 9 millio
Byelorussians, which puts them in the same league a
many European sovereign states; and there are mor
Kazakhs, Tatars and Azerbaidzhanis than there ar
Scots, Danes or Norwegians. Twenty-two Sovie
nationalities each number over a million (see Tabl
8.1). Small compared with the Russians they may be
but they are by no means negligible.

There is also a great variety of language types
(8) contrary to popular usage, we are not dealin
here with 'dialects', but with language groups whos
members are as diverse as German and Chinese
(Indeed, the list includes German and a variety o
Chinese.) The Indo-European family is by far the mos
numerous, including as it does the Slavs (Russians
Ukrainians and Byelorussians), but there are others
The Baltic group comprises Lithuanian and Latvian
related historically to the Slavonic but not mutuall
comprehensible or anything near. Moldavian is
Romance language, closely related to the Romania
spoken across the border. (Indeed, the onl
substantial difference is that it is written in th
Cyrillic rather than the Latin alphabet.) Armenia
forms a distinct branch of the Indo-European family
and has had its own script and a rich literatur
since the middle of the present millennium. Th
Iranian branch is most conspicuously represented b
Tadzhik, the only one to be recognised as th
official language of one of the fifteen Unio
Republics, but there are others, notably in th
Caucasus; one of them, Ossetian, is the language o
its own ASSR (Autonomous Soviet Socialist Republic,
subordinate administrative division). Even that doe
not exhaust the list; although not defined as Sovie
languages, Polish and German are spoken by over
million each, and Yiddish, though transcribed fo
cultural reasons in the Hebrew alphabet, is a Middl
German dialect.

The next largest family is the Turkic (o
Altaic). This includes Uzbek, Kazakh, Turkmen
Kirgiz and Azerbaidzhani, all the languages of Unio
Republics (four in Central Asia and one i
Transcaucasia). These have reasonably clos

affinities with Turkish, though others, like Chuvash and Yakut further north, are more aberrant. There are many other smaller Turkic and Mongolic groups scattered from Central Russia to Siberia, from Dagestan in the Caucasus to the Pamirs. Another family, known usually as Uralic, (9) includes Finnish as its major non-Soviet member; in the USSR, its chief representative is Estonian, but there are many others - Karelian, Nenets, Khanty, Mari, etc. - in Siberia and the Far North. Georgian (the mother tongue of such notorious figures as Stalin and Beria), and the official language of the Georgian SSR, has its own script and ancient literature; it is the largest member of the Caucasian family, which includes locally important languages like Avar and Lesgin, and has no known affinities with any other language family. The Palaeoasiatic or Palaeo-Siberian languages do not really constitute a family at all, for there is little evidence of any genetic relationship. They are spoken over a wide area, but the populations are small and scattered; they include the Chukchi, Itel'men and Yukagir. Finally, there are small populations whose main representatives are elsewhere, such as the Semitic family (Arabs in Central Asia and Assyrians - more properly, Aramaic speakers) and the Dungans or Chinese Muslims.

The developmental level of the languages varies also. As already observed, Armenian and Georgian have their own scripts and literary cultures, much older than the Russian (as they are not slow to point out) and still flourishing. The languages of the Baltic Republics developed late (19th century, for the most part), but are now used across the full range of activity, using the Latin alphabet. The major Turkic languages (and Tadzhik) were written (if at all) in the Arabic script before the Revolution, though the level of illiteracy was so high that this made little difference to the population at large; for most purposes, Arabic, Persian, Turkish or (latterly) Russian were used instead. After the Revolution, moves were made towards standardisation (creating half a dozen standard languages from a series of more than twenty distinguishable Turkic dialects), and the creation of a Latin alphabet. This was later replaced by Cyrillic, with extra letters or diacritics to deal with sounds not found in the Slavonic languages. Most of the other languages, of whatever group, lacked a written form completely. Many were devised by the Academy of Sciences of the USSR, all based on Cyrillic, and now have an extensive literary use. (10) Some were invented, but seem not to have caught on. In Karelia, for example, the closely akin Finnish was already available, and most tended to use that or Russian instead of written Karelian. Written Yukagir, likewise, never came into use; there are only a few hundred Yukagir, they are widely scattered and outnumbered by Russians locally. For literary purposes, Russian is used instead. Most of the small groups without a written language use Russian for this purpose, but others are in use also (notably Georgian, Lesgin, Avar and Azerbaidzhani in the Caucasus, Tadzhik in Central Asia, etc.).

One factor affecting the status and development of a language may well be the proportion of Russians in the area. In most of the ASSRs and National Regions within the RSFSR (the Russian Federation), the titular nationality are outnumbered by Russians, and in one (the Bashkir ASSR) by Russians and Tatars. In the exceptions (Chechen, Ingush, North Ossetian, Tatar and Tuva ASSRs) the Russians are still a substantial minority. This is not so, however, in the ASSRs in the other Union Republics. There are even two Union Republics where the titular nationality forms a minority. In one of them (Kirgizia) it is still the largest single group, but in Kazakhstan the Kazakhs account for 36 per cent, the Russians over 40 per cent. (This is a rather different situation, however; Russians predominate in the north of the Republic, Kazakhs in the south.) In all Union Republics, except for Georgia, Armenia and Azerbaidzhan, there is a significant Russian minority – over 20 per cent in the Ukraine, 10-12 per cent in the Central Asian Republics (indeed, in some Central Asian cities, like Tashkent and Dushanbe, Russians are in a majority), over 12 per cent in Moldavia, and much higher in the Baltic Republics – over 32 per cent in Lithuania, for example (see Table 8.2).

This pattern is changing, however, and shows wide variations from place to place. Broadly speaking, there has been an increase in the proportion of Russians living in the western Republics; between the Census of 1970 and 1979, the Russian percentage of the population rose from 19.4 to 21.1 in the Ukraine, from 10.4 to 11.9 in Byelorussia, from 24.7 to 27.9 in Estonia, from 11.6 to 12.8 in Moldavia, and so forth. But in Central Asia the proportions went down – from 12.5 to 10.8 in Uzbekistan and from 11.9 to 10.4 in Tadzhikistan, for example. In the Transcaucasian Republics, the much lower percentages dropped still further – 10 per cent

Table 8.2: Composition of Populations of Union Republics: Members of Titular Nationality and Russians as Percentage of Populations, 1970-1979

Republic:	1970		1979	
	Titular nationality	Russians	Titular nationality	Russians
R.S.F.S.R.	82.8	82.8	82.6	82.6
Ukraine	74.9	19.4	73.6	21.1
Byelorussia	81.0	10.4	79.4	11.9
Lithuania	80.1	8.6	80.0	8.9
Latvia	56.8	29.8	53.7	32.8
Estonia	68.2	24.7	64.7	27.9
Moldavia	64.6	11.6	63.9	12.8
Azerbaidzhan	73.8	10.0	78.1	7.0
Armenia	88.6	2.7	89.7	2.3
Georgia	66.8	8.5	68.8	7.4
Uzbekistan	65.5	12.5	68.7	10.8
Kazakhstan	32.6	42.4	36.0	40.8
Tadzhikistan	56.2	11.9	58.8	10.4
Turkmenia	65.6	14.5	68.4	12.6
Kirgizia	43.8	29.2	47.9	25.9

Note: Numbers do not add up to 100%, since other nationalities are not counted.

Source: 1979 Census, Munich bulletin (see Note 7 below).

to 7 per cent in Azerbaidzhan, 2.7 to 2.3 in Armenia, 8.5 to 7.4 in Georgia. The shifts either way are modest, but clear enough (see Table 8.2).

The changes can be attributed in part to marked differences in birth-rates. Between 1959 and 1970, the population of the USSR increased by 15.8 per cent. The Russian increase was lower (13.1 per cent), as was that of the Byelorussians and Ukrainians (14.4 and 9.4), Lithuanians and Latvians (14.6 and 12.1) and, strikingly, the Estonians (1.8.). The rate was much higher in the Caucasus (Armenians 27.7 per cent, Georgians 20.5 per cent and Azerbaidzhanis 49 per cent) and in Central Asia, most of the major nationalities there approaching or surpassing the 50 per cent mark. By the next Census in 1979 the rates had slowed down somewhat, but broadly the same pattern was maintained - 8.5 per cent for the country

Table 8.3: Union-Republic Nationalities as Percentage of Total USSR Populations, 1959-1979, and Annual Growth Rate

	% total population			Annual growth rate	
	1959	1970	1979	1959-70	1970-79
Russians	54.6	53.4	52.4	1.3	0.9
Ukrainians	17.8	16.9	16.2	1.1	0.7
Byelorussians	3.8	3.7	3.6	1.2	0.5
(Slav group:	76.2	74.0	72.2)		
Lithuanians	1.11	1.10	1.09	1.2	0.8
Latvians	0.67	0.59	0.55	0.2	0.07
Estonians	0.47	0.42	0.39	0.2	0.1
(Baltic group:	2.25	2.11	2.03)		
Moldavians	1.06	1.12	1.13	1.8	1.1
Azerbaidzhanis	1.41	1.81	2.09	3.7	2.5
Armenians	1.33	1.47	1.58	2.3	1.7
Georgians	1.29	1.34	1.36	1.7	1.1
(Caucasus:	4.03	4.62	5.03)		
Uzbeks	2.88	3.80	4.75	4.0	3.4
Kazakhs	1.73	2.19	2.50	3.5	2.4
Turkmens	0.48	0.63	0.77	3.9	3.2
Kirgiz	0.46	0.60	0.73	3.8	3.1
Tadzhiks	0.67	0.88	1.11	4.0	3.5
(Central Asia:	6.22	8.10	9.86)		

Note: Nationalities are grouped geographically rather than linguistically.

as a whole: Russians 6.5 per cent, Ukrainians 3.9 per cent, Armenians 16.6 per cent, and Uzbeks, Kirgiz, Tadzhiks and Turkmens all showing an increase of over 30 per cent in nine years. (See Table 8.1 and Table 8.3 for annual growth rate.)

What emerges from this welter of figures is not only that the Central Asian and Caucasian peoples are maintaining a high rate of growth, but that the Russians are well on the way to becoming a minority in the country as a whole; since 1959, they have dropped from 54.6 to 52.4 per cent. They are still, of course, by far the biggest single nationality and nothing is likely to alter that; but already, most children in school, and young men in the armed forces, are non-Russians.

In theory, this is not supposed to matter in a multinational state of 'brother-peoples' all with equal rights; much is made of this in official propaganda. (11) But in reality it would be astonishing if the Russians were not anxious about the decline in their own position, for geopolitical considerations are bound to enter the picture. In the west, the traditional route for invasion in modern terms, they are strongly placed; but in Central Asia, with these huge increases among the traditionally Muslim peoples, their position is being eroded, and the spectre of Islamic revivalism looms across the frontier. Some may argue for Russification as a security measure - it has been tried before in other parts of the country - but this seems hardly feasible even if it were desirable. The reconciliation of diversity and unity, the creation of a <u>Soviet</u> nationality that can embrace the various languages and cultures in a higher loyalty, has always been officially on the agenda of the USSR: geographical realities give it an added urgency. The aim of creating 'a culture national in form but socialist in content' is still much quoted, though usually without mentioning that its author was Stalin - an attempt, perhaps, to recognise the objectives without the methods he used.

Policy and Practice in Education

Of the various markers of identity, one of them, citizenship, does not apply here, since all are citizens of the USSR, regardless of nationality or place of abode. Another, religion, is not recognised officially, being disapproved of by the Soviet state and specifically separated from the school by the Constitution. Language plays an obvious major role, at least unofficially; at any rate, maps and directories of 'peoples of the USSR' are based on linguistic data, and peoples tend to be classified according to language families. (12)

This is not definitive, however, as some members of each nationality give some <u>other</u> language as their mother tongue. In the case of the major Union Republic nationalities, this proportion is quite low in Central Asia (ranging from 1.3 per cent for Turkmens to 2.5 for Kazakhs), in the Caucasus (from 1.7 for Georgians to 9.3 for Armenians), the Baltic Republics (from 2.1 for Lithuanians to 5 per cent for Latvians) and Moldavia (6.8). It is higher, however, among non-Russian Slavs - 17.2 for Ukrainians, 25.8

197

for Byelorussians. Among some of the smaller nationalities, the proportion is much higher; only 46.8 per cent of the Yukagir, for example, claim Yukagir as their <u>native</u> language, and three-quarters of Jews (who count as a nationality in the USSR) speak Russian, not Yiddish, even though the same word (<u>evreiskii</u>) is used officially for both the language and the nationality. (13) It can not be assumed, incidentally, that the 'other' language is necessarily Russian. This is the case with most of the Jews, Yukagir, Ukrainians and some at least of the Baltic peoples; but in Central Asia and the Caucasus it is more likely to be one of the neighbouring major languages. (It should also be noted that there is little correlation between the proportion giving another language as the mother tongue and the proportion of Russians in the local population. This does fit with some of the smaller groups and in the Ukraine and Byelorussia; but in the Baltic Republics, where the proportion of Russians is also high, this is not the case.) Even among the Russians, a minute percentage (0.1 per cent) give another language as their native tongue.

Closely related though it is, then, language is not the determinant of identity or ethnicity. The Russian term for ethnic group (<u>natsional'nost'</u>) also means nationality, and this is shown on every Soviet citizen's internal passport. When this is issued at the age of 16, the recipient has to declare his or her 'nationality', and it cannot be changed thereafter. Normally, this will be the nationality of the parents; in the case of mixed marriages (which are increasingly common), the child chooses. The passport, incidentally, does not have to be produced to the Census enumerator; once again, the individual simply declares his nationality. In the Soviet Union, then, identity is what the person says it is. The same holds good for language; respondents are asked what their first language is, and what other they also speak fluently (if any). Thus, there is a rough guide - necessarily so, since it relies so heavily on self-reporting - to the incidence of language retention or shift, and of bilingualism. (Trilingualism, which is quite common in some areas, is thus not recorded at all, which is rather a pity.) Allowance must be made, therefore, for error, approximation and interpretation.

Officially, any Soviet citizen can elect to use any Soviet language - mother tongue, Russian or any other - for all purposes, including education. (14) It is hard to believe that this was ever intended literally, for the practical constraints must be obvious. (15) For one thing, not all peoples have a written language, and many others are too few in numbers to support schooling beyond the elementary levels. For the major nationalities - those of the Union Republics, plus the Tatars - instruction in the vernacular through the whole range of schooling is at least feasible, but even for them this is likely to be available only to those living in the particular republic, not to those living in other parts of the country.

Bernard Comrie, in his classical study of Soviet languages, (16) divides them usefully into six categories according to the extent of their use. His classification may be summarised thus: -

1. Languages with no written form, spoken by very small populations already bilingual in one of the larger languages (e.g. Aleut, Khinalug).
2. Languages with a written form, used to some extent in publication, but not as a medium of instruction (e.g. Yiddish, Koryak, Kurdish).
3. Languages used quite extensively in publication, and as media of instruction in the first few classes of school; thereafter, instruction shifts to another language, though the first may be kept as a subject of study (e.g. Chukchi).
4. Languages used for a wide range of publications (including technical) and as media of instruction throughout school, though not usually in further or higher education (e.g. most ASSR languages such as Abkhaz, Tatar, Komi).
5. Languages with the full range of publication, used as media for the whole educational system, including higher education (often alongside Russian), and as governmental and administrative languages (again, often alongside Russian) (e.g. the languages of the 14 Union Republics other than the RSFSR).
6. Russian, used for all functions and as lingua franca.

Although Russian is not technically the official language of the USSR, it functions as though it were. It may be chosen as the medium of instruction almost anywhere, and commonly is, even in many areas with a viable vernacular system. Otherwise, it is taught in non-Russian schools as a subject. As the medium of communication between different parts of the country, and with the outside world, it enjoys a special position, and it is hardly surprising that the authorities have been aiming to develop full functional bilingualism throughout the Union. Such an aim is far from realisation. In 1970, only among a handful of nationalities, mostly in the west, did over half the population claim to speak Russian fluently as a second language. By the time of the 1979 census, there had been considerable advances (see Table 8.4). The number of native Russian speakers had risen from 141 million to over 153 million (of whom 16 million were non-Russians), and the number claiming second-language fluency was up from nearly 42 million to over 61 million. The total percentages claiming fluency had risen to over half among the Byelorussians, Kazakhs, Lithuanians, Tatars, Chuvash, Bashkir and a few others, and very close among Ukrainians, Uzbeks and Moldavians. The Uzbek increase, from under 15 per cent to nearly 50 per cent in nine years, does not seem possible, and suggests that the enthusiasm of the party Secretary, Rashidov, overcame the scrupulous handling of statistics. (17) There may have been other cases, albeit less obvious, but generally there does seem to have been an advance towards effective bilingualism. The policy continues, from constant propagandising on behalf of Russian to plans (announced in 1980 and confirmed in 1984) to pay much more attention to the supply and quality of teachers of Russian in non-Russian schools. (18) There is some way to go yet; moderate competence in Russian is widespread but one can still meet older people and children with virtually no Russian at all, and less than a quarter of the non-Russian population, as yet, claims second-language fluency.

Numbers are not the only constraint upon parents' choice of language for their children's schooling; so, obviously, is the ethnic composition of the local population. In practice, the choice is normally between the major local language and Russian. The extent to which native-language instruction is actually chosen varies considerably. In Kazakhstan, for instance, a high proportion of Kazakhs prefer Russian-medium schooling for their children; but this is not typical of Central Asia, where the vernacular is much stronger, especially in Uzbekistan. (19) In the rural Ukraine, some 80 per cent of the children are taught in Ukrainian, but in Kiev itself the figure is only 20 per cent, the rest opting for Russian. (Ukrainian is used officially, of course, and in Kiev the public signs are either bilingual or in Ukrainian only; but most people there

Table 8.4: Bilingualism and Language Retention: Major Nationalities - Percentage Claiming Fluency in Russian as a Second Language, and Own Nationality as First Language (Census returns, 1970 and 1979)

	% claiming fluent Russian as second language		% giving language of own nationality as first language	
	1970	1979	1970	1979
Russians	0.1	0.1	99.8	99.9
Ukrainians	36.3	49.8	85.7	82.8
Byelorussians	49.0	57.0	80.6	74.2
Lithuanians	35.9	52.1	97.9	97.9
Latvians	45.2	56.7	95.2	95.0
Estonians	29.0	24.2	95.5	95.3
Moldavians	36.1	47.4	95.0	93.2
Azerbaidzhanis	16.6	29.5	98.2	97.9
Armenians	30.1	38.6	91.4	90.7
Georgians	21.3	26.7	98.4	98.3
Uzbeks	14.5	49.3	98.6	98.5
Kazakhs	41.8	52.3	98.0	97.5
Tadzhiks	15.4	29.6	98.5	97.8
Turkmens	15.4	25.4	98.9	98.7
Kirgiz	19.1	29.4	98.8	97.9
Tatars	62.5	68.9	89.2	85.9
Chuvash	58.4	64.8	86.9	81.7
Peoples of Dagestan	41.7	60.3	96.5	95.9
Bashkir	53.3	64.9	66.2	67.2
Mordvin	65.7	65.5	77.8	78.6

Source: 1979 Census, Munich bulletin (see Note 7 below).

speak Russian, with a Ukrainian accent.) In Armenia, by contrast, less then three per cent of children attend Russian-medium schools, Armenian being used everywhere. The University of Erevan, for example, has an introductory one-year language course for foreign students, as does the Lumumba University in Moscow, but the language is Armenian, not Russian. (20)

The fact that there are many Russians living in the Ukraine and few in Armenia may have something to do with it, but it cannot be the whole story. The Ukraine has a large population, but there is a long tradition of using Russian among the educated urban population; indeed, the Ukrainian language was long referred to as 'little Russian' as opposed to 'great Russian', and was regarded as partly peasant dialect, partly as a language of poetry and fiction - not unlike the position of Lowland Scots, except that Ukrainian now has official status as well. Ukrainian and Russian are quite close linguistically, which makes one more easily penetrable by the other - again, not unlike Scots vis-à-vis English. Armenian is in quite a different situation. It is totally distinct linguistically, even in its script, and though there are fewer speakers - about four million - the population is compact and provides a stronger base for the language. There is also a long tradition of literary use, a high level of urbanisation, and a degree of sophistication and self-confidence lacking in some other areas. The strength of a language, and its status in the educational system, depends upon factors other than numbers, important though these may be.

In so far as a policy of pluralism is being followed, it applies to language and little else. Young Azerbaidzhanis, Uzbeks and Tadzhiks may be taught in their own languages, and may study Islamic art forms and architecture. But they will not be taught about leaders of resistance to Russian imperialism in the nineteenth century; these conquests, though of course imperialist in their time, are presented (if at all) as 'historically progressive' in that they later made the creation of the USSR in its present form possible. Nor is there any allowance - not officially, at any rate - to 'traditional' attitudes towards, say, the role of women. True, there appear to be some concessions now and again, like the soft-pedalling on 'scientific atheism' in Muslim areas, or the survival there of the occasional single-sex teachers' college; but these are tactical concessions, not an acceptance in principle of an alternative value system. The medium of teaching may be a matter for local variation, but the general aims of the system are not; the content of teaching, and the social values contained therein, are centrally determined. There is no suggestion that this principle is even open to discussion.

Developments and Perspectives

In the days of the Russian Empire, official policy towards the nationalities veered between Russification and neglect, and sometimes managed both simultaneously, assiduously trying to assimilate the Poles while leaving the Finns more or less alone. Count Sergei Uvarov was not alone in assuming the superiority of Russian culture, but he was unusually active in trying to spread its blessings among the 'lesser breeds'. He was even more unusual in taking an interest in the eastern languages and literatures, fostering them as subjects of study in the universities. But he saw no inconsistency in this; there was no question of encouraging cultural autonomy among the subject peoples, or of compromising on the primacy of Russian language and culture. (21)

Modern Soviet policy has been interpreted by some observers in a similar light. True, the Academy of Sciences designed scripts for many of the minority tongues, and vernacular education is widespread where formerly there was none. At the same time (as already noted), the Russian language is strongly encouraged, and teachers of Russian in the national schools are one of the two priority categories for recruitment. (The other is labour training.) It has been argued that this, like the use of the Cyrillic alphabet for most minority languages, indicates a long-term policy of cultural imperialism, vernacular schooling being merely an interim concession. (22)

Indeed, there are some, Isayev among them, (23) who talk rather vaguely about an eventual 'convergence' of all the Soviet peoples into a single new language community. He makes much of the fact that people from most nationalities have moved to other parts of the country (without mentioning that for some whole groups, especially in Stalin's time, there was no choice in the matter). There has been a good deal of conventional mobility, and of mixed marriage, both of which can encourage linguistic homogenisation. But, looking at the linguistic pattern nationwide, it is hard to see what 'convergence' could mean other than assimilation. The Russians, certainly, are on the way to becoming an overall minority, but they are bound to remain the largest single group by far for the foreseeable future, they live in varying but substantial numbers in every part of the country, and their language is the lingua franca of the whole of the USSR as well as the tongue of its largest component. Isayev mentions linguistic borrowing but this concerns vocabulary rather than structure, and is (unsurprisingly) from Russian to the other languages. It is hard to see what real difference it makes to Russian to have a Georgian word for toastmaster or a Siberian word for a kind of sledge, any more than the adoption of a few words like slogan, whisky or galore can be said to have Gaelicised the English language. Convergence, unless it does mean assimilation or Russification, is hardly a realistic concept.

But Russification is hardly realistic either, at any rate on a national scale. There has been some mixing of populations, but not universally or evenly. The proportion of Russians has been rising in the Baltic republics, Byelorussia and the Ukraine, and in the RSFSR itself the proportion of non-Russians has been going up. But some other parts, notably the Caucasian republics and Central Asia, have become less mixed, partly at least the result of the differential birth rates. Also, Muslim sentiment seems to be on the increase in Central Asia, reinforcing a sense of cultural identity. Assimilation, even if it were the intention of the authorities, does not seem to be a practical option.

But the authorities strenuously deny that this is the intention. There is nothing inconsistent, they argue, in fostering the spread of Russian as a <u>second</u> language and at the same time encouraging the minority cultures and, where necessary, devising alphabets for their languages. Nor would they accept that using Cyrillic instead of Arabic for some of the Asian languages was intended to cut them off from their cultural roots. As Musaev points out, (24) some traditional scripts fit the needs of their languages well (like Georgian) and were retained, but Arabic script was a clumsy vehicle for the transcription of Turkic languages. After all, Kemal Atatürk introduced the Latin alphabet in place of the Arabic for Turkish itself, and for the same purpose of making literacy more accessible. (25) As for the encouragement of Russian learning, this is to meet the obvious need for a common medium of communication, but does not, it is argued, preclude the retention and development of the minority languages (a point alluded to in the 1984 guidelines). (26)

In support of this, it has been pointed out that the policy of closing and amalgamating small schools in remote areas has been modified to take account of social and cultural factors as well as economic considerations. The financial arguments for amalgamation may be strong, but when a school is an essential focal point for the survival of a community or even a nationality, these arguments may be overridden. (27) The publication of books and journals in the minority languages is also mentioned

204

as an indication of pluralism. Actually, the picture here is uneven, and could reflect demographic patterns, cultural strengths, and the degree to which they are in contact with Russian just as much as cultural policy. (28) Of the 30-odd languages used in publication, there has been a decline in the number of copies printed in Ukrainian, Byelorussian, Kazakh, Moldavian, Kirgiz, Estonian, languages of Dagestan, Osetin, Tatar and some of the smaller groups. There are few surprises here (except perhaps for Kirgiz), since all are languages liable to considerable penetration by Russian (or, in the case of some smaller groups, by other major languages). On the increase are Uzbek, Georgian, Azerbaidzhani, Tadzhik, Armenian and some others that might be expected in view of the coalescence of populations already noted; more surprising in this category are Lithuanian, Latvian and some of the smaller Uralic peoples, all from areas where the Russian presence is large and growing. In the case of the first two, it may be that cultural distinctiveness, plus a long-standing and well-developed level of educational attainment, may account for the departure from what would be expected from demographic trends.

There is no doubt that the various groups do exhibit substantial differences in educational attainment, and that this had been greater in the past. Nathan Kravetz, (29) comparing the proportions in each group attaining complete secondary or higher educational qualifications, found wide disparities. The Russians, however, did not appear at the top of the league. They did better than average, but were outranked by others. Higher educational qualifications, for example, were held by an extraordinary 40 per cent of Jews in 1970, by 10.5 per cent of Georgians, 7.5 per cent of Armenians, 6.8 per cent of Tatars (in Uzbekistan) and 6.8 per cent of Estonians. The Russians had 5.9 per cent and Latvians 5.6, just over the national average. Just under came the Azerbaidzhanis, Yakut, Lithuanians and Ukrainians. Most of the Turkic peoples tended to come out much lower, but so did the Moldavians (2.2 per cent). The patterns for completion of secondary schooling were not dissimilar.

Kravetz tried to link the differences to levels of urbanisation and to the proportions claiming fluency in Russian as a second language. Urbanisation does seem to be a factor in many cases, but the link with knowledge of Russian was less convincing. It could be that access to Russian proved to be an advantage where the indigenous cultures were relatively weak, as with the Tatars of Uzbekistan, but mattered less where they were strong, as in Georgia or Armenia. Other factors must have been at work.

Religion, or at least the traditional religious background, may have been one of these. Nicholas Hans suggested, as a general hypothesis, that the formal educational attainment of a group could be correlated with its religious affiliation (actual or traditional) in the following descending order: Jewish, Protestant, Catholic, Orthodox, Muslim. (30) Zvi Halevy and Eva Etsioni-Halevy (31) sought to apply this to Soviet nationalities, and by and large did confirm such a connection (though they had few traditionally Protestant or Catholic groups to work on), at least until recently, when the Muslim peoples began to close the gap. Actual observance is officially discouraged, but this could be one of these cases where religion can serve as a convenient shorthand for a cluster of social attitudes. For example, the religious base of what is still called the 'Protestant work ethic' used to be clear enough; but in the modern USA, Catholics, Jews and even the occasional atheist can cheerfully subscribe to it. Likewise, most Muslim societies have their views about the special place of women in society, though not all go as far as Saudi Arabia in forbidding women to drive cars or work with men. How far these attitudes are a necessary outcome of the teaching of the Qur'an is for others to debate; but they have become part of traditional Islamic culture, and may survive independently of the survival of actual belief. Even now, one hears of girls in Central Asia being withdrawn early (and quite illegally) from school 'lest too much knowledge make them less obedient wives.' (32) Apparently, the development of a common set of Soviet values is still not complete.

The 'Hans hypothesis' may have had some validity, but decreasingly, for the discrepancies between the different peoples have been lessening. For whatever reason (a commitment to equality, or concern at the political vulnerability of Central Asia, according to one's preferences), the authorities seem to have been diverting resources and imposing a quota system on higher education. (This has also been tried in the USA, with mixed results.) That a quota system is in operation seems clear from Kravetz's study of developments during the 1970s (when the system was still expanding). The greatest increase was among some of the Central Asian and Turkic peoples, especially the Chuvash, Bashkir,

Tatars, Tadzhiks, Kazakhs and Kirgiz; the Byelorussians, Lithuanians, Latvians, Uzbeks, Turkmens and peoples of Dagestan were still above the average for growth; the Estonians, Moldavians, Ukrainians and Russians were on or just below the national average, and the Armenians substantially below. At least there were net growth rates, however minimal; as for the two previously advantaged groups, the Georgians and the Jews, both experienced a net reduction in admissions (drastic in the case of the Jews - nearly 40 per cent). The number of Jews in the USSR has fallen (see Table 8.1) partly because of emigration and, more commonly, assimilation; but generally the figures are consistent with a policy of positive and negative discrimination.

But a quota system is·unlikely to be the whole story. Negative discrimination is relatively easy; if the Georgians and Jews are reckoned to be disproportionately advantaged, cutting back on their numbers is administratively straightforward - always provided, of course, that one is prepared to put up with the waste of resources and the annoyance on the part of the groups themselves (especially the Jews, whose position has been deteriorating in Soviet society in any case, exacerbated by a good deal of surviving anti-Semitic sentiment, against which education has traditionally provided the only protection). But positive discrimination is much more difficult; there is little point in special admission to higher education if those thus favoured retain the handicaps that made special treatment necessary in the first place. (This has also emerged in the USA.) Remedial programmes are possible, but in the long run the only stable solution is improvement of the whole school system further down, a much longer-term process. There are signs that this has been happening, though the effects seem as yet to be uneven.

Overall, then, there seems to be a long-term policy of equalising the educational opportunities of the various nationalities, even at the cost of holding back some of the more advantaged. This need not mean Russification. Some cultures are, as we have seen, more susceptible to Russian influence, especially when there is a high proportion of Russian settlement; in these cases, the very process of educational advancement may favour further exposure to Russian cultural norms. This seems to be less true, however, where the indigenous culture is advanced and well-established, as in the Baltic republics. Other cultures, notably those of the

Caucasus and some of Central Asia, seem to be at least holding their own, reinforced by demographic trends. In these circumstances, homogeneity (or assimilation, or 'convergence') seems unlikely. Those who emphasise the multinational nature of Soviet society (33) (conveniently able to quote Lenin in support) can argue that multinational education is the logical objective; the alternative is likely to make for tension and conflict.

But at least linguistic pluralism, for all the practical complications, is straightforward at least in theory. But cultural identity need not stop at language, and can extend to social customs and values. So far, there seems not the slightest chance of that kind of pluralism being entertained; the official objective remains 'culture national in form but socialist in content', even if the steps in that direction are taken cautiously these days – especially in Central Asia, with the spectre of Islamic revivalism looming across the frontier. Whether the social norms conveyed in the Soviet educational system prove strong enough, or flexible enough, to underpin the unity of the country amid all the forms of diversity remains to be seen, and should be a matter of some interest in the West. For, however different the context, the fundamental issue of reconciling unity with diversity, defining the claims of each, and relating this to educational policy and practice, concerns the rest of us also.

Notes

1.   Slovene is fairly closely related to Serbo-Croat, but the two languages are not readily mutually comprehensible. Macedonian is much closer to Bulgarian, a highly aberrant member of the Slavonic group in certain basic grammatical features (such as the loss of case inflection and the possession of a definite article). Croatian and Serbian have some minor phonological and lexical differences, but are generally mutually comprehensible; there are also dialectical differences that cut across the Serbian-Croat divide.

2.   For discussion, see R. Bell and N. Grant, Patterns of Education in the British Isles (Allen & Unwin, London, 1977).

3.   See E. Haugen, J.D. McLure and D.S. Thomson (eds.), Minority Languages Today (Edinburgh University Press, Edinburgh, 1981).

4.   N. Grant, 'Language and education: an international survey', Teaching English, vol. 19,

no. 2 (Spring 1986), pp.9-14.

5. E.g. Peter Borby (ed.), <u>Bilingualism:</u>
<u>Psychological and Educational Implications</u> (Academic
Press, New York, 1977); E. Glyn Lewis, <u>Bilingualism</u>
<u>and Bilingual Education</u> (Pergamon, Oxford, 1981);
Derrick Sharp, <u>Language in Bilingual Communities</u>
(Arnold, London, 1973); Hugo Baetens Beardsmore,
<u>Bilingualism: Basic Principles</u> (Tieto, Cleveland,
1982).

6. For discussion, see Julian Dakin, Brian
Tiffen and H.G. Widdowson, <u>Language in Education</u>
(Oxford U.P., Oxford, 1968); T.P. Gorman (ed.),
<u>Language in Education in Eastern Africa</u> (Oxford U.P.,
Oxford, 1970); N. Grant, 'Education and language' in
J. Lowe, N. Grant and T.D. Williams (eds.), <u>Education</u>
<u>and Nation-Building in the Third World</u> (Scottish
Academic Press, Edinburgh, 1971).

7. <u>Naselenie SSSR po dannym perepisi</u>
<u>naseleniya 1979 goda</u> (Politizdat, Moscow, 1980),
from which all figures are drawn unless otherwise
stated. Some of the more detailed analyses are
adapted from <u>The All-Union Census of 1979 in the USSR</u>
(Radio Liberty Research Bulletin, Munich, 1980).

8. For a full treatment of the languages of
the USSR (including their linguistic structures,
functions and status) see Bernard Comrie, <u>The</u>
<u>Languages of the Soviet Union</u> (Cambridge U.P.,
Cambridge, 1981).

9. Also known as Finno-Ugric, from its major
European members, Finnish and Hungarian.

10. K.M. Musaev, <u>Alfavity yazykov narodov SSSR</u>
(Nauka, Moscow, 1965).

11. M.J. Isayev, <u>National Languages in the</u>
<u>USSR: Problems and Solutions</u> (Progress Publishers,
Moscow, 1977).

12. E.g. <u>Karta narodov SSSR</u> (Moskva, 1965).

13. <u>Evrei</u> (Hebrew) is used for Jew; since <u>zhid</u>
is an offensive version, the Yiddish language is also
called <u>evreiskii</u> (literally, again, Hebrew). To get
round the resultant confusion, what is known
elsewhere as Hebrew is rendered in Russian as <u>ivrit</u>
(the Hebrew version).

14. Constitution of the USSR, Article 121.

15. For a valuable case-study, see Frances
Cooley, 'National schools in the Yakutskaya ASSR:
some language issues' in J.J. Tomiak (ed.), <u>Soviet</u>
<u>Education in the 1980s</u> (Croom Helm, London &
Canberra, 1983), pp.278-305. For an overview, see
Glyn Lewis, 'Bilingualism as language planning in the
Soviet Union' in J.J. Tomiak (ed.), <u>Western</u>
<u>Perspectives on Soviet Education in the 1980s</u>

(Macmillan, 1986), pp.75-96, and Wolfgang Mitter, 'Bilingual and intercultural education in Soviet schools', ibid., pp.123-137.

16.   Comrie, The Languages of the Soviet Union, pp.27-8.

17.   The First Secretary of the Communist Party in Uzbekistan, Sh. R. Rashidov, was well known to be strongly committed to encouraging knowledge of Russian. This may well have influenced the Census enumerators, or at any rate the collation of returns. Certainly a leap from 14.5% in 1970 to 49.3% in 1979 is hard to accept at face value.

18.   V.K. Rozov, 'Sotsial'no-ekonomicheskie problemy pedagogicheskogo obrazovaniya i povysheniya effektivnosti ispol'zovaniya pedagogicheskikh kadrov', Sovetskaya pedagogika, No. 2, (1980), pp.97-102; 'Proekt TsK KPSS: Osnovnye napravleniya reformy obshcheobrazovatel'noi i professional'noi shkoly', Pravda, 4 January 1984.

19.   See W.K. Medlin, W.M. Cave and F. Carpenter, Education and Development in Central Asia: a Case Study on Social Change in Uzbekistan (Brill, Leiden, 1971).

20.   Personal observations, Kiev and Erevan, 1976.

21.   Cynthia H. Whittaker, The Origins of Modern Russian Education: an Intellectual Biography of Count Sergei Uvarov, 1786-1855 (Northern Illinois U.P., 1984), pp.189-212.

22.   John Gunther, Inside Russia (Penguin, 1965).

23.   Isayev, National Languages in the USSR.

24.   Musaev, Alfavity yazykov.

25.   The Arabic alphabet, like the Hebrew, is suited to the structure of a Semitic language, which it evolved to express. The consonants are all-important, vowels less so; indeed, short vowels are normally omitted for most purposes. They can be indicated by diacritic points, but this is not usually necessary, and only three vowels (a, i, u) are recognised in writing anyway. It is thus less suitable for non-Semitic languages, especially Turkic, which has a wider range of vowels, and in which vowel-harmony is grammatically important. Also, calligraphic conventions (reinforced by the authority of the Qur'an) make the Arabic script aesthetically beautiful, but difficult to adapt to printing for easy reading. This, at any rate, was the view taken by Kemal Atatürk when he changed Turkish writing from Arabic to Latin in 1924. In the Soviet Union, the later change from Latin to Cyrillic was a

much less fundamental step, since both alphabets are of essentially the same type, with separable letters and equal symbolic value for consonants and vowels (as in Greek, their common parent).

26. <u>Pravda</u>, 4 January 1984.

27. Oral communication from Deputy Minister of Education of the RSFSR, Glasgow 1982.

28. <u>Narodnoe khozyaistvo SSSR v 1985 godu: statisticheskii ezhegodnik</u> (Moscow, 1985), pp.548-9. By far the largest number of titles and copies, however, are in Russian.

29. Nathan Kravetz, 'Education of ethnic and national minorities in the USSR: a report on current developments', <u>Comparative Education</u>, vol. 16, no. 1 (March 1980), pp.13-24.

30. Nicholas Hans, <u>Comparative Education</u> (Routledge & Kegan Paul, London, 1958), pp.103-5.

31. Zvi Halevy and Eva Etsioni-Halevy, 'The "religious factor" and achievement in education', <u>Comparative Education</u>, vol. 10, no. 3 (1974), pp.193-200.

32. E.g. <u>Uchitel'skaya gazeta</u>, 27 January 1973; <u>Kommunist Tadzhikistana</u>, 8 June 1973; <u>Turkmenskaya Iskra</u>, 2 February 1972.

33. F.G. Panachin (ed.), <u>Sovetskaya mnogonatsional'naya shkola v usloviyakh razvitogo sotsializma</u> (Pedagogika, Moscow, 1984).

Chapter Nine

STUDENT RESPONSE TO COMMUNIST UPBRINGING IN SOVIET
HIGHER EDUCATION

George Avis

Introduction (1)
The main aims of Soviet higher education are: (i) to
offer advanced subject teaching in the humanities,
sciences and technology for the purpose of producing
highly qualified specialists for the national
economy, and (ii) to ensure that these graduates have
the necessary views and skills in the ideological,
political, social and moral realms to enable them to
become leaders in their work collectives and, in the
oft-quoted phrase of Leonid Brezhnev, 'politically
literate and ideologically convinced fighters for
the cause of Communism'. The Soviet graduate, then,
should be a dedicated professional worker in his own
field and a highly principled and informed political
activist displaying exemplary sentiments of
collectivism, patriotism and internationalism. (2)
It is not then surprising that a fundamental
distinguishing feature of Soviet higher education is
the importance it attaches to that system of
practical and theoretical instruction known as
'communist upbringing' (<u>kommunisticheskoe vospitan-
ie</u>). In the process of this upbringing every student,
no matter what his or her particular course of
academic study may be, is expected to develop a
strong commitment to the specialised vocation he is
being trained for and to acquire the requisite
philosophical, political, social and moral values
and mode of behaviour of good socialist leaders of
men, educators and activists. Indeed, Soviet
authorities go so far as to assert that communist
upbringing, since it inculcates a Marxist-Leninist
scientific view of nature and society, is a
prerequisite for academic learning itself. (3)
    The target or focus for all this educational and
ideological attention is the Soviet student. But what
do students in the Soviet Union actually think of

ideological instruction? Do students satisfy the official attitudinal and behavioural norms? How do they react to the pressures put upon them to match up the ideals prescribed by their mentors? Does, in short, communist upbringing work? These are the sort of questions addressed in this chapter.

A basic problem is that while the effectiveness of academic training may be readily assessed by looking at indices of student performance, the genuine assimilation of attitudes and prescribed behaviour patterns is difficult to measure. To an outside observer the life of Soviet colleges and universities resembles more or less that of similar institutions the world over. The teaching of familiar academic disciplines dominates the scene. Even compulsory ideological instruction takes the form of discrete social science subjects such as History of the Soviet Communist Party, Marxist-Leninist Philosophy and the like - a programme which is analogous to compulsory general education courses in the higher education curricula of many countries. The acquisition of knowledge and reasoning ability is assessed by traditional methods of testing and examining. Much less visible is the process of communist upbringing whereby attitudes, values, enthusiasm and activism are supposed to be inculcated. And because it is less in evidence, its successful implementation is more problematical from a pedagogical point of view. Knowledge is one thing, conviction is another, and action yet another. That is why representative anonymous surveys of the views and perceptions of Soviet students both about their vocational commitment and about their lengthy ideological training can be of considerable interest since they provide at least suggestive evidence of the efficacy of official upbringing methods. The main focus of what follows will be restricted to recently published empirical studies which reflect the results of the most representative large-scale surveys of Soviet students conducted in the last decade or so by leading research centres in this field. (4)

Vocational Orientation

The strength of students' dedication to their specialism, that is to their future professional role in Soviet economic life, is considered a touchstone of their successful assimilation of the values imparted by communist upbringing. It has been assessed by Soviet sociologists using several indicators. Academic performance, failure and transfer provide some indication of commitment, of course. Other more direct measures of student attitudes in this area have included surveys to elucidate students' motives for choosing a given specialism (i.e. profession), their views about the desired features of work in general and of their own future profession in particular, their level of satisfaction with the choice of vocation they have made, and their willingness to make the same choice again.

In the All-Union Survey of 1973-1974 first-year students were asked: (i) when they had decided on getting a higher education, (ii) when they had chosen to study their particular specialism, (iii) what motivated their choice of specialised VUZ (acronym for vysshee uchebnoe zavedenie - higher educational establishment - to be used hereafter) at the time of entry, and (iv) what their plans were for their immediate future as students. The results of the survey reveal that the decision to aim at higher education is taken well before any particular course is contemplated. That is, social motivation or the desire for graduate status precedes the purely vocational motivation of acquiring expertise for a specific profession. (5) The Soviet researchers suggest that if these two decisions are taken early on and if the size of the time gap between them is small, then this constitutes a broad indicator of clear vocational orientation. Students of medicine would appear to be surer of their vocation in this respect, as are would-be teachers both in the humanities faculties of universities and in pedagogical institutes. (6) The choices made by agricultural students are also close in time but both are left late, indicating considerable initial doubts about the whole idea of higher training. More than one-third of all the students decided they would like to have a higher education three or more years before entry to a VUZ, and another third a year or more before, while about 25 per cent only made their minds up in the year prior to entry. But when it came to choosing a vocational specialism, more than one-half of the respondents admit to leaving this decision until some time during the preceding twelve months. (7)

Table 9.1 presents some data from the All-Union Survey on the extent to which certain motives were influential in the selection of a particular VUZ. (In the context of the Soviet system of higher education this is synonymous with selecting a career

214

Table 9.1: Motives for Choice of VUZ, (a) First-year Students at Entry by Type of VUZ (All-Union Survey, 1973/4)

Motives	All VUZs	Polytech- nical Institutes	Agricultural Institutes	Pedagogical Institutes	Medical Institutes	Universities Humanit. Facs.	Nat. Sci. Facs.
				Students considering motive important (%)			
VUZ specialism matches own abilities and inclinations	69.7	51.8	66.5	77.3	79.6	85.7	76.9
VUZ specialism offers interesting work in the future	48.9	37.4	49.2	44.4	50.1	48.1	42.2
No other choice	18.1	25.3	18.2	16.8	10.7	17.6	14.0
Entry less competitive	8.4	11.5	10.3	7.0	3.6	3.8	4.8
Recognition of national economy's need for graduates with VUZ specialism	37.1	36.3	58.4	33.2	41.9	21.2	28.2

Note: (a) The Russian acronym VUZ denotes any type of higher education establishment, whether university or specialised institute.

Sources: L. Ya. Rubina, Sovetskoe studenchestvo: sotsiologicheskii ocherk. (Mysl', Moscow, 1981), p.88; M.N. Rutkevich and F.R. Filippov (eds.), Vysshaya shkola kak faktor izmeneniya sotsial'noi struktury razvitogo sotsialisticheskogo obshchestva (Nauka, Moscow, 1978), p.193.

specialism.) These results indicate that the intrinsic interest of the vocation concerned and its compatibility with personal inclinations and abilities are dominant considerations in the minds of most new students (48.9 and 69.7 per cent of them, respectively). Among those who state that these motives were important university, medical and teacher-training students score highest; and so, not surprisingly, do those whose career plans were clearly formulated two to three years in advance. Also represented to an above average extent here are the children of parents who themselves are graduate specialists. (8)

On the other hand, a sizeable minority of respondents are motivated by mainly opportunistic considerations of the moment - easier access, the lack of other choices or other reasons not included in the table such as proximity of the VUZ to home, the availability of student hostel accommodation and so on. As we saw above some of this group are among those young people who regard higher education from an essentially non-vocational standpoint, that is as a means of personal development and fulfilment. But the main reason given by the researchers is the absence of any firm vocational orientation. Noticeably low proportions of engineers (approximately one-half) cite the 'positive' motives as influencing them most, while over one-third frankly admit to the 'wrong' ones. Of the latter subgroup some ten per cent had tried at an earlier date to be admitted to a different VUZ in order to study a different subject. (9) This pattern of behaviour no doubt partly reflects the decline in the relative popularity of engineering and technical higher education among Soviet youth which has bedevilled Soviet student recruiters since the early seventies. Yet student teachers and agriculturalists also rely on opportunistic motives in quite high proportions, despite scoring well, as it were, on the positive reasons. The key variable here, according to the authors of the study, is whether the choice of specialism itself was made early or late. Some 50 per cent of the engineers, for example, did not choose engineering until the last minute! The somewhat tautological conclusion drawn is that the later aspiring students make this crucial decision, the more likely they are to be swayed by ad hoc considerations. In the International Survey some years later it was similarly found that Soviet engineering students chose their specialism late, and so did future economists and teachers, with little variation between the different regions of the USSR surveyed. (10)

Awareness of national needs, the altruistic motive in the set, is not very highly developed in the sample. Medical and agricultural students seem to be most conscious of the relevance to the public good of their essentially practical and applied sciences. Conversely, university students, who are expected to become teachers and researchers, and pedagogical institute students rate this motive rather low. It may be that at this early stage any thoughts about their future upbringing role are somehow dampened by loyalty to their particular subject or by the low prestige of teaching. Curiously enough, the researchers, while commenting on the responses to the other items, fail to develop any discussion on this rather important one.

Thus far we have examined the personal motives and intentions of inexperienced students in order to gauge in an indirect fashion the strength of their vocational aspirations. Their reactions are not absolutely clearcut and unequivocal. And this is understandable since subjective factors and immediate circumstances inevitably affect responses. What is clear is that the respondents do not exhibit a strong sense of higher education as professional training. Yet, nor are they overenthusiastic about devoting themselves to the pursuit of knowledge. The same uncertainty about both the academic and vocational functions of higher education was displayed by RSFSR students in the International Survey whose authors were nonplussed to discover that as many as one-fifth of the Russian students polled, though involved in a highly vocationalised system, did not regard as an important function of higher education the acquisition of professional skills. And the same proportion expressed the opinion that raising one's educational level was not of much importance either! Those who felt that these two purposes were very important constituted only just over 40 per cent of the respondents in both cases - well below the percentages from the Baltic republics and the other socialist countries. This 'passivity' of the Russians was, surprisingly, blamed on the fact that the sample was weighted towards students from Russian provincial VUZs. (11)

A genuine sense of vocation in students, of course, may not be present initially but may develop later on. Similarly, firm career intentions can dissipate during the course as students learn more of the realities of the chosen occupation or if the

217

Table 9.2: Desirable Features of a Job – Student Views in USSR, Sverdlovsk, RSFSR and Baltic Republics, 1973-1979

A job should	USSR (1973/74)		Sverdlovsk (1973/77)		RSFSR (1977/79)	Baltic Reps. (1977/79)
	1 Year	V Year	1 Year	V Year		
1. be of great use to society	63.3	56.0	63.0	44.1	56.7	39.6
2. aid personal development	63.1	66.3	60.1	48.0	-	42.1
3. enable one to mix with people	50.1	40.3	51.4	43.2	43.9	39.4
4. give chance to be creative	47.6	47.2	-	-	27.0	47.7
5. be respected by family and friends	41.8	37.3	43.2	26.5	47.8	20.7
6. bring one success in life	17.9	24.8	10.4	7.5	12.2	13.3
7. provide good salary	14.0	27.2	14.7	15.6	18.3	17.2
8. enjoy public recognition	10.7	19.9	17.1	12.6	6.7	13.5
9. offer interesting work	-	-	-	-	54.4	58.9
10. fully utilise one's abilities	-	-	-	-	50.2	50.1

Students stating feature as very important (%)

Sources: M.N. Rutkevich and F.R. Filippov (eds.), Vysshaya shkola kak faktor izmeneniya sotsialnoi struktury razvitogo sotsialisticheskogo obshchestva (Nauka, Moscow, 1978), p.176; L. Ya. Rubina, Sovetskoe studenchestvo: sotsiologicheskii ocherk (Mysl', Moscow, 1981), pp.105-106; F.R. Filippov and P.E. Mitev (eds.), Molodezh' i vysshee obrazovanie v sotsialisticheskikh stranakh (Nauka, Moscow, 1984), pp. 103-104.

training for it proves uncongenial, or both. Table 9.2 contains results from a number of major surveys of the 1970s showing students' expectations with regard to a job and, in the case of the earlier studies, how these expectations can differ between the beginning and end of a course. The USSR figures indicate that final-year students develop a more realistic or instrumental attitude to employment. The social utility of work loses some of its attraction and takes second place to self-development as a desirable feature. The significance of good wages, success and public recognition rises appreciably.

A banal cautionary note or two should perhaps be sounded here. As with all opinion measurement, expressed views do not necessarily represent convictions, and convictions do not necessarily determine behaviour. Nor, for that matter, does seemingly correct behaviour always imply the existence of the right attitudes and motives (such 'formalism' is constantly criticised in the Soviet Union). Moreover, just as it is difficult to deny that virtue is a good thing, so it may have been difficult for respondents in these surveys to disagree with propositions that a field of work should ideally be of great benefit to society and promote personal growth. One might conclude, indeed, that viewed from this perspective the proportions of positive responses to these items are not impressive, ranging as they do from only 40 to no higher than 66 per cent across the table. The authors of the All-Union Survey themselves point out that some students who rated these features as very important will have internalised the attitudes only superficially. They call, therefore, for a strengthening in VUZ upbringing work. (12) And although it is clear that they implicitly treat the items concerned as being more laudable or more 'socialist', at the same time, nevertheless, they attempt to play down the instrumental tendencies of senior students by suggesting that public recognition, being successful and earning good money should not really be regarded as negative aspirations (though they are generally thus regarded in the Soviet Union) when they occur in a socialist society where social classes are non-antagonistic. (13) Indeed, Filippov specifically proposes that better career prospects and salaries for graduate engineers would improve the vocational orientation of final-year engineering students and encourage them to take up jobs in production. (14)

The Sverdlovsk data in the table are of especial

interest because they are taken from a longitudinal study by Rubina and her associates and thus reveal the degree of attitudinal change in a single cohort of students over the period of their course. A noticeable decline has taken place in virtually all the indices. Not only does this confirm the trend towards greater realism, but the differences between the years are large enough to hint at a generalised loss of morale. Rubina, however, does not address herself in her interpretation of the data to this swing, merely stressing the continued prominence of the 'positive' features in the hierarchy of responses. (15)

The figures in the remaining columns are extracted from the main International Survey report and do not differentiate between years of the course, but other sources, which do, make it clear that this later survey, on the whole, confirms the general picture of the earlier ones. (16) There are distinct differences between the Russian and Baltic patterns of response. Social usefulness, in particular, appeals less to the Balts, it seems. The Russian students rate creativity much lower than those in the earlier studies featured in the table, but they regard the respect of friends, success and good wages as somewhat more important. As in the other surveys (although this is not recorded in the data here) the researchers noted an increase in the importance accorded to remuneration among final-year Soviet students and a decline in that accorded to the social utility of work in their case, too. (17) In general, again, the more students learn about or gain experience of their future profession, the less, it seems, they are inclined to esteem it. The same broad trend was confirmed in a study of Leningrad University students in 1976 with reference to specific careers they were being trained for. (18)

Finally, Soviet students have been asked at the beginning and end of their course direct questions about their degree of satisfaction with their chosen specialism-vocation. Table 9.3 presents data for the proportions of first- and fifth-year students in the USSR, Sverdlovsk, and the RSFSR who expressed satisfaction, the first two samples combining complete and partial satisfaction in one figure, while the Baltic republics results refer to complete satisfaction expressed by all students surveyed. The USSR survey reveals that the respondents in the early seventies may well have had their satisfaction with their chosen vocational study enhanced by their VUZ course, since nearly all the final-year percentages

Table 9.3: Student Satisfaction with their Choice of Vocation (Specialism) by Type of VUZ and Year of Course - USSR, Sverdlovsk, RSFSR and Baltic Republics, 1973-79

| Type of VUZ and Year of Course | Students satisfied with choice of vocation/specialism (%) (a) | | | |
	USSR (1973/74)	Sverdlovsk (1973/77)	RSFSR (1977/79)	Baltic Republics
Engineering				
First Year	79.5	89.1	55.7	
Final Year	81.1	79.3	35.5	31.2
Agriculture				
First Year	88.5	90.5	70.8	
Final Year	87.2	80.2	50.7	44.3
Pedagogical				
First Year	78.8	80.3	61.8	
Final Year	83.8	86.3	38.8	37.0
Medical				
First Year	91.5	93.8	79.4	
Final Year	93.6	92.8	64.4	67.7

Note: (a) The percentages for the USSR and Sverdlovsk combine both 'completely satisfied' and 'partly satisfied' responses. Those for the RSFSR and Baltic republics refer to 'completely satisfied' students only.

Sources: M.N. Rutkevich and F.R. Filippov (eds.), _Vysshaya shkola kak faktor izmeneniya sotsial'noi struktury razvitogo sotsialisticheskogo obshchestva_ (Nauka, Moscow, 1978), p.194; L. Ya. Rubina, _Sovetskoe studenchestvo: sotsiologicheskii ocherk_ (Mysl', Moscow, 1981), p.114; F.R. Filippov and P.E. Mitev (eds.), _Molodezh' i vysshee obrazovanie v sotsialisticheskikh stranakh_ (Nauka, Moscow, 1984), p.84.

are higher than those in the first year of the course. The same senior students, however, when asked if they planned to go on and actually work in their chosen profession in the future, were less positive by several points than their younger contemporaries. (19) (This may not be as paradoxical as it may seem, since in these comparisons different cohorts are involved and, in addition, the final-year group does

221

not include those students who have transferred or dropped out during the course and who presumably by their conduct demonstrated dissatisfaction and lack of commitment to their chosen studies. It should be borne in mind, too, that the increased overall percentage in the final years may conceal a swing from complete to qualified satisfaction.)

The data for the late seventies in the table, including the end phase of the Sverdlovsk longitudinal study, reveal a much changed pattern of responses with regard to strength of vocation. They confirm the trends highlighted by the other indicators discussed above, namely that disenchantment with one's specialism and future job develops throughout the VUZ course. Enthusiasm becomes seemingly much dampened among RSFSR students whose feelings of complete satisfaction drop by an average of 20 per cent between the first and final years of the course, mainly as a result of more students registering just qualified satisfaction. And the proportion of the really dissatisfied almost doubles for all types of VUZ reaching as much as one-fifth among engineers and trainee teachers. (20) The lack of vocational commitment among the Baltic students in all subjects is surely a cause of concern to the higher education authorities there, although the proportion acknowledging actual dissatisfaction proved smaller than that of their Russian counterparts. There is no comment at all, however, from the authors with respect to this. (21)

The finding that one in every six teachers and one in five engineers are decidedly unhappy about their chosen occupation by the end of an expensive vocational training is a worrying phenomenon in the Soviet context. It implies that a considerable number of students must be studying in Soviet higher education with no liking for or interest in what they are doing and that in their working career they will perform indifferently in the three years of their compulsory work placement (if they bother to turn up for it!) and then in all probability take up an entirely different kind of work. (22) The loss in purely economic terms must be enormous and the failure of communist upbringing measures is quite obvious.

The follow-up question posed to the RSFSR and Baltic students as to whether they would be prepared to choose the same vocation again brought confirmation of what looks like widespread uncertainty and ambivalence among senior students about their original choice of studies and career.

(23) No more than about a half of the engineers and teachers would definitely make the same choice, some 60 per cent of the agriculturalists and 70 per cent of the medical students. By comparing the 'fully satisfied' percentage with that of the 'would definitely repeat choice' group we see that between 8 and 14 per cent of the partly satisfied students are still convinced that their original choice was right. The opposite tendency occurs with the Balts. The proportions of them who would definitely choose the same vocation are down by two to six points on those of the fully satisfied.

Academic Ideological Instruction

Throughout their <u>VUZ</u> course students of all disciplines follow compulsory lecture and seminar courses in certain social science subjects. This cycle of teaching starts with 120 or more hours in the first year devoted to the History of the Communist Party of the Soviet Union. In their second and third years students move on to Marxist–Leninist Philosophy and Political Economy. The former comprises courses in dialectical and historical materialism which are intended to give the student the necessary equipment for a scientific outlook and the dialectical method of perceiving and transforming the world. These can take up from a minimum of 90 to 200 class hours for most students and 300 hours for those who specialise in philosophy. For medical, agricultural, pedagogical, arts and culture <u>VUZs</u> extra philosophical topics are added such as ethics, aesthetics and the foundations of scientific atheism; in other types of <u>VUZ</u> these delights are optional. Political Economy occupies 140 to 250–300 hours, the higher volume being reserved for economics and law students, while the political economy specialists receive up to 400 hours' tuition in it. The culmination of the whole social science programme is an 80-hour course in Scientific Communism – a study of the development of socialism in the Soviet Union, the other socialist countries, and in the world at large – which since 1974 has merited state-examination status. (24)

To a great extent all these courses are of an academic nature. Students attend lectures, read the materials assigned to them and give the answers required of them in examinations. Whether student attitudes and convictions and behaviour are radically affected by such theoretical instruction is debatable. In research carried out in 1975 at four

223

Leningrad VUZs by Lisovskii students were asked what sources they used frequently for information on current domestic and international affairs. (25) Their social science lectures and seminars were placed only fifth with 18 per cent saying 'frequently' and some 39 per cent saying 'occasionally' - well behind such sources as friends, television, radio and the press, and just ahead of the family. Only a small proportion cited foreign radio broadcasts and newspapers as a frequently used source of information, but they were just as popular as an occasional source as the official ideological instruction. So much so that the author comments, 'The balance between the information sources cannot but cause alarm. Can one speak of effective political activism (among students), despite (their) high marks in the social sciences, when faced with this?' (26) In reply to another question 85 per cent of the sample said that they preferred to discuss topical political matters with their friends, just 38 per cent said with their social science teachers, and a miserable 14.5 per cent with their representatives in the student Komsomol and trade union organisations. (27) Lisovskii uses this finding to accuse social science lecturers of being out of touch with the socio-political interests of their students and to suggest that every VUZ should have a permanent sociological unit for monitoring student orientations in this area. (28) He reveals, too, the finding that those students who occupied elected positions in VUZ organisations were most intent on working in the future in party organisations, teaching in a VUZ or technical college or doing postgraduate work, and others who were very active in a socio-political sense stated their preference of working in government, trade union and other public organisations in administrative and managerial positions, as well as in party organisations. Their socio-political activity was motivated by the need for recognition and career promotion, 'evidence more of a pragmatic attitude to socio-political work than of a high level of internal activism'. (29)

Socio-Political Practice

Soviet higher schools have always stressed the formation in future graduates of socio-political activism. The country's graduate workforce is expected to provide not merely professional management in their fields, but also political, ideological and social leadership within their work ideological and social leadership within their work collectives and in the community at large. Students are given the requisite knowledge and skill training to make them competent organisers, speakers, propagandists and political information officers. In the past this type of training took different forms in different VUZs; it was neither universally uniform or systematic, nor did it encompass the whole student body. However, from the beginning of the seventies a tightening-up and standardisation of instruction in communist upbringing is to be observed. It was highlighted by two particular decrees: 'On Measures for the Further Improvement of the Country's Higher Education' (1972) and 'On the Work of the Moscow Bauman Higher Technical School and of Saratov Chernyshevsky State University in Raising the Ideological and Theoretical Level of the Teaching of the Social Sciences' (1974). A major step was taken in the academic year 1971/2 when the Ministry of Higher Education and the Central Committee of the Komsomol established a standard programme of socio-political training for all VUZs known as 'socio-political practice' (obshchestvenno-politicheskaya praktika) or SPP. Soviet students are now obliged to undergo this programme of instruction and practical activities designed to last throughout their VUZ course. Every year students are assessed individually on their SPP activism and their performance is noted in their personal record. (30)

The basic structure of SPP is set out in the Komsomol-produced handbook for students. (31) SPP is supervised by the VUZ administration, public organisations, and the teaching staff of the social science and other faculties. Practical work for SPP is based on the knowledge acquired by students in social science lectures and seminars. Every student must carry out annually at least one project on a theme taken from his social science curriculum. This project might include: (1) preparing a summary or text of a lecture on a topical problem in Marxism-Leninism and then delivering it to a student or outside audience; (2) writing a scholarly paper and presenting it to the student research circle or at a conference; (3) participating in research conducted by the various departments in the social science faculty. The best student work is then entered for the All-Union Competition for student work on problems of the social sciences, history of the Komsomol and the international youth movement. During the industrial practice period of their course students are expected to engage in a programme of political and educational work at their enterprises and to join in socio-political, cultural, sporting and other activities and events.

Outside the academic course structure and in non-academic time SPP can involve practical skill training in the so-called Public Service Faculty and Young Public Speaker School, participation in national propaganda campaigns, and student construction brigades during the summer vacation. Other assignments to fulfil SPP requirements could be serving as an elected Komsomol, trade union or academic group leader, running a Komsomol education class or giving political information talks, taking part in various societies and clubs, or working outside the VUZ in schools, housing estates, police juvenile departments and so on. Assessment is based on reports received about individual students from the organisations and bodies involved and on an interview and discussion at a meeting of the students' academic group.

Lisovskii in his 18-VUZ survey in 1979 found that 75.4 per cent of students participated in SPP, while one in four were inactive. When asked what prevented socio-political work from being effective over half of the students cited 'formalism', 29 per cent said that their academic group was not united enough, and 24 per cent blamed lack of organising skills among the students. Only 14 per cent mentioned academic workload and just one in ten thought that SPP was irrelevant to their academic and vocational interests. (32) The degree of participation, however, may vary considerably within the overall figure. In the time budget of students socio-political activities rank low with only a minority devoting much time to them. In her Sverdlovsk longitudinal study Rubina confirms this order of priorities in actual time use and shows, too, that the proportion of active participants in SPP declines from about 51 per cent in the first year to 38 per cent at the end of the course. (33)

So, if the rates of participation in SPP can look impressive, the amount actually being done can be less so. And the quality of the experience or its effect on the student may not be what was intended. In the 1979 Leningrad study referred to above it was discovered that roughly half of the students who engaged in SPP got little enjoyment out of it. (34) Rubina, again, supports this finding and identifies a particular 'hard core' of about 30 per cent of students who have a confirmed negative attitude to SPP. 'These students', she claims, 'do not regard socio-political work as important for their future job, get no satisfaction from it, and devote little time to it'. (35)

Another research study carried out by Leningrad sociologists in the late seventies looked at student motives for SPP activism by year of course. The social importance of SPP motivated 48 per cent of freshmen to participate but only 35 per cent of senior students. An analogous pattern applied with the vocational importance of SPP, except that the decline in numbers citing this motive was even sharper, from 48 per cent to 16 per cent in the final year. At the same time, as we noted above with regard to vocational orientation, instrumental motives for SPP activism - personal prestige, advancement, and material reward - become more dominant. And the proportion of students claiming that they only took part in SPP because they were forced to (sic!) rose from four per cent to 30 per cent over the years of the course. (36)

Reactions such as these help us to see the quantitative indicators of SPP activism in a more realistic light. They seem to reflect a pervading attitude among Soviet students about the place of socio-political activity in their life and work as a whole. Published data on the early to mid-seventies showed that first-year students put SPP almost at the bottom of their plans for enjoying VUZ life (see Rubina, Sovetskoe studenchestvo, p.91). At the end of the decade the relative value accorded to it by Soviet students in the International Survey can be assessed in Table 9.4. Once more these official measures to implement communist upbringing are seen to be largely rejected in favour of personal and cultural life, as well as academic studies, in the minds of Soviet young people. This phenomenon is not explained away by the authors but simply accepted with the comment, 'of course, objectively speaking, socio-political activities cannot have as great a significance as the fundamental activities of life (work, family and so on)'. (37)

Conclusion

In this paper we have examined some of the ways students in Soviet higher education perceive and react to the demands made upon them by official organisational structures, the formal requirements of their academic/vocational courses, and by programmes of socio-political taining. The evidence we have adduced has consisted of selected data from

Table 9.4: Student Views on the Importance of Various Activities, RSFSR and Baltic Republics, 1977-1979

Type of activity (and overall ranking) (a)	Degree of importance (% of students)							
	Very great		Fairly great		Not very great		Insignificant	
	RSFSR	Baltic	RSFSR	Baltic	RSFSR	Baltic	RSFSR	Baltic
Academic study to master specialism (3)	23.9	45.7	37.4	43.6	16.2	9.8	15.3	0.9
Socio-political work (6)	7.3	11.0	25.3	39.5	37.2	40.9	23.9	8.6
Being with friends (1)	32.1	50.2	43.1	42.1	14.6	7.2	3.3	0.6
Hobbies (4)	14.6	35.7	27.3	40.4	31.3	19.9	21.7	4.0
Physical culture (7)	9.1	25.0	21.3	36.4	28.4	31.7	40.3	6.9
Theatres, concerts, exhibitions, reading (2)	29.7	45.0	38.0	44.7	25.9	9.6	5.3	0.7
Boyfriend/girlfriend	-	55.9	-	29.0	-	9.6	-	5.5
Family life (5)	23.9	-	17.0	-	11.0	-	36.9	-

Note: (a) Overall ranking is based on the combined percentages of the columns 'very great' and 'fairly great', and refers here to the RSFSR students only. The ranking of the Baltic students' responses is essentially the same.

Source: F.R. Filippov and P.E. Mitev (eds.), Molodezh' i vyshshee obrazovanie v sotsialisticheskikh stranakh (Nauka, Moscow, 1984), p.115.

what are acknowledged by Soviet sociologists to be the most authoritative and representative surveys of Soviet students in recent years. By and large, the results we have discussed here are repeated in many smaller, more localised empirical researches in this field. The stimulus for this type of research is the need felt by the Soviet authorities to assess the effectiveness of a costly educational process which they regard as vital for the achievement of their economic, political and social goals. For the manner in which future Soviet graduate managers, organisers and leaders conform to, cope with, accept or resist the above-mentioned demands has far-reaching implications for the success of manpower planning, national economic and social development, and the overall ideological and political control of the populace.

Our focus has been somewhat 'negative', that is to say we have concentrated on the extent to which expressed attitudes and declared behaviour have fallen short of official expectations and claims. In this we have reflected in some measure the greater frankness and realism with which 'negative' findings of sociological fieldwork are now reported both in scholarly writings, including the sources we have drawn on here, and in contemporary Soviet commentary in general. It must be recognised, nevertheless, in the light of the ideals aimed at and the considerable amount of 'positive' data in the studies under discussion, that much has been achieved by Soviet higher education.

Yet one cannot but suspect on reviewing the materials above that Soviet higher education faces an impossible task in its attempts to instil required values and convictions. To begin with it comes upon the scene too late, as it were. The influences of students' pre-VUZ life have probably had a decisive effect on their way of thinking and acting long before their entry. And VUZ authorities have neither the resources, nor the flexibility and subtlety of approach to investigate the 'starting position' of each individual student in order to counter, if necessary, prior incorrect socialisation and to devise a more relevant programme of communist upbringing. Nor can the higher education system do much about broader economic and social factors which can radically affect student motivation and aspirations such as labour shortage, wage differentials, the varying prestige of occupations, the consequences of universal secondary education, the 'feminisation' of certain professions, family mores, traditional patterns of working, and so on.

These drawbacks are compounded, moreover, by what sometimes appears to be a refusal on the part of Soviet higher education authorities to take into account the psychology of young people at a time of considerable upheaval in their work and life experiences. The processes of maturation, youth's natural unsureness of self, its desire to achieve adulthood and independence, prompting the rejection of values imposed by others and of paternalistic injunctions - all this is seemingly ignored when a planned mass system of vocational and ideological training is applied to young people in Soviet higher education. It is clear that their emotions are not being engaged in the process of communist upbringing. And, in the end, of course, the success of the upbringing enterprise cannot readily be assessed by the educators.

The empirical evidence of student attitudes which we have been exploring indicates a relative failure of ideological training. The vocational commitment of a sizeable proportion of Soviet students actually worsens while they are at <u>VUZ</u>. Their attitudes to their studies, <u>VUZ</u> life and future work tend to become more instrumental and their motivation more personal rather than altruistic and collectivist. As they mature, Soviet students, like students everywhere, (38) become surer of themselves and hence less conformist <u>vis-à-vis</u> official <u>VUZ</u> requirements. This is not so much a matter of opposition as of adopting coping strategies. Completing the academic course is the main thing; and communist upbringing is not viewed by Soviet students as having a great deal of relevance to their future personal and professional life. And, paradoxically, in thinking this way they are following the imperatives embodied in the structure and ethos of a higher education system in which academic instruction has primacy. Ultimately, for Soviet higher education establishments and their academic staff, the producing of highly qualified graduate specialists (with or without a strong sense of vocation) takes precedence over producing ideologically committed, politically well-informed activists and organisers. Were the priorities to be reversed, Soviet higher education would have to undergo a drastic transformation.

Notes
1.   This chapter is taken from part of a paper

presented by the author at the Third World Congress for Soviet and East European Studies, Washington, D.C. (October 30 - November 4, 1985) with the title: 'Soviet Students: Lifestyle and Attitudes'. The full paper appears in the selected proceedings of the Congress educational panels, J. Dunstan (ed.), Soviet Education Under Scrutiny (University of Birmingham, 1987).

   2. A.A. Abakumov, N.P. Kuzin, F.I. Puzyrev, and L.F. Litvinov (comps.), Narodnoe obrazovanie v SSSR, Obshcheobrazovatel'naya shkola: sbornik dokumentov 1917-1973 g.g. (Pedagogika, Moscow, 1974), p.101.

   3. V.P. Elyutin, Vysshaya shkola obshchestva razvitogo sotsializma (Vysshaya shkola, Moscow, 1980), p.271.

   4. We utilise data taken from three major questionnaire surveys of full-time students:

(i) The first survey (hereinafter referred to as 'the All-Union Survey'), organised by the Institute of Sociological Research of the USSR Academy of Sciences, took place in 1973-74 in the following six regions of the Soviet Union: Moscow, Sverdlovsk, Novosibirsk, Odessa, Estonia, and Krasnodar. It involved the administering of an anonymous questionnaire to a total sample of 7200 first-year students and 7955 final-year students, selected by a mixture of stratified random sampling and quota sampling to give large sub-samples of students from polytechnical, agricultural, pedagogical, and medical institutes, and from humanities and natural science faculties in universities. Despite the large numbers in the sample, the sampling procedures were such that the findings of the survey can be generalised only for each subject cohort within the regions concerned. The main report of the results obtained was published in M.N. Rutkevich and F.R. Filippov (eds.), Vysshaya shkola kak faktor izmeneniya sotsial'noi struktury razvitogo sotsialisticheskogo obshchestva (Nauka, Moscow, 1978). Further analyses are to be found in M.N. Rutkevich, M.Kh. Titma, and F.R. Filippov, 'Izmeneniya v sotsial'nom sostave i professional'noi orientatsii studenchestva v SSSR,' in T.V. Ryabushkin and G.V. Osipov (eds.), Sovetskaya sotsiologiya, T.2, Dinamika sotsial'nykh protsessov v SSSR (Nauka, Moscow, 1982), pp.111-41, and in L.Ya. Rubina, Sovetskoe studenchestvo: sotsiologicheskii ocherk (Mysl', Moscow, 1981).

(ii) The second survey (which we shall subsequently call 'the International Survey') was also conducted by the Academy's Institute of Sociological Research and constituted the Soviet contribution to a large-scale study conducted in 1977-79 (some sources give 1977-78) in the East European socialist countries of Czechoslovakia, Hungary, Poland, Bulgaria, GDR, and in four union republics of the USSR, namely the RSFSR and the Baltic republics of Latvia, Estonia, and Lithuania. The Soviet sample comprised 2310 first-year and 1661 final-year students studying in 13 towns and cities of the European part of RSFSR, and 11,680 students in Baltic VUZs, chosen by means of cluster sampling. The fullest account of the survey as a whole (omitting, however, the Polish results) is given in F.R. Filippov and P.E. Mitev (eds.), Molodezh'i vysshee obrazovanie v sotsialisticheskikh stranakh (Nauka, Moscow, 1984). Earlier short reports are contained in F.R. Filippov, 'Formirovanie popolnenii sotsialisticheskoi intelligentsii (K itogam mezhdunarodnogo sravnitel'nogo issledovaniya)', Sotsiologicheskie issledovaniya, no. 2 (1980), pp.87-98, and in Rutkevich, Titma and Filippov, 'Izmeneniya v sotsial'nom sostave'.

(iii) The most ambitious study of student views carried out by Leningrad University sociologists took place in 1979 among a sample of some 4065 students in 18 VUZs including four universities, in several regions of the RSFSR and in the Ukraine, Belorussia, and Turkmenia. The Soviet reports of this survey contain little or no information about the methodology used, sampling procedures, or the size of sub-samples. The most detailed selection of results was published in V.T. Lisovskii (ed.), Obraz zhizni sovremennogo studenta: sotsiologicheskoe issledovanie (Leningrad State University, Leningrad, 1981). Additional materials from the survey are also to be found in V.T. Lisovskii and V.A. Sukhin (eds.), Chelovek i obshchestvo, vypusk 20, Problemy povysheniya uspevaemosti i snizheniya otseva studentov (Leningrad State University, Leningrad, 1983).

We rely heavily on the following chapters/sections of the main reports cited above: M.Kh. Titma and L.Ya. Rubina, 'Sotsial'no-professional'naya orientatsiya i zhiznennye plany studenchestva', section 3 of Rutkevich and Filippov, Vysshaya shkola kak faktor, pp. 154-231; M. Titma, 'Sotsial'naya aktivnost' studentov' and 'Sotsial'no-professional'naya orientatsiya studentov', chapters 5 and 6 respectively of Filippov and Mitev, Molodezh'i vysshee obrazovanie, pp.76-93 and 93-118. The relevant Leningrad University materials, however, are contained in numerous contributions by different members of the research team in the works cited above.

5. Titma and Rubina, 'Sotsial'no-profession-al'naya orientatsiya', pp.156-61, 191-5; Rubina, Sovetskoe studenchestvo, pp.84-92, 112-13. The same finding was confirmed in the later International Survey (see Filippov, 'Formirovanie popolnenii', p.94).

6. Titma and Rubina, 'Sotsial'no-profession-al'naya orientatsiya', pp.156-7, 191-2; see also pp.211-12, 216.

7. Ibid., p.157.

8. Rubina, Sovetskoe studenchestvo, pp.88-9.

9. Titma and Rubina, 'Sotsial'no-profession-al'naya orientatsiya', pp.158-9, 204; Rubina, Sovetskoe studenchestvo, p.89.

10. Titma and Rubina, 'Sotsial'no-profession-al'naya orientatsiya', pp.192-3; Filippov, 'Formiro-vanie popolnenii', p.94.

11. Titma, 'Sotsial'no-professional'naya orientatsiya studentov', pp.95-7; Rutkevich, Titma and Filippov, 'Izmeneniya v sotsial'nom sostave', p.129; Filippov, 'Formirovanie popolnenii', p.94.

12. Titma and Rubina, 'Sotsial'no-profession-al'naya orientatsiya', p.158; Rubina, Sovetskoe studenchestvo, p.108; see also Filippov, 'Formiro-vanie popolnenii', pp.92-4.

13. Titma and Rubina, 'Sotsial'no-profession-al'naya orientatsiya', p.179; Rubina, Sovetskoe studenchestvo, pp.108-9. See also Titma, 'Sotsial'-no-professional'naya orientatsiya studentov', pp.116-17, and Rutkevich, Titma and Filippov, 'Izmeneniya v sotsial'nom sostave', pp.132-3.

14. Filippov, 'Formirovanie popolnenii', pp.96-7.

15. Rubina, Sovetskoe studenchestvo, pp.105-10.

16. Filippov, 'Formirovanie popolnenii', p.94; Rutkevich, Titma and Filippov, 'Izmeneniya v sotsial'nom sostave', p.130.

17. Titma, 'Sotsial'no-professional'naya orie-ntatsiya studentov', pp.105, 108; Rutkevich, Titma and Filippov, 'Izmeneniya v sotsial'nom sostave', p.135.

18. G.A. Zhuravleva, 'Professional'naya nap-ravlennost' kak vazhneishaya kharakteristika otnosh-eniya studentov k trudovoi deyatel'nosti', in Lisovskii, Obraz zhizni, p.52.

19. Titma and Rubina, 'Sotsial'no-profession-al'naya orientatsiya', p.196.

20. Titma, 'Sotsial'naya aktivnost' studentov', p.84.

21. But for strong critical remarks about the alarmingly weak vocational orientation of Soviet students questioned in this survey see Filippov, 'Formirovanie popolnenii', p.94-6.

22. Zhuravleva, 'Professional'naya napravlennost', pp.55-9; G.A. Zhuravleva, 'Ukhod studentov iz vuza po sobstvennomu zhelaniyu', in Lisovskii and Sukhin, Chelovek i obshchestvo, vypusk 20, pp.58-60.

23. Titma, 'Sotsial'naya aktivnost' studentov', p.85.

24. Elyutin, Vysshaya shkola, pp.274-7. State examinations are now (1986) being extended also to the subject of Marxism-Leninism.

25. V.T. Lisovskii, 'Formirovanie lichnosti sovremennogo studenta (opyt sotsiologicheskogo issledovaniya v vysshei shkole. 1966-1975 g.g.)', unpublished dissertation for the degree of Doctor of Philosophical Sciences, University of Leningrad, 1976, p.211.

26. Ibid., p.212.

27. Ibid., p.213.

28. Ibid., p.214.

29. Ibid., pp.228-9.

30. M.B. Zimina, 'Soderzhanie obshchestvenno-politicheskoi praktiki, metodika ee provedeniya i organizatsii', in V.P. Agafonov (ed.), Obshchestvenno-politicheskaya praktika studentov (voprosy teorii i metodiki) (Vysshaya shkola, Moscow, 1980), pp.14-18.

31. O.I. Karpukhin and I.S. Mostyka (comps.), Komsomol v vuze (Molodaya gvardiya, Moscow, 1981), pp.178-82.

32. Lisovskii, Obraz zhizni, p.175.

33. Rubina, Sovetskoe studenchestvo, pp.138-9.

34. Lisovskii, Obraz zhizni, p.149.

35. See Rubina, Sovetskoe studenchestvo, pp.138-43.

36. N.V. Kuz'mina and V.A. Yakunin, 'Rol' organizatorskoi deyatel'nosti dekanatov v preduprezhdenii otseva i akademicheskoi neuspevaemosti studentov,' in Lisovskii and Sukhin, Chelovek i obshchestvo, vypusk 20, p.149.

37. Titma, 'Sotsial'no-professional'naya orientatsiya studentov', p.113; see also Rutkevich, Titma and Filippov, 'Izmeneniya v sotsial'nom sostave', pp.136-7.

38. It is difficult to make valid comparisons between the empirical materials discussed here and the results of Western research into attitude change

and political socialisation among students in higher education. Unlike their Western counterparts Soviet students are exposed to a systematic and thorough programme of ideological instruction, exhortation and other activities throughout their academic career which is intended to inculcate specific officially approved attitudes and socio-political activism. Failure to assimilate such attitudes is castigated as being detrimental to the social and economic aims of Soviet society, and it may also affect students' future career prospects.

It is interesting, however, to compare the responses to more or less the same questions by Soviet students and students in other socialist countries which were included in the International Survey whose data have been utilised in the present essay (see Note 4). For example, complete satisfaction with their chosen specialism appeared to be even less widespread among respondents in Bulgaria and Hungary than among senior Russian and Baltic students (see Table 9.3 above), although the figures for Czech students were slightly higher. This applies to all the subject groups except engineering students where even the Czechs are less satisfied. As for the proportions of students who would definitely make the same choice of specialism, once again the students from the other socialist countries recorded much lower percentages than the Russian students on the whole (Titma, 'Sotsial'naya aktivnost' studentov', pp.84-5). Conversely, the importance of academic study to master one's specialism and of socio-political work was emphasised overall much more by the Czech, Bulgarian and Hungarian students than by the Russian ones (see Table 9.4). But, generally, although they employed a standardised questionnaire and were dealing with samples drawn in countries with similar socialist political systems, the researchers found that comparisons were frequently vitiated by differences in the cultural, economic and social backgrounds of the students.

INDEX

236